Joe Quigley, Alaska Pioneer

Joe Quigley, Alaska Pioneer
Beyond the Gold Rush

CHERYL FAIR

McFarland & Company, Inc., Publishers
Jefferson, North Carolina

ISBN (print) 978-1-4766-7927-3
ISBN (ebook) 978-1-4766-3874-4

LIBRARY OF CONGRESS AND BRITISH LIBRARY
CATALOGUING DATA ARE AVAILABLE

Library of Congress Control Number 2019056329

© 2020 Cheryl Fair. All rights reserved

No part of this book may be reproduced or transmitted in any form or by any means, electronic or mechanical, including photocopying or recording, or by any information storage and retrieval system, without permission in writing from the publisher.

On the cover: Joe Quigley at a cairn on Wickersham Dome close to Quigley Ridge. Some say that Joe built this monument alone, but generally cairn building was a group project. Taken around 1912 when the pointed capstone was still in place—see page 151 (National Park Service DENA 3512). Background: a photograph of the Denali range and Mount McKinley (Christopher Boswell/Shutterstock)

Printed in the United States of America

McFarland & Company, Inc., Publishers
Box 611, Jefferson, North Carolina 28640
www.mcfarlandpub.com

To all those with a roving disposition

Acknowledgments

Many people helped me to complete this book. My husband George Hagegeorge made it possible for me to spend time writing, encouraged me to tell the story of Joe Quigley, and patiently listened as I talked through my discoveries and ideas. My cousin Kim Talboo contributed her genealogical research findings and commiserated with me from the project's inception to completion. Patty Quigley Voldbaek shared her father Ken Quigley's treasure trove of memorabilia, giving new insight into Joe Quigley's life. Some cousins that I've known for my entire life, and some that I met recently through researching Joe Quigley, all kindly shared their stories and photographs: Katheryn Jean Graham Campbell, Jim Cooper, Lonnie Fair, Mary Fair, Tom Johnson, Phil Lasher, Teri Morgan, and Rebecca Campbell Quintana all shared their family photographs, genealogy research, and family memories with me.

Erik Johnson, historian for Denali National Park and Preserve, was the first person outside of my circle of family and friends to encourage me to write Joe Quigley's biography and was very helpful with referrals and networking. Erik led me to author/historian Tom Walker, who became my unexpected mentor. His encyclopedic knowledge of the exact time and place I was researching consistently amazed me, and his generosity in sharing that knowledge has been invaluable. William "Willie" L. Iggiagruk Hensley graciously responded to my enquires and helped guide me down the right path. His sense of humor and inspiring example opened up my mind to new ways of looking at history. Jane Haigh's biography of Fannie Quigley was the spark that convinced me to write this book. Jane kindly shared her research findings with me and answered many of my questions. Tom Buntdsen shared his research and relayed personal stories of Joe Quigley that were passed down to him through his work with the Alaska Mining Hall of Fame. Some of the Alaskans who kindly shared their knowledge and support for this project include Kim Arthur, Becky Butler, Virgil Campbell, Linda Conley, Bill Cotter, Simon Hamm, Helen Hegener, Joanne Oehring, Diane Purvis, Jennifer Raffaeli, Rosemarie Speranza, Denice Swanke, and Joan Tovsen.

I am fortunate to be surrounded by a group of very talented and generous friends who offered advice and practical help on this project. Thank you to Rahne Alexander, Skizz Cyzyk, Michael Faulkner, Linda Franklin, Mitch Holson, Scott Johnson, Nora Lockshin, Josephine Ma, Jonathan Mayo, Paula Millet, Arwen Nuttall, Marie-Rose Phan-Le, Melyssa Polen, Brandon Rohrbaugh, Cynthia Sanders, Jen Talbert, Joe Tropea, and Kristin Weisman.

Thank you to Robbie Franklin, Steve Wilson, and Susan Kilby of McFarland for giving me the opportunity to tell the story of Joe Quigley's life.

Table of Contents

Acknowledgments   vii
Introduction: Searching for Joe Quigley   1

1. The Chilkoot Pass and Fortymile River   5
2. "Just a small family"   16
3. "A roving disposition"   22
4. The Last Frontier   31
5. Rocking on the Bars   35
6. Eldorado   43
7. Fairbanks   50
8. Kantishna   55
9. Joe and Fannie   62
10. Hard Rock   67
11. "An accurate observer of nature"   73
12. Community   80
13. The Great Mountain   86
14. Struggle   95
15. Postwar Resurgence   99
16. Expansion   109
17. Celebrity   118
18. Flight   124
19. Back Home   129
20. Cave In   138

21. Cashing Out		144
22. Still Rovin'		155
23. Seattle		162
Chapter Notes		169
Bibliography		185
Index		189

Introduction:
Searching for Joe Quigley

One day while sitting at the kitchen table with his usual crossword puzzle and beer, my father started talking about places he wanted go, saying that Alaska was on the top of the list. I was playing on the floor, and my mother was folding laundry, but we were listening. I was watching him as he sharpened a carpenter's pencil with his penknife, and almost as an afterthought he said, "I had an uncle that went to Alaska and discovered gold." That statement got my attention, but there was no more to the story that day.

Years later, in the 1990s after my father had passed away, I felt ready to learn more about my family's stories and began doing genealogy research. I found that the uncle who went to Alaska was my great grandmother's younger brother, Joseph Buffington Quigley. I had very limited information about his life, and the story remained on the back burner until 2017 when my husband became interested in genealogy, which then rekindled my interest in the subject. Since my previous foray into researching the story of my great-great uncle, information had become much more accessible and the mysterious Joe Quigley was emerging from the shadows of my consciousness to became the focus of my family research.

I started with a Google search in July of 2017, which led me to a short documentary on YouTube about Denali National Park and Preserve that included pictures of Joe and Fannie Quigley. It felt surreal to see what looked like still shots from a film of the Old West and realize that they were photographs of someone from my family. I immediately emailed my cousin Kim Talboo, an avid genealogist who grew up in Pennsylvania near where the Quigley family originated. By the next day our investigations brought us to Jane Haigh's book *Searching for Fannie Quigley,* and we continued to look for more information about our ancestor. I wrote to Denali National Park and Preserve to see if they had any photographs of Joe, which led me to correspondence with park historian Erik Johnson, who directed me to the Denali archives and the University of Alaska, Fairbanks, which had a wealth of information and photographs.

As soon I learned that Joe Quigley and I shared a May 9 birthday and a love of photography, I was completely hooked on the story. Learning of the impact he had on Alaska history, and the many years he had spent in the Far North as a miner before, during, and after the great Klondike Gold Rush, I was surprised that a definitive biography had not been written about him. It occurred to me that I could do something to bring Joe Quigley's story to light, and I knew that to do it right would take something longer and more detailed than a blog entry, something deeper than a compilation of genealogical facts and documents, and something beyond another retelling of the story of the gold rush.

The more I looked into the story of my great-great uncle, the more I felt like I was getting to personally know the

Cheryl Fair with her father, Frank Fair, in front of their home in Maryland in 1957, around the time that Cheryl first heard of her father's great uncle Joe Quigley, who "went to Alaska and discovered gold" (photograph by June L. Fair, 1957, author's collection).

Alaska wilderness, Joe Quigley, and the people in his world. I set out to learn more about turn-of-the-20th-century Alaska, Denali National Park and Preserve, and the mining community. I read many archived documents, old newspaper articles, and books on Alaska history including Tom Walker's book *Kantishna Mushers, Miners, Mountaineers* which had a wonderful portrayal of Joe Quigley that inspired me to continue my search for the details of Joe's life.

Feeling that Alaska Natives must be crucial to the story of any Alaska pioneer, I searched for information about the interaction between the influx of prospectors to Alaska and the indigenous people. Living on the East Coast of the United States, I found that I was at a disadvantage, but I began my search where I live. I contacted the Baltimore American Indian Center and the Smithsonian Museum of the American Indian to find that there was very little information available on Alaska Native history at either place. I was directed to the Smithsonian affiliate in Anchorage and the Alaska Native Heritage Center, but I still did not find an individual available to speak with me about the specific historical information I was looking for. Erik Johnson suggested that I contact Alaska Native rights activist, professor, retired politician, and author of *Fifty Miles from Tomorrow* William L. Iggiagruk Hensley. I contacted Hensley, an Inupiat who very patiently answered my questions. I quickly learned that Alaska Native culture is much more diverse than I'd realized, with many languages and cultures represented, and that the people who were in the interior of Alaska, where Joe Quigley settled, were Athabascan.

Joe Quigley's character comes to life in his letters to family and friends. He was an articulate man with a good sense of humor, a strong sense of responsibility, and a tendency to underplay his own achievements. Another major source for Joe's biography was the 14-page transcript of an interview with Joe done by Hazel Lindberg in 1953 when Joe was 84 years old. When Rosemarie Speranza, of the Alaska and Polar Regions Collections and Archives, Elmer E. Rasmuson Library, University of Alaska, Fairbanks, sent me the document, I read Joe's story in his own words, and his personality came through clearly. In my mind, I could hear his western Pennsylvania accent and speech patterns that I recognized from my father's storytelling, and I saw his wry sense of humor coming through in his description of his own experiences. That document became a key element for my telling of the story of Joe Quigley's remarkable life.

During my research I was surprised to find that Joe Quigley was not included in the Alaska Mining Hall of Fame. I contacted the president of the organization, Tom Bundtzen, to nominate Joe as an inductee and the situation was rectified on November 6, 2018. Joseph Buffington Quigley was honored at an induction ceremony held in Anchorage.

Each time I approached anyone in Alaska by email or phone for help with this project, they responded with enthusiasm and practical help. Authors whose work I admire, librarians, historians, and record keepers of all kinds have given generously of their time and knowledge, and it has been an unexpectedly uplifting experience. I feel great appreciation for the chain of people and events that brought Joe Quigley's inspiring story to me, and I feel fortunate to be the person to pass the story on to others.

Chapter 1

The Chilkoot Pass and Fortymile River

In the spring of 1891, more than five years before the famed Klondike Gold Rush, Joe Quigley started off on the trip of a lifetime. He was 21 years old and had spent almost seven years on his own, growing from someone who "didn't know whether to hire on as a man or a boy"[1] to a "six-foot and then some" man who was "all bone and muscle."[2] He had, through his various jobs on the road, developed many of the skills he would need to succeed on the next leg of his journey. His intense awareness of the power of life within himself, tremendous determination, and sense of urgency to move forward spurred him on, and he was about to master one of the most rugged trails in the world.

Investing his hard-earned savings in a trip to Alaska was a huge gamble, but Joe had the confidence and optimism to imagine a bright future in the Far North. Venturing into the gamble of gold mining, Joe started off with the intention of going to Juneau where he'd heard there were gold mines. He was fortunate enough at the beginning of the trip to find potential mining partners who were going to the goldfields in the Yukon. As he later remembered it Joe said, "I went up on a steamer to Juneau, where I had heard there were mines, but I saw a party getting ready to go into the Interior of Alaska, I partnered up with him, and we went together. Billy Kaufman." Joe and Kaufman joined up with Lew Pierce, Charley Framton and some others and "took a year's outfit ... minimum necessities."

Joe understood that he would need a partner. Being a prospector is a dangerous job, but there is safety in numbers. Having grown up in a large family and a tight-knit community, he knew how to weigh the value of himself as a work partner and how to find people to fill in the gaps. In the unknown territory he was entering, conditions were harsher than even a hard-working outdoorsman such as Joe was accustomed to. Sharing and cooperation were essential for survival.

Severe cold threatened Far North travelers in the winter, and mosquitos tortured them in the summer. Due to permafrost, water drainage is prevented, and water stands on the ground. When spring thaw happens, overland travel becomes a nightmare of bogs, or muskegs, also called muskeg swamps. Muskegs are a mixture of acidic soil, water and partly dead vegetation, frequently covered by a layer of various types of moss. Rather than grassland or meadows, the Far North has tussocks, which are tall grasses that grow in clumps, and thickets, or dense groups of trees or tall shrubs. The large amounts of standing water breed more than 35 different species of especially large mosquitos.[3]

Juneau was a mining town that sprung up when hard rock gold was discovered there in 1880. Hard rock mining, or quartz mining, refers to mining techniques used to excavate hard minerals that contain precious metals, as opposed to placer mining which is the mining of stream beds for deposits of minerals. The most famous mining operation in Juneau was begun by John Treadwell 17 years before the big gold rush. The Treadwell Mining Complex was ultimately composed of four different mines, and in 1889 Treadwell sold his stake in the company for $1.5 million and moved to California.[4]

All sorts of people with a "roving disposition" were attracted to Juneau, using it as a launch pad to Alaska and the Canadian Yukon. Most were there to try their luck with placer mining. Adventurers, fortune hunters, and frontiersmen came to Juneau in pairs and small groups. Some brought no more than a rucksack, a gold pan, a shovel and a vial of mercury.[5] Placer gold was known as "poor man's gold" because the people who looked for it had no time or money to develop lode deposits.[6] As with all boom towns, whenever a prospector struck it rich, camp-followers were quick to come in to "mine the miners." People providing the necessities and satisfying the desires and whims of the gold miners made up the citizenship of the towns. By 1890 Juneau had a population of just over 1200 and these people ranged from good people trying to make an honest living to the unscrupulous who took advantage of the miners' weaknesses or naïveté.

Joe Quigley's group, which included Billy Kaufman, Lew Pierce and Charley Framton, chartered a small fishing boat for the 115-mile trip from Juneau to Dyea. In the Far North, getting from one place to another was a constant problem to be solved. Locations with enough population to provide help, provisions, or companionship were far distant from each other. In the places where individuals of this group originated from, provisions and people could be right next door for a city dweller or just a few miles on foot or by horse for rural folks. In the northern latitudes where they were traveling, what would have been a simple errand back home would take days or weeks and an enormous amount of energy. Transportation methods in the Far North were seasonal. The vast area has a network of rivers and streams that are natural highways, and those waterways were often the fastest, and sometimes the only, way to go long distances. Travelers would follow the wa-

Chapter 1. The Chilkoot Pass and Fortymile River

terways as far as possible in the desired direction, then leave to cross mountain ranges at the most favorable points, and return to the streams again as soon as the water became available. In the winter dog sleds were employed. In the summer the course was similar except that boats were used, and the shallowness of the water would limit the distance that boats could go. Once one was on the ground, hiking or riding a horse would have been the only choices available get to the desired destination. Joe and his companions relied on their own legs for any travel beyond the water.

The chartered fishing boat they were in hit bad weather and had a two-week delay. In our time of instant gratification, it is hard to imagine what it must have been like for the group to have a two-week delay after coming so far on their journey, but they knew there was no choice and made the best of it. Joe recounted, "We struck head winds and bad weather en route to Dyea and pulled into Sunset Cove, the weather continued bad…. Couldn't venture out again for fourteen days … made camp on shore"[7] Camping for two weeks in bad weather while anticipating their long-awaited journey into unknown territory must have been frustrating, but they were aware that, as always, mother nature was the ultimate authority and that they would not be moving forward until the weather allowed the boat to continue.

It was March or April by this time and there is an old axiom that there are three seasons in Alaska: winter, the Fourth of July, and autumn. The temperature often goes below freezing at night on the water during early spring, and large, strong gales and storms are common. Fortunately, the coastline offers an unusual number of protected waterways for boats to take shelter. Sunset Cove was somewhere between Juneau and Dyea and was a local place name that fell out of use later.

After the weather delay, the party arrived in Dyea and saw a wood frame building that was a combination store, residence and barn, with a nearby garden, and was called the Healy and Wilson Trading Post. It was the only business there. In the mid–1880s, John J. Healy had been a hunter, trapper, soldier, prospector, whiskey trader, editor, guide, Indian scout, and sheriff, and he was living in Montana Territory when he heard about the early pre–Klondike Yukon gold strikes and headed north. Healy was known as an unsociable man of sour disposition. He did not offer credit at his trading post, but he did maintain lower prices than other suppliers who did.[8] Healy and his brother-in-law Edgar Wilson opened the trading post at the convergence of the Taiya River and Taiya Inlet on the south side of the Chilkoot Pass. The business became an important supply and information point for prospectors who were heading into the Yukon basin before the Klondike Gold Rush. It was located just downriver from a Tlingit village and was a place where Alaska Natives and First Nations peoples gathered to get work helping prospectors pack their outfits over the Chilkoot Pass.[9]

Historically, the Chilkoot Pass was a trade link between the coastal Tlingit and interior Athabascan Indians, and it was crucial to the trade network involved in the mid to late 19th-century Western fur industry. The Chilkoot Trail was one of only three year-round passages to the Canadian interior, which made it an important entryway for explorers, pioneers, and prospectors in the last quarter of the 19th century.[10] In 1873 George Holt was the first white man to cross the Chilkoot Pass, making the journey to the upper Yukon. In 1879 the Chilkats turned back three prospectors when they tried to go over the Chilkoot Pass, and a year later armed U.S. Navy personnel persuaded the Chilkats to open the trail to prospectors. Arthur Krause made a sketch map of the Chilkoot Pass when he crossed it in 1882, and a year later, in 1883, Lieutenant Frederick Schwatka of the U.S Army led a military reconnaissance across the Chilkoot Pass and descended the Yukon River to its mouth on a raft. In 1884, John J. Healy and Edgar Wilson established a trading post at the head of Taiya estuary, marking the beginning of Dyea.[11] The number of prospectors using the Chilkoot Trail gradually increased after prospectors discovered gold in the late 1880s on the Stewart and Fortymile rivers, upper tributaries of the Yukon River.

Joe Quigley and the rest of the party began relaying their supplies up the Dyea River towards the Chilkoot Pass. Dyea is very close to Skagway, and in modern times is within the limits of the Municipality of the Skagway Borough. The area has a unique climate, sandwiched between the wet, temperate rainforest and the dry Yukon exterior.[12] Drier than other towns in southeast Alaska, it has only 26.1 inches of precipitation annually, but it is known for its winds. The name Skagway derives from the Tlingit word which means "where the water bunches up," referring to the white caps that are common in the Northern Lynn Canal. The weather experienced at different elevations varies dramatically.

The Chilkoot Pass is a small gap in a massive mountain range that divides the Yukon Valley from the north Pacific Ocean. To say that this route is difficult and dangerous is an understatement. The pass itself can only be reached after a 1000-foot climb up a 35-degree slope that is completely encased in ice for most of the year, with avalanches being a threat in the spring.[13] The 26-mile trail is very steep and shoots up about 1000 feet in the last half mile. Joe's party brought tools, equipment, and supplies, including snowshoes and a sled. A typical "year's outfit" weighing nearly a ton had to be carried in heavy 100-pound packs, requiring repeated trips up to the top of the pass. There were no regulations yet about what to take, but in 1887, because they feared mass starvation the Canadian government required miners to take a year's worth of minimum necessities. That load became known as "a ton of goods" because food for a year weighed more than 1000 pounds, and when clothes and equipment were added, the weight was easily doubled.[14]

Chapter 1. The Chilkoot Pass and Fortymile River

Although the rivers had melted enough to be flowing, the temperature of the April air was still hovering near freezing. Each person in the party trudged through the hard currents, crossing and re-crossing the river, carrying heavy loads of gear and supplies, struggling to keep their footing while wading through waist-deep frigid water and fighting against the ice floating around their bodies. In Joe's words, there were "still chunks of ice in water in April 1891 … water to waists, and sometimes above, hard to hold footings. If it had not been for the packs on your back you wouldn't have held footing." The journey required an intense physical connection with nature and there was no respite for the weary or the weak-willed. Many people who made the attempt would hire "packers," usually Alaska Natives, to carry the massive burden that even minimal preparation required. The packs for Joe Quigley's group averaged 80 to 100 pounds each,[15] and the men carried their own packs, discovering that the weight of their load was helping to keep them from being swept away by the rushing ice water. Losing one's footing and falling in the water could be deadly, and hypothermia was a serious risk.

Hypothermia occurs when the body temperature drops to dangerous levels. The symptoms can include hallucinations that cause the victims to do things like abandon a sled with survival gear to go off toward an imaginary warm cabin. People with hypothermia have been known to take off their clothes because of a symptom called "paradoxical undressing," and their bodies are found partly or completely unclothed with abrasions and bruises on the knees, elbows, feet and hands.[16] Hudson Stuck, who traveled extensively in the Far North, wrote that "the strong cold brings fear with it. All devices to exclude it, to conserve the vital heat, seem feeble and futile…. Yet the very power of it, and the dread that accompanies it, give a certain fearful and romantic joy to the conquest of it."[17] Joe Quigley was young and physically fit, and he had an iron will and a decent share of good luck to get him through. He also had the forethought to take precautions against frost and other dangers to ensure his survival.

Much of a Yukon prospector's life was centered on rivers and streams, and extreme weather was a given. The challenge of carrying their belongings across the freezing stream over and over during the beginning of the trip was more than most of the would-be gold miners could take. They began to understand that the arduous journey to the goldfields was only the start and that they would not be able to survive the first winter in the arctic wilderness. They could sense the threat of death and permanent bodily damage looming. It was spring, and they feared the possibility of avalanches, knowing that when a massive slab of snow comes roaring down the mountain at 80 miles an hour, escape is unlikely. Frostbite was a constant threat as well. Freezing tissues could cause a person to lose their fingers, toes, nose, or ears. Each torturous slog through the frigid water and climb up the perilously steep trail made the climbers wonder if it was worth it. Joe said in an interview that by the second day all but four of the men began to turn back, and "we bought what we could of their outfits, though we didn't have much money with us." Years later during the big gold rush, many people on the trail had to turn back and lost all of their belongings.

Many of the people who chose to enter the Klondike through the Chilkoot Pass had sunk all of their hopes and all of their money into the effort. Some had given up their homes and had nowhere to return to, or they had borrowed money to make the trip, having no way to pay the debt if they didn't find gold. For many, finding gold in the Klondike held the promise of an instant change in social status during a time of economic depression and their hopes hung on a successful search for the sought-after treasure. Those whose spirits or bodies could not take the strain would hope to salvage something from the things they'd brought with them and would try to sell their outfits to the people who could continue.

By the time all of the gear and supplies were at the top of the Chilkoot Pass, Joe Quigley, Billy Kaufman, Lew Pierce and Charley Framton were alone. "We couldn't use our sleds or snow shoes, so they were only a liability until we got over the pass, and we had to pack them up the steep trail along with everything else."[18] By Joe's recollection, they had cut some 700 steps into the ice to reach the summit. Several years later, in 1897 during the peak of the big gold rush, the stairs cut into the ice would be called "the Golden Staircase." That sobriquet was memorably illustrated by Eric E. Hegg's iconic 1898 photograph depicting a string of prospectors, tied together by rope, bent over with huge packs on their backs, struggling to reach the top. This image had such impact on the mind of the brilliant comic, actor and filmmaker Charlie Chaplin, that when he made the film *The Gold Rush* nearly 30 years later in 1925, he recreated the scene perfectly. In 1891 when Quigley, Kaufman, Pierce and Frampton were making their climb, the small party was alone, and there were no journalists watching and waiting with cameras.

On May 9, 1891, on his 22nd birthday, Joe Quigley was on the border between the Alaska Territory and Canada, standing at the top of the Chilkoot Pass, looking toward Summit Lake below him, knowing that the frontier was not by any means closed. "We landed on top of Chilkoot Pass May 8, 1891 and found the snow on the sunny side of the hill too soft for travel so we walked back and forth on top of the divide until the night got cool enough to harden up the trail. On my twenty-second birthday, May 9, we started relaying our outfits on the sleds down to Summit Lake that day."[19] He dove into the biggest adventure of his life by sliding all of his worldly belongings down a 3000-foot mountain into a place he'd dreamed of with a spirit of expectation and optimism that would keep him going through years of working in conditions that would test even the hardiest bodies and souls.

Chapter 1. The Chilkoot Pass and Fortymile River

The men had carried tools and nails with them, and now they had to build a boat that could carry them with their equipment and supplies down the river for the next leg of the trip, which involved travel by water. "The next day we went down to the head of Lake Linderman. There we built camp and saw pit, and cut logs, and built 21 feet on bottom, double ender boat, floored so it would carry quite a load. I had had experience with building boats, so we got along fine."[20] Having grown up next to a river, Joe had experience with small boats and that proved to be helpful for the travelers.

They had to cut enough logs to build a boat, then use the whipsaw to cut the logs into planks. A whipsaw had a blade up to 14 feet long and was made to be used by a two-person team. The procedure for whipsawing started with either digging a pit deep enough for one person to be under the log or building a trestle frame tall enough for one of the team to stand under. The second person stood on top of the logs to be cut. The saw blade teeth were angled and sharpened so as to only cut on the downward stroke. On the return stroke the burden of lifting the weight of the saw was shared equally by the two-person team. Joe had some boat building experience, but none of them knew how to whipsaw. This is not a thing that can be easily learned unless the two people on the team have a natural rhythm together, and the group had difficulty with it. They had all been told that two men could saw 250 board measure a day in good timber, but they felt that it was impossible for them. They also didn't know how to file their saw correctly, even though they had files with them.

Through persistence, the four men managed to build a 21-foot-long double-ender, floored boat. A "double-ender" boat has an outboard rudder, as opposed to a "canoe stern" boat that has an inboard rudder. Their shiplap boat was built with overlapping timbers. Grooves were cut into the top and bottom of the boards to fit the panels tightly together to keep out the water. Years later, when the stampede came through, Joe and his friends would be considered "old-timers" or "Sourdoughs"[21] and hordes of new "Cheechakos"[22] would emulate them. In the early years, when Joe's party was building their boat on the shores of Lake Lindeman, there were plenty of natural resources. It was a time of learning and paving their own way. These prospectors in 1891 had no idea that less than six years later the surrounding forest would be stripped of timber from the thousands of stampeders on their way to the goldfields.

Quigley, Kaufman, Pierce and Frampton launched their newly-built boat loaded with their supplies and gear and "ran down the Linderman River."[23] They were lucky to miss the rocks and go on to Lake Bennett without incident. The next leg of the journey from Lake Bennett to Miles Canyon was quite a distance, about 100 miles, but it went smoothly. The party tied up above Miles Canyon and climbed up on the bluff to inspect the canyon and White Horse Rapids, mapping a course they hoped to follow. Joe saw that there was a place in the White Horse Rapids that seemed smoother, and they all agreed to steer for that. The currents were very fast and they stayed right on the crest for miles, then shot through Whitehorse Rapids quickly, then on through the somewhat slower Squaw Rapids. The party made it through Five Finger Rapids and also had what Joe described as "a smooth and pleasant trip" from Squaw Rapids to Fortymile, where they camped on shore along the way.[24]

The Yukon is a massive 2000-mile-long river and the party had successfully traveled close to 600 miles to Fortymile in the boat they constructed on the shores of Lake Bennett. Their planning and attention to detail paid off in a smooth shot through the rapids, but this was not something to be taken for granted. A few years later during the big stampede, there were so many accidents that the North-West Mounted Police began to assign each boat a number and record the names of the passengers to notify the next of kin and identify bodies if the boats capsized. In the first days of the rush down the Yukon River more than 100 boats were torn to pieces in the White Horse Rapids, killing at least ten people. Those who survived the disasters lost most of their supplies and were trapped between the Coast Mountain passes and the unknown territory of the goldfields.[25]

Joe and his companions poled their boat up the Fortymile River to Nugget Gulch on Bonanza Bar. It was often necessary to pull the loaded boat upriver with ropes as they waded. The rivers in the Far North are like highways and the seasons determine the method of travel. After spring breakup, boats were the best method of travel, but once the water was frozen, dog sleds were the preferred method of transportation. The water systems in the area tend to be wide and shallow, and when the water became too shallow to paddle or sail, they would pole the boats. Poling is back-breaking work that requires the person to stand and propel the boat by using a long pole, touching the end of the pole to the river bottom and pushing against the current. It is a different skill than paddling or rowing and requires good balance, but it can extend the range of the boat, reducing the amount of hiking and backpacking necessary.

They knew that there were two basic types of gold deposits: lode deposits and placer deposits. They understood that gold-bearing quartz veins ran through the ground and that erosion loosened gold particles and washed them into the rivers and streams. They were there to do placer mining, to separate the heavy gold particles from the lighter sand and gravel. Lode, or hard rock, mining took more work and capital than any of them had at this time. The simplest way to approach placer mining was to pan for gold. The men would first dip the pan into the stream and bring up a combination of water, sand and gravel, swirl the pan around, letting the water slosh out along with the lighter sand. As the lighter materials leave the pan, the motion causes the heavier minerals, such as gold, to sink to the bottom, ideally leaving gold nuggets at the bottom of the pan.

Chapter 1. The Chilkoot Pass and Fortymile River

A more effective method of placer mining was to use sluice boxes. Since the miners were working on the shores and gravel bars of the creeks and rivers, the power of water could be harnessed to help them separate the gold they found from the dirt and gravel. They would build wooden troughs, called sluice boxes. After they shoveled some sand, gravel and water into the box, a series of riffles in the bottom of the box would agitate the slurry of water and gravel, allowing small particles of the heavier gold to fall out of the solution. This was an efficient way to collect the gold while allowing the waste material to fall out of the end of the box. An alternative to building the long sluice boxes on site was to use a portable unit called a rocker that the miners would carry with them. The rockers were compact, boxy sluices operated by rocking the unit from side to side. This process of rocking the portable sluices, while working on the gravel bars of the creeks, was called "rocking on the bars." Unless they could rock out an ounce a day, they put their rocker in the boat and moved on to the next new bar.

Landing in a place with a name like Nugget Gulch, finally getting to do some prospecting, and finding a little gold must have given them a feeling that they had truly arrived. Nugget Gulch didn't quite live up to its name, but they were still excited to find some gold. Joe reminisced, "Right about then, we found some coarse gold in Nugget Gulch, and then began prospecting the Gulches that ran into the 40-Mile, and all were pretty good. Franklin Gulch, further up was pretty good too. We were on pretty poor ground on Nugget Gulch, and there weren't many nuggets in that spot."[26] Every time they would dip their pans in the water, they hoped to find large quantities of the precious metal that would change their lives. Each time they would bring up just enough to keep their hopes up, and each time they would brush themselves off and start over, hunting for the next big thing. When prospectors came to the Yukon to seek gold, they didn't know how long it would take to strike it rich, or if they ever would. Some inner voice drove them on and gave them the resilience to bounce back from each disappointment.

A practical man who was accustomed to things manifesting in their own time, Joe soon realized that he needed to make a living by more than just prospecting for his own gold. He met some old-timers who had been in the area for a while and he worked for them while learning more about prospecting and mining. He made enough money to buy minimal provisions and supplemented his diet by hunting. In the short time he had been there, he'd learned about which game was the best to hunt. Recounting the experience, he said, "I had enough to go down 40-Mile and buy bacon and beans and tea and rice, and a little ammunition for my .30–40 Winchester ... fine moose meat, plenty of caribou, and if you go back in the mountains plenty of bighorn sheep. Sheep is the best of all, finest kind of meat and no gamey or mutton flavor. Bear is excellent in the right season and away from fish as food. Meat taken up until September 20th is excellent." Game meat was a major part of everyone's diet in the Far North, and to be a knowledgeable hunter could mean the difference between life and starvation. Some sections of the wilderness had very little game, making survival without provisions questionable.

Even though Joe was an experienced hunter, he found that hunting in the Far North was different than in other places he'd lived, and he learned an important lesson early on. Shortly after he came to Fortymile country he'd hunted for several days before he saw a caribou. There was snow on the ground and the temperature was well below zero. It was late in the afternoon and he was a long way from his cabin, so after he killed and dressed the caribou, he rolled it over on its stomach and packed snow around it so the birds couldn't pick at it. Joe left the carcass to come back and get it the next day. When he returned and rolled it over the stench was overwhelming. He realized that he hadn't let the body cool off and having it almost airtight with snow had insulated it, keeping it warm and spoiling the meat. Joe chalked it up as a lesson: "That was another thing I learned not to do!"[27] A survivor, Joe learned not to repeat his mistakes, and he earned a reputation as a superb hunter.

Years later Grant Pearson said of Joe Quigley, "He was one of the best hunters and rifle-shots in the country, and he had a lot of patience. If Joe couldn't get close enough to the game, neither could anyone else. He first spotted his game through his field glasses and would take special notice to determine whether it was in good condition. Then, after watching to find out which way it was headed, he would get the wind direction and plan his approach. When you heard his rifle speak you could bet your money it was a hit and one that wouldn't spoil too much meat." Pearson went on to describe a specific hunting trip when he and Joe spotted a bull caribou. After watching the caribou for some time Joe remarked, "We won't get any closer. I'll take him from here." The caribou was 400 yards away. Joe took a rest across an outcropping of boulders, where he could see only the top of the animal's back. "When that fellow moves it'll be downhill, and we'll lose him," Joe said. "I'll break his back, that won't spoil much meat." Joe shot and the caribou disappeared. Pearson reminisced, "We went over and sure enough his back was broke. Joe surely called his shot!"[28]

Joe continued doing labor for other miners and persisted in searching for his own big payoff. He talked about meeting miners in the area and the work he did: "I rocked on the bars awhile. They were pretty well rocked out, so I found Old Man Adam Malden, on Nugget Gulch and he needed help on handling his boxes so he took me in as partner." This is where he first met Skiff Mitchell who came down to see Old Adam. "Skiff was a big, Skookum fellow then … black mustache and black hair."[29] Skookum is a Chinook word that people in the Far North and the Pacific Northwest often used to describe someone strong, powerful, significant, and impressive. Skiff Mitchell was a California lumberman who had come to the Klondike in 1886. Ten years later, Mitchell bought Discovery Claim #1 on Eldorado Creek from prospector Jay Whipple for a very low price. Mitchell made a fortune from the claim and lived on the proceeds for the next 50 years.[30] Skiff Mitchell was one of the rare lucky ones.

Living and working alone in the snow-covered wilderness presented a multitude of challenges. There were no nearby stores, and even with careful planning and impressive resourcefulness, a trip to get supplies was inevitable. Joe told of a trip trudging through the snow for more than 200 miles to obtain the necessities of life. "After the freeze-up in Fall 1891 I freighted provisions on sled, up the 40-Mile, about forty miles, and then over the divide seventy—eighty miles, then to the headwaters of the 60-Mile River. I traveled alone with a sleigh, necking it. I didn't even have a little dog."[31] Dragging a sled full of goods over rough territory with no roads required strength, stamina and specialized knowledge. Keeping the load balanced so that the sled didn't nose into the snow or become uncontrollable on the downhill slopes was a concern that had to be addressed while fighting the cold, working with as little as four hours of sunlight, and finding the way without the help of modern equipment.

Joe's exceptional ability to walk quickly and tirelessly for long distances was remarked upon by many throughout his life. Covering long distances on foot became essential for the life he had chosen and his hiking skills would serve him well in the future. He was not a complainer and had a tendency to understate things, but Joe must have been wishing for a dog team to help with the work of pulling the heavy sleigh during the long trek. Everything Joe had accomplished and endured up until this point had prepared him for the life of extremes he had taken on, and by the end of his first year in the Far North, he realized that he had what it took to continue on his chosen path. He had already, at age 22, achieved things that very few could, and Joe Quigley was in it for the long haul.

Chapter 2

"Just a small family"

On May 10, 1869, at Promontory Summit, Utah, the wood-burning Central Pacific Jupiter and the coal-burning Union Pacific engine number 119 faced each other on the track. There was a strong breeze blowing as the crowd gathered around to watch the last rail being placed and the last, specially made "golden spike" driven. The event had been delayed for two days on account of the weather, and expectations were high. More than 20 newspapers had at least one reporter there to write their account of the joining of the rails of the first transcontinental railroad across the United States.[1] This connection of the eastern and western United States by rail inspired celebrations nationwide and instilled in millions of people expectations for expansion and hope for a vast bright future.

One day earlier, in rural western Pennsylvania, on May 9, 1869, 49-year-old Robert Orr Quigley and his wife, 45-year-old Mary Graham Oliver Quigley, became the parents of their 13th child, Joseph Buffington Quigley. Perhaps the general air of expectation for a more connected and prosperous future, brought by the much-publicized completion of the transcontinental railroad, foreshadowed the fact that as the boy grew, he would feel compelled to travel across the continent and spend his life prospecting for gold.

Joe Quigley's wry sense of humor is evident in an interview conducted in 1953 when he was 84 years old. Described by the interviewer as "having a merry twinkle," Joe said, "It was just a small family. I had seven brothers and six sisters. I was next to the youngest. I have nieces and nephews older than I am."[2] Joe was the second youngest of Robert and Mary Quigley's 14 children, and by the time he was born into the large family, some of his siblings were old enough to be his parents. Family patriarch Robert came from a well-established Pennsylvania pioneer family whose ancestors arrived in America from Ireland in the 1700s and included men who fought in the Revolutionary War. His wife Mary was also of Irish heritage, and the couple owned a productive farm in Armstrong County, Pennsylvania, providing a good life for their sizable brood.

The Quigley farm was in East Franklin township located on the Allegheny River in Western Pennsylvania, 12 miles upstream from the town of Kittanning and about 45 miles northeast of Pittsburgh. Thirteen years before Joe was born, Robert Quigley purchased 180 acres near the river and created a working farm there. Although western Pennsylvania is not designated by the commonwealth as an official region, it is distinctly different from the eastern part of the state and has maintained its own identity because it is separated from the east by the Appalachian Mountains. The township of East Franklin was made a legal entity 12 years after Robert and Mary established the family farm there. In addition to several branches of the Quigley family, the township population included quite a few other Scots-Irish Presbyterians, and the church was active in the area, with congregations established in 1801 and 1811. Schools had long been important to the community and by 1811 there was at least one log schoolhouse, which taught first through eighth grade. As the area developed, Robert's brother David Cook Quigley was elected to be the school director in 1872 for a two-year term.[3] The Quigley children all attended schools in the area through the eighth grade. For further education they would have to travel away from their community.

Not all of the Quigleys were farmers and settlers. Some inherited the same wanderlust that brought the family to the United States from Ireland and in later generations drew some on a quest for adventure. Robert O. Quigley's brother, Benjamin Cook Quigley, who was born in 1829, went off for the California God Rush of 1849 and never returned. Records show that Benjamin Quigley worked in the grocery business and as a street inspector in San Francisco until his death in 1906. There is no mention of any success as a gold miner, only that he "was a California forty-niner," making him one of 300,000 people who went to California to seek gold.[4] Robert and Mary's children grew up hearing the story of their uncle Benjamin.

By the time Joe Quigley was born in 1869, the tidy little farming community of East Franklin was well established. By 1870, the population for East Franklin township was just under 3000 people. Most of the people were born in the United States, and the immigrants in the area were generally from Ireland, England, or Germany. In 1876, when Joe was seven years old, most of the families in the area made a living through agriculture, but there were a few other occupations listed in the record-books, including ten carpenters, seven merchants, six miners, five teachers, four blacksmiths, a gunsmith, a ferryman, a physician, a shoemaker, a daguerreotypist (photographer), and a wagonmaker.[5] Although it wasn't listed, I am certain that there must have been at least one bootlegger. In 1873 the people of East Franklin township had voted 61 for and 101 against granting licenses to sell intoxicating liquors.[6]

The farm life in the rolling hills of mid–19th-century western Pennsylvania that Joe Quigley was born into was a cooperative process that involved the family and also depended on the community. Neighbors exchanged services, labor, and goods, and everyone knew everyone else. The old cemeteries in the area have the same dozen surnames repeated on the headstones, showing a couple centuries of the same families working together and marrying each other. The community was tight-knit. Farmers kept scrupulous records of what they owed each other and would periodically "settle up" and begin again. Little cash changed hands, even though work and goods were calculated in cash value equivalents. The average Pennsylvania farm family possessed a range of skills that would be unusual and impressive by today's standards. Both adults and children did farm work, and that labor built remarkable physical stamina. Agriculture remained the dominant industry in Pennsylvania through the 1860s, but the industrial revolution was changing things.[7]

Robert and Mary Quigley's children were of the generation that would learn to work on the farm but adapt to new technology, leaving their parents to the business of full-time farming. This time of bridging the old ways and the new ways was the genesis for Joe's skill set. He learned many of the things that would give him an advantage later when he went to the Far North. His grasp of mechanics and construction, and his logging and carpentry skills, including how to build a log cabin and a boat, were especially valuable, while his intellectual curiosity and business sense made it possible to turn those skills into success.

The oldest of the children, Benjamin, was named for the aforementioned "49er"[8] uncle and was born on April 1, 1847. Benjamin left the farm when his brother Joe was only two years old, marrying Hannah Gould in 1871 and working as a house painter in Butler, Pennsylvania. Benjamin was also listed on the 1900 census as a sucker rod manufacturer, working in a factory that made parts for oil drilling machines. Pennsylvania had an oil boom in the 1860s which peaked by the early 1890s. This was a time of economic shift in Pennsylvania, moving from farming to the industrialized harvesting of natural resources.

Also leaving the agricultural life, the second Quigley child, John, who was born in 1848, married Alice Jane Mateer in 1877 and left for Oakmont, Pennsylvania, where he worked as a carpenter. The couple had seven children, which seems like a very large family now, but was only half as large as John's family of origin and reflected the changing times. Children in the previous generation were generally considered an economic asset, but that concept was changing as infant mortality rates lowered and the shifting economy required less help with agricultural work, making children a financial liability. As people's lives became more cosmopolitan, it became impractical to have a large family.

Emmaline Delene Quigley, Joe Quigley's older sister, was born 18 years before Joe, in 1851. Emma lived on the Quigley farm until she married at age

30, when Joe was 12 years old, so she likely had a hand in raising young Joe and was certainly an influence on him. A woman who was not married by the age of 30 was generally considered an old maid, so it may have been a relief to the family to see Emma marry John Fair in 1881. John was 20 years older than Emma and had contracted a serious illness at the age of two that disabled him permanently, causing him to walk with a cane for the rest of his life. Unable to work as a farmer or serve as a soldier, he taught school for 17 years before leaving the area in 1865. He worked as a clerk with mercantile firms in Pennsylvania and New Jersey until 1872 when he moved back home to Pennsylvania and opened his own general mercantile store in Adrian, Pennsylvania.

General stores in rural areas during that time served as meeting places for people to socialize and do business as well as buy supplies. The store was three miles from the Quigley farm, was the only business in Adrian, and also served as the post office. The Quigley family had been patrons of the store for nine years in 1881 when Emma married John, and after their marriage, Emma

Store owners and customers in front of Fair General Mercantile, Armstrong County, Pennsylvania, 1905. Emmaline Quigley Fair is sitting in the doorway, her husband John Fair is sitting at left, and their son Lawrence Homer "Irish" Fair is standing behind him. Three miles from the Quigley farm, the Fair store was also the post office and was the only business in Adrian, Pennsylvania. The Quigley family frequented the store from the time it opened in 1872. When Emmaline Quigley married John Fair in 1881 she became the postmistress for the area (photographer unknown, author's collection).

ran the store with John and was the post mistress.[9] John Fair was elected justice of the peace for two terms in 1880 and 1886.[10] The couple were central to the community and helped establish St. Mark's Lutheran Church in Adrian, Pennsylvania. While John was in his fifties and Emma was in her 30s, the couple had three children. First was James Franklin Fair, and then, in 1885, twins Carrie B. Fair and Lawrence Homer Fair. Family ties were strong in the community and the children were close to both the Fair and Quigley sides of the family, learning traditions from both. Lawrence earned the nickname "Irish" because he was known for dancing the Irish jig. Lawrence had seven children with Cora Henry, and their second-youngest son, my father, Frank Fair, was called "Quig" because of his strong Quigley family resemblance. When they grew up and moved away from the area, Frank and his siblings would refer to visits to see their father in Pennsylvania as "going back to Ireland."

Quigley sisters Pauline, Mary, Martha, Jane, and Rosanna were born in 1849, 1853, 1856, 1859, and 1861, respectively. Martha Quigley never married and was 13 years older than Joe, still living on the family farm, when Joe left in 1884. In 1900, when their mother died, Martha was the only one left living on the farm with their father, Robert. Years later, Joe Quigley named one of his mines "Martha Q" after his sister and gave her a pin made of gold nuggets.

One older sibling who may have played a pivotal role in Joe's life but came to a sad end was James Sharron Quigley, born September 15, 1854, 15 years before Joe. By 1885 James had moved to Ulysses, Nebraska, with his wife Sarah and three of their children, Christopher, Robert, and Emma. A fourth child, Mary, was born in Nebraska in 1886. By 1900 the family had moved from Nebraska to Prairie, Oklahoma, where James was a farmer, and then, four years later, back to western Pennsylvania. It seems likely that James was lured out west by the Homestead Act, wanting to own land and settle in a new territory, but it hadn't worked out the way he planned.[11] After his return to Pennsylvania, James' life took a tragic turn when in 1906, while working for the railroad, an accident caused his arm to be amputated.[12] After that he deteriorated into alcoholism and eventually went to jail for bootlegging in 1912.[13] Sarah left James in 1907, the year after his accident, and they were legally divorced ten years later, in 1917.[14]

Joe's older brother, Robert O. Quigley, was born in 1860 and became a woodworker for an oil well supply company.[15] Oil drilling and coal mining were important parts of the western Pennsylvania economy at the time. Joe stayed in touch with Robert and listed him as his official family contact until Robert's death in 1922. The youngest of the Quigley children, Lee David, was born in 1872 and worked security for the federal government on the Monongahela River locks and dam number 3. Even though they were raised on a farm, the Quigley siblings all adapted to changing times by working in non-agricultural jobs.

Chapter 2. *"Just a small family"*

Seven years older than Joe, his brother William Huston Quigley was born in 1862 and was a well-respected teacher. William taught schools in Armstrong County, Pennsylvania, in the 1920s and 1930s. Among his students were my father Frank Fair and his siblings. William was known by the students as a strong disciplinarian, and my father often told stories about corporal punishment being doled out by his teacher. Frank's education was very similar to that of the Quigleys and Fairs from earlier generations. They all attended a one-room schoolhouse where children in grades one through eight, including siblings of different ages, would be in the same room learning at the same time. The older children would help teach the younger children and much of the learning was done through repetition and memorization. Teaching in this environment required a strict behavioral code to keep order.

During those times people tended to have large families, with the children working on the family farm, and many families could not afford to send all of their children to high school. The life of a rural child included walking long distances each day to get to school or arriving by horse since there was no public transportation. It was common for a child to end his formal education at age 14 and either do farm work for a living or go on to some kind of vocational training or apprenticeship. Even young children worked then. Rural children worked on the family farm and children living in cities or towns worked selling newspapers and food, shining shoes, or laboring in mines or factories.[16] Rural schools had a somewhat shorter school year than urban schools so that the students would be available as farm laborers. The one-room schoolhouses in Armstrong County, Pennsylvania, traditionally closed for the summer in late April.[17]

Older than Joe by four years, Lincoln Johnson Quigley was born in 1865, as the Civil War ended. Their father, Robert Orr Quigley, Sr., signed up for the U.S. Civil War draft registration two years earlier, on July 1, 1863, at age 44. Naming his son after both President Abraham Lincoln and succeeding president Andrew Johnson reflected the Quigley family political leanings. Although the exact year he left Pennsylvania is not known, Lincoln Quigley traveled west and is listed as a registered voter in 1896 in Pasadena, California, where he married Marietta Mulkey, a teacher from Oregon, that same year.[18] Lincoln was a carpenter and by 1910 moved with his wife and two sons, Vernon Orr Quigley and Lloyd Lincoln Quigley, to Jackson, Oregon, and by 1920 to Vancouver, Washington. After moving west, Lincoln (called "Link" or "Abe" by his family) remained close with his brother Joe. Lincoln's wife "Etta" and their children Vernon and Lloyd also stayed in contact with Joe over his years in the Far North.

Chapter 3

"A roving disposition"

When tall, lanky Joe Quigley was 15 years old and had finished school "all the way through McGuffey's readers,"[1] he had to make a choice as to which direction his life would take. He could go off to high school in another town, learn a trade, work on his parents' farm, or he could possibly get a labor job nearby. He felt hemmed in by having a large family in such a sparsely populated place and longed for something more. Naturally restless and adventurous, he was sure that something more exciting and satisfying could be found far away from the familiar confines of Armstrong County, Pennsylvania, and he made the choice to head downriver in an old boat.

Joe left the life of a western Pennsylvania farm boy in 1884, beginning the process of working his way across the continent. Although young people were expected to work either on family farms or at a job, they generally lived with their parents until marriage. The median age for white males to leave home in 1880 was 22.[2] Fifteen was young to be on his own, but it was not unheard of. He had already mastered many survival and work skills because of the place and time where he grew up. Living in a rural area near a river and forests, he knew boating, fishing, and hunting, and he was accustomed to walking long distances. He already knew how to build a log cabin, was a good carpenter, and had experience clearing land and handling timber. Like all children raised on a farm, he had done heavy work since he was young and was physically strong.

Joe didn't offer details that would tell us if his parents approved of his cross-county journey. He simply said, "I was of kind of a roving disposition and fifteen years old when I quit that part of the country and they didn't see me for about forty years."[3] It seems reasonable to think, that when 15-year-old Joe Quigley left Pennsylvania and spent three years in Nebraska, that at least part of that time was with his brother James, although Joe is not listed as part of James Quigley's household in the 1885 Nebraska state census. When Joe recounted the story of his travels, he didn't mention James. He said only that he spent three years in Nebraska as a blacksmith's apprentice.

The lumber industry was booming in the United States due to the de-

Chapter 3. "A roving disposition"

mands of the Industrial Revolution, the flourishing railroad industry, and the settling of the Great Plains where the demand for lumber was far greater than the quantity of trees, so it is not surprising that Joe's first job while on the road was in a lumber yard. Somewhere downriver, between Kittanning and Pittsburgh, he found a place that was hiring. He was already taller than most grown men, "six feet and then some," and he "wasn't sure whether to hire on as a man or a boy."[4] When he came into the lumber yard looking for a job, he gave his name as J. B. Quigley. Joe's father Robert O. Quigley, Sr., had listed him as Buffington on the census and later referred to him as Buffington in his will. It seems that Joe preferred not to use his middle name much after he left home. He generally signed letters "J.B. Quigley" and preferred to be called "Joe" by friends.

Joe was hired in the shipping department for 18 cents an hour to work 11 hours a day, with the admonition from the boss that "if you're no good you don't last very long."[5] He was happy to be making some money, but he quit later. This was the beginning of a seven-year journey from Pennsylvania to the Far North.[6] Joe later found out that the lumberyard owner's name was John B. Quigley, but he unrelated to Joe's family as far as he knew. Joe worried a bit that the man may have thought that he made up the name to get the job. The reality of the situation was that even though Joe was the size of an adult, he was still a naive kid, and even though the lumberyard was away from Joe's hometown, it wasn't far by a well-traveled adult's standards. It's also likely that the owner of the lumberyard was a distant relative, one that Joe wasn't aware of.

Young Joe had ventured out into the world during a time of social unrest. Labor relations were very tense, as business practices and laws did not always match up. At the same time that 15-year-old Joe Quigley was hired to work 11 hours a day for 18 cents an hour (the equivalent of about $4.39 in 2018), the labor movement was in full swing. In 1884, the year Joe left Pennsylvania, the Pittsburgh-based Federation of Organized Trades and Labor Unions in the U.S.A. was calling for an eight-hour workday. One of the forces that influenced the formation of the FOTLU, the Knights of Labor, was an organization looking for cooperation between the owner class and the working class. A few years later, in 1890, Joe Quigley's cousin, William H. Quigley, was active in the Knights of Labor and became the secretary for his local chapter.

Joe was in the Midwest during the time that Chicago was the center of labor unrest, and the air of an uprising for the working man influenced Joe during his teenage years as an itinerant laborer. On a national level, radical labor organizers in the Chicago area had ties to a German language newspaper, *Arbeiter-Zeitung*, which complained of wealthy businessmen living opulently while workers suffered and unemployment rose. Labor organizations around the nation mobilized for "Emancipation Day," and Chicago's

Eight-Hour Association and the Knights of Labor prepared for the largest strike in city history. On May 1, 1886, the national eight-hour strike day, as many as 60,000 workers left their jobs. There was a violent clash between the striking workers and the Chicago police, with police killing several workers.[7]

That clash triggered one of the most significant organized labor events ever a few days later on May 4, when what began as a peaceful pro-worker rally at Haymarket Square became violent. An unknown person threw a bomb at police and the police opened fire. Eight police officers and an unknown number of civilians were killed or injured. The aftermath of the riot set off a "national wave of xenophobia"[8] as police rounded up foreign-born radicals and labor organizers, resulting in a controversial trial in August 1886 and the conviction of eight men. Seven of the men were given death sentences; four of those were hanged.

Joe Quigley's adolescence occurred during a strained and turbulent time in the United States. Because of his sheltered upbringing, he may not have been aware of the level of classism and racial intolerance that permeated the country until after he was on the road. Tension had built during the Reconstruction era after the Civil War, when federal laws protecting the rights of African Americans who had formerly been slaves were put into effect. The laws did not offer genuine equality because of a series of state and local statutes, known as Jim Crow laws, around the country that allowed segregation. The era of segregation continued for another 100 years after the end of the Civil War. Unchallenged acts of racism were common, and an atmosphere of intolerance for immigrants and people of color continued. Joe came from a community of family farms, mostly owned by white families of Irish and German descent, and his family was against slavery, siding with the Union during the Civil War. The bloodiest battle ever fought on American soil, Gettysburg, took place less than 200 miles from his family's farm, but that had happened nearly 20 years before he was born, and young Joe Quigley's mind was on his own adventures.

As he was of Irish extraction Joe was likely aware of past mistreatment of the Irish and possibly subject to some persistent anti–Irish prejudice. It seemed as if each wave of immigrants suffered prejudicial treatment as they tried to assimilate into life in the United States. In the mid–19th century, bigotry against the Irish was at its peak. Centuries of British rule had left Ireland in extreme poverty. Potatoes were easy to grow, highly nutritious, and the only practical crop to grow in the tiny plots of land doled out by wealthy British Protestant landowners. The population was heavily dependent on their potato crops and by 1845 the potato blight had begun, ruining the crops and causing a horrific famine. The massive poverty and starvation caused half of the population of Ireland to die. Many of the surviving population emigrated, giving up their homes in order to survive. By 1852 when the po-

Chapter 3. "A roving disposition" 25

tato blight ended, two million starving Irish had become part of the largest single-population movement of the 19th century (with Germans running a close second) and most of them landed in the United States.

Newcomers to the United States were often treated badly, and this group of Irish were not only poor, but the majority were Catholic, which stirred tensions and anti-papist sentiments. The new Irish immigrants were generally relegated to the most menial jobs for low pay, and some working-class Americans saw the Irish as outsiders who were stealing their jobs. The discrimination against the massive wave of Irish was open and hostile, with job listings including the words "No Irish Need Apply" and ape-like depictions of Irishmen commonly appearing in publications.

By the 1880s and 1890s an influx of immigrants from China and southern and eastern Europe came as the Irish were moving up the social ladder in the United States. Bigots had new groups to fear and hate, and they now felt that since the Irish were from the British Isles, they were more able to assimilate into the American way of life.[9] So by 1884 when Joe Quigley went out on his own traveling the country, the fact that he was a healthy white male probably gave him advantages that outweighed any lingering bigotry against his Irish name and background.

By 1880 there were more than 300,000 Chinese immigrants in the United States with many working as laborers in the mining industry and building the railroads. In 1882, two years before Joe began his travels, the United States Congress passed the Chinese Exclusion Act, which was the first act in U.S. history to restrict a specific ethnic group. Ironically, in 1885 the Statue of Liberty arrived in New York Harbor with her message of acceptance, only a few months before the Rock Spring, Wyoming, mining incident occurred, where 150 white miners brutally attacked Chinese coworkers, killing 28, seriously injuring 15, and forcing several hundred more to leave Rock Springs. The miners at the Union Pacific coal mine had been struggling to unionize and strike for better working conditions for years, but the railroad company thwarted their efforts at every turn. The railroad initially brought the Chinese workers in as strike breakers and the Chinese were not interested in unionizing. This frustrated and angered the white miners who impulsively violently mobbed Rock Spring's Chinatown. Most of the residents of Chinatown tried to escape, abandoning their homes and businesses as they saw the angry mob approaching. Those that didn't escape were brutally beaten and murdered.[10] Joe found that anti–Chinese sentiments were still prevalent as he traveled across the country and when he arrived in the Far North.[11] This was an era of prosperity and adventure for some but a tenuous, precarious time for others.

After quitting the Pennsylvania lumber yard job, Joe floated down the Alleghany River in an old boat to Pittsburgh, then went west, "beating my way on a freight train part of the way."[12] Pittsburgh was about 50 miles down the Allegheny River from the Quigley farm, and life there couldn't have been more different than rural life in Armstrong County. The iron and steel industry developed rapidly after 1830 and Pittsburgh was the hub of that industry. By the 1880s Pittsburgh was a burgeoning urban environment and may have been overwhelming to a 15-year-old farm boy. It is possible that Joe already had something in mind that was not available in Pittsburgh, or perhaps it was a little too close to his origins to satisfy his wanderlust, but he didn't intend to stay. The train yard was close enough to the river for Joe to have gone directly there if that was his intention.

Skulking through the train yard avoiding the railroad guards and looking for an open boxcar door was quite an escapade for a 15-year-old on his own, far from home. Running alongside a moving train and pulling himself up into the open door of a boxcar, Joe hopped the train, heaving a sigh of relief and joy as he headed west. Hopping a train was dangerous and illegal, but a free way to go a long distance fast. There was some chance of violence among the transient population that frequented the boxcars, but a bigger fear was the train yard guards who were known to sometimes beat an illegal rider nearly to death. The practice of train hopping was relatively common after the Civil War, continued to be popular up through the Great Depression of the 1930s, and was part of what it took for Joe Quigley to feel free in 1884.[13]

It seems logical to think Joe intended to go to see his brother James in Nebraska, although it is possible that he just ended up there through the circumstances of his journey. Either way, he did land in Nebraska, where he stayed for three years as an apprentice blacksmith. There were no trade schools at the time, and boys learned to be blacksmiths by working with an experienced smith. Sometimes they had a contract or formal arrangement with a master blacksmith, which, by the late 1800s, when Joe was an apprentice, would have included a small wage.[14] Blacksmiths work with iron and steel by heating the ore in a furnace until, at temperatures higher than 1000 degrees, it becomes soft enough for shaping by hitting it with a hammer or chisel on an anvil. An ancient craft, blacksmithing was a highly marketable skill in the United States during the late 1800s and it was a reasonable trade for a young man to learn. Joe used the skills he learned as an apprentice later but was not ready to settle down in Nebraska and work as a blacksmith, so after three years he left, continuing on his westward trek. He was now 18, disciplined, and still lanky but physically very strong. He was looking forward to seeing what the world had to offer him as a grown man.

During the time that Joe was learning to be a blacksmith in Nebraska and later working at logging camps on the West Coast, westward expansion of the United States was reaching its zenith. Since President Abraham Lincoln had signed the Homestead Act in 1862, citizens had been claiming land west of the Mississippi. There were homesteaders and ranchers throughout

Chapter 3. "A roving disposition" 27

the Midwest and West. South Dakota, North Dakota, Montana, Washington, Idaho and Wyoming all became states. Mining was also drawing people westward. The restless, individualistic prospector types continued on to other areas after the mid–19th-century California Gold Rush. Silver, copper, zinc, lead, and gold called to hopeful fortune seekers, and boomtowns across the western United States grew.

While Joe Quigley had drifted toward the Northwest coastal states, a peak event in the settling of the West, the Oklahoma Land Rush, happened on April 22, 1889. Nineteen days after taking office, President Benjamin Harrison took two million acres of land back from Native American tribes, breaking the agreement between the tribes and the federal government, and put it into the public domain. Joe Quigley's brother James Sharron Quigley seems to have been part of the land rush. James, with his wife and children, left Nebraska about the same time that Joe did, and he then appears in the 1900 United States census as a homeowner and head of household in Prairie, Oklahoma. Joe may have gone to Oklahoma when his brother did, or he may have headed north toward Washington and Oregon.

The American Indian Wars, or First Nations Wars, were still happening during the time that Joe was traveling through the American West. Indians viewed the Oklahoma Land Rush, and other changing policies, as campaigns to take their land, and some sought answers from spiritual guidance. In the winter of 1889, a Paiute man named Wokova brought back a ceremonial dance called the Ghost Dance. The dance was meant to bring about a transformation that would bring about a reunion of the people and the dead in a "world without death, sickness, or old age."[15] Government officials feared that the Ghost Dance ceremonies would incite violence and sent military troops to Pine Ridge, South Dakota. On December 15, 1890, agents tried to arrest Sitting Bull, mistakenly thinking that he was the leader of the Ghost Dance movement. Sitting Bull resisted arrest and he was shot at close range, an event which furthered tensions. Two weeks later, on December 29, 1890, on a hill above Wounded Knee Creek, United States troops massacred hundreds of Native American men, women, and children. Twenty-nine soldiers died. This was one of the last battles between the United States troops and Indians and is considered to be the end of the era.

Manifest Destiny was a widely held 19th-century doctrine that white settlers were destined to expand across North America. It was a controversial philosophy that gave a sense of entitlement to the people who wanted control of the land in the West, and the tensions brought about by it had led to destruction of the Native population. The phrase "Go west young man and grow up with the country" was popularized by Horace Greeley in 1865 to encourage westward expansion. Twenty-five years later, in 1890, the director of the U.S. Census Bureau announced that the frontier was closed because the population density now had more than two people per square mile. This information was used to justify taking an additional six million acres in the Oklahoma panhandle called the Cherokee Strip to open up to settlers in 1893. To venture westward and conquer new territory was now part of the American dream, and although Joe Quigley was acting out of his own internal restlessness rather than any deep-seated belief or cause, he was living that dream. Joe's personal drive was not to dominate people or control vast amounts of land. He was a natural pioneer with a perpetual urge to make new discoveries, and he had a compulsion to explore and investigate and to match himself against what the environment offered.

When Joe made it to the Pacific Northwest, he worked in logging camps "logging by bull teams, felling and bucking timber."[16] A bull team was generally composed of six to eight yoke of oxen and was used to haul logs from the forest to the lumber mill. Lumber production on Puget Sound had a huge surge, starting in 1848, because of the California Gold Rush, and business continued to thrive. Sawmills there provided building materials to San Francisco and other boomtowns, and by the mid–1850s there were more than two dozen mills there, many of them having been built by San Francisco investors. To keep the mills running efficiently, lumber companies often established mill towns where they could be away from the control of the government, competitors, and organized labor. The logging camps were separate from the mill towns and were fairly primitive. There was usually a camp consisting of utilitarian bunkhouses and mess halls. A main building was divided into two rooms, one for sleeping and one for cooking. The life in camp was simple and most of the workers were single men.[17] Living the tough logging camp life from the ages of 18 to 21 was preparing Joe for a much more challenging and exciting future.

During his stint in the logging industry, Joe worked as both a feller and a bucker. Fellers worked in pairs and cut the trees by hand, using axes and crosscut saws. The feller must work in a way that ensures the trees fall in the proper direction to prevent breakage and land in the correct position for being hauled. Once the trees were felled, buckers stripped the bark from the logs and sawed them into suitable lengths. Other workers would place the logs onto oiled skids and haul them to the main skid road, where they would be dragged by bull teams of oxen to the mill. By 1890, when Joe was in the logging industry, bull team logging was being replaced by new technologies that used engines to haul the logs, but Joe was hired to do it the old-fashioned way, with oxen.

Working as a logger was not a life that Joe Quigley could be content with. Some of the other hardy, restless men that Joe met in the logging camp had allowed their wanderlust to draw them north, and Joe felt a kinship with those individuals. He had been saving his money "all along the way" during

Chapter 3. "A roving disposition"

the time since he left his parents' farm, and when he "heard about Alaska from fellows working in logging camps who had been up and into the interior,"[18] he focused his energy on getting to the Far North to see what he could find.

In 1880, bedrock gold had been discovered, and Juneau, Alaska, was formed. Each year, from 1880 onward, prospectors tended to show up in Juneau in twos and threes with minimal equipment and big dreams.[19] In 1891 when Joe decided he would throw in his lot and head for the Far North, the chaos of the 1896 stampede was still years away. Decades later, a *Pittsburgh Press* article quoted Joe's brother William Quigley as saying, "Joe left his home near Kittanning, PA, when a young man, his mind filled with stories of Alaska and gold."[20] William was seven years older than Joe and could remember the time when Joe left home to head west, but according to Joe himself, his true motivation for leaving was simply "a roving disposition."[21] Joe spent seven years working his way across the United States before heading north to Alaska, so perhaps looking for gold was just an excuse, or validation, an easy-to-explain reason for his wanderlust.

Things had changed a great deal since Joe Quigley left home seven years earlier. He was beginning a new phase of his life and leaving not just easy access to family but the familiar culture of his homeland. The years between 1884 and 1891 while he was making his way across the continent were an exciting time for a young man in the United States to be alive. The year that Joe left the family farm, the first post-season games in baseball were held between the National League champions and the American Association champions, the capstone was positioned on the Washington Monument, and a new president, Grover Cleveland, was elected. As Joe moved west, Edison completed the prototype for the commercial phonograph and began working on the first motion picture camera, the rotary dial for use on telephones was invented by Almon Brown Strowger, and Nicola Tesla invented the Tesla coil. But no matter how marvelous new inventions were, nature was still more powerful and awe inspiring. In 1887 the deadliest flood in American history happened, killing 2,209 people in Johnstown, Pennsylvania, about 50 miles from the home that Joe Quigley had left a few years earlier. Joe was getting ready to let go of the last vestiges of connection to the people and places that he had known and face natural forces that no human could control.

Both men and women went to Alaska for more than riches; they wanted freedom from the structures and rules that bound them in their current lives. They were willing to brave the elements to gain an opportunity to change their lives completely. Some were running away from debt, bad relationships, or the law. All of them were running to something, and that something was a feeling of freedom to be an individual of their own invention. On a practical level it was easier for a single man to uproot his life and start over than it was for a family or a single woman. Consequentially, the influx of non-indigenous people into Alaska included more single men than women or families. It was a physically arduous and expensive endeavor to go to the Far North, but Joe had his hard-earned savings and no emotional ties holding him back. He was 21 years old, at his physical peak and ready to prove that he could handle whatever came his way.

CHAPTER 4

The Last Frontier

In 1891 when Joe Quigley went to Alaska, being able to do what it takes to survive was a matter of life and death on a daily basis. Alaska was known as a world of glaciers, sea life, rivers teeming with fish, beautiful forests and mountains abundant with wildlife, bitter cold, and vast snowy landscapes. The immense Yukon River and its tributaries spread through the mountain ranges of Alaska and Canada's Yukon Territory creating a beautiful yet hostile environment where a person could prove their strength and stamina. This environment was immensely attractive to adventurers and fortune seekers throughout history.

The Far North had always offered valuable natural resources, including precious metals, and those natural resources sustained the indigenous people of Alaska for more than 15,000 years. Alaska's Native people are divided into 11 distinct cultures, speaking 11 different languages and 22 different dialects.[1] The word Alaska is derived from the Aleut word Alaxsxaq or Alyeska, meaning "mainland."[2] Before the Europeans came, some of these groups were enemies and there were wars, but there was also trade and intermarriage between the different cultures. Each group had control of its own culture. Things changed when the Europeans came to Alaska because the European interest was in taking control of the land rather than assimilating into the culture that was already there. Colonialism included some cases of enslavement of Alaska Native, and generations of exploitation. The European interest disempowered the indigenous people of Alaska by undermining the Alaska Native culture.

The indigenous people of Alaska began losing control of their own culture in 1741 when Russian explorers commanded by Danish explorer Vitus Bering and German naturalist Georg Wilhelm Steller appeared on Bird Island in the Shumagin Islands. Russian fur traders soon came in, decimating the sea otter population. The Europeans also brought Old World diseases such as smallpox, to which the indigenous people had no immunity, killing about 80 percent of their population.[3] Directly after the fur traders came the missionaries. Although some missionaries and educators worked respectfully with and on behalf of Native communities and cultures, others believed that the success of their efforts depended on the destruction of traditional ways. Ultimately, the missionaries were responsible for thousands of Alaska Native children being exported from their villages to boarding or mission schools far away from home. The price of a Western education included severance from family and culture and punishment for speaking their own languages or honoring their cultural traditions.[4]

European interest in Alaska came from several sources. There were Spanish claims, dating as far back as the 15th century, to the late 18th century, with various naval expeditions to explore the area and claim it for Spain. Spanish explorers visited Russian settlements and Unalaska (the largest city of the Aleutian Islands), but there was no Spanish colonization.[5] King Charles II of England gave exclusive trading rights over the entire Hudson Bay drainage basin to "the Governor and Company of Adventurers of England trading into Hudson Bay" through a royal charter in 1670, but their operations were limited to a few forts and posts around the shores of the James and Hudson bays.[6] The British became interested in expanding into Alaska when, during his final voyage of exploration in 1778, British captain James Cook sailed along the West Coast of North America from California to the Bering Strait and discovered what came to be known as Cook Inlet. This exploration encouraged the British, and by 1845 the Hudson's Bay Company had a post at Fort Yukon.[7]

In 1865 the Russian-American Telegraph was an undertaking by the American-owned Western Union Telegraph Company to lay an electric telegraph line from San Francisco to Moscow. The project was abandoned in 1867, but the exploration brought detailed reports of Alaska's vast resources, and that information was used by Senator Charles Sumner to help convince the United States Congress to appropriate money for the purchase of Alaska.[8] U.S. Secretary of State William H. Seward signed a treaty with Russia for the purchase of Alaska for $7 million on March 30, 1867.

More than a century later, Alaska Natives are still recovering from the impact. On the occasion of the Smithsonian 150-year cession celebration, Alaska Native political activist William L. Iggiagruk Hensley described the situation: "It is with mixed emotions that I stand here to discuss the transaction that took place between Russia and the United States 150 years ago, in the time of my great grandfather. I am virtually certain that he was totally unaware of this event that was to have such a profound effect on the future of our people and that of all the other cultures that occupied virtually all of the 586,400 square miles of what is now called Alaska."[9] Edouard de Stoeckl for the Russians and President Andrew Johnson for the United States signed their names for the purchase of the land of Alaska, which was already occupied by people who were oblivious to the impending invasion.[10]

Chapter 4. The Last Frontier

The exchange of control over Alaska was controversial. Despite the price of two cents an acre, the Alaskan purchase was ridiculed in Congress and in the press as "Seward's folly" and President Andrew Johnson's "polar bear garden."[11] For a territory of the United States to be granted statehood, it has to be proved that the area has a large enough resident population and a way to sustain itself economically.[12] The discovery of gold in the Yukon Territory during the late 19th century inspired tens of thousands of people to come to Alaska, bringing about a boom in mining, fishing and trapping. There was also knowledge of oil in Alaska from at least as far back as 1836, when geologist Alfred Hulse Brooks made a report confirming that Hudson's Bay Company officer Thomas Simpson's observations of seepages at Cape Simpson were oil.[13] So although there were skeptics, the potential economic viability of Alaska was proven. In 1946 Alaskans voted in favor of statehood in a referendum and Alaskan delegates began to lobby Congress for statehood.[14] Alaska was granted statehood by a proclamation signed by President Dwight D. Eisenhower on January 3, 1959.

Over a period of about 200 years, Alaska went from being the home of about 100,000 indigenous people, with a relatively small number of Russian inhabitants, to approximately 50,000 indigenous people out of a total population of 229,000, at the time of cession. By 2010, Alaska's total population was more than 700,000, with less than 15 percent of the citizens being American Indian or Alaska Native.

Born two years after the United States purchase of Alaska, and dying just a few months before statehood was granted, Joe Quigley spent his entire life in Alaska between the time the United States gained control of it and the time it became a state. To a great extent, Alaska defined Joe Quigley's life, and Joe held a unique place during a pivotal time in Alaska's development and history. One of the few prospectors to arrive in the Far North before the gold rush of 1896, he came into the area as a 21-year-old Cheechako. He developed his survival skills and attitudes about partnerships and community in one of the harshest environments in the world during his years in Fortymile country. By the time he led the rush to Kantishna in his mid–30s, Joe was a Sourdough who shared his knowledge and taught his skills to others. When he retired to Seattle at age 69, he was an old-timer and still considered Alaska his true home.

Joe Quigley seemed to enjoy the idea that Alaska was its own place, separate from "the States," and that his home in Kantishna was completely unique. He liked to sign his letters "J. B. Quigley, Kantishna, Alaska."[15] Joe invested blood, sweat and tears into Alaska, and Kantishna was Joe Quigley's place in the world. When he and Jack Horn arrived in the area in 1905, they expected to find their fortune there, brought their friends to live and work in the area, and created the Kantishna Mining District. Joe married there, lived off the land there for more than 30 years, and nearly died there. Some of the Kantishna land features are named after Joe Quigley, and some have names that he gave them. Joe knew the foothills of North America's tallest mountain intimately and any complete account of Denali National Park or Kantishna mining history includes Joe Quigley's name.

Chapter 5

Rocking on the Bars

From the winter of 1891–1892 until the spring of 1893 Joe lived a solitary life in the wilderness of the Far North. Every prospector in Canada had to buy a mining certificate to work. Joe had his certificate and was working a couple of claims on Glacier Creek, which is a tributary of the 60-Mile River. He also built a log cabin, sawed lumber for sluice boxes and made himself "comfortable for winter."[1] Joe was an excellent carpenter and capable of building a log cabin by himself, first by chopping down enough trees of similar size, and then by preparing the ground where the cabin would sit. He would notch the logs to fit together, and after the basic room was built by stacking logs, the door and windows were cut out, and the gaps between the logs were filled with mud and moss. The essentials were a roof that didn't leak, a heat source for warmth and cooking, and something to sleep on. The typical miner's cabin was a very simple, small one-room structure with a stove and a metal chimney.

Joe was a subsistence hunter, not a sport hunter. He often went out into the wilderness without a rifle and sometimes found himself in trouble because of it. One day he was out prospecting and had an experience with a couple of bears that he never forgot. Joe had packed his lunch and headed over to the McKinley River to do some prospecting. He stopped to "eat lunch, build a fire, and boil the billy for some tea."[2] Boil the billy was a phrase of English or Scottish origins that Joe used to describe boiling water for tea. A billycan is a lightweight cooking pot or bucket, used for cooking over a campfire. As he was eating, he noticed two large bears. Alaska has several types of bears and these two were extremely large brown grizzly bears. Grizzlies are terrifying creatures, between eight and ten feet long, up to four feet tall at the shoulder, and they can weigh more than 1000 pounds. Each claw on their paws is the length of an adult human finger, and their teeth can be three inches long. Standing on their hind legs, some bears are more than ten feet tall and can eat 100 pounds of food a day. Bears can have a sense of smell seven times more acute than a bloodhound, and one paw swipe can kill an animal as large as a moose.

At that time, Joe didn't carry a rifle when prospecting. He ignored the bears because he thought "they wouldn't bother me unless I bothered them; those big bears are as hard to stalk as deer. They don't hunt you."[3] As he was eating his lunch, Joe heard something behind him and turned to look. To his surprise, the two bears were coming right for him at a "near-trot" and were suddenly only about 100 feet away. Joe was defenseless and did the only thing he could do; he climbed the closest tree, leaving his pack on the ground. Once he got in the tree, he realized that it had a "rotten heart" and was too weak to hold the limbs with his weight on them. At the height of about ten feet, he stopped for fear of breaking the limbs and falling to the ground.

The bears circled the tree, pausing now and then to look up at Joe with what seemed to him to be "a calculating and hungry look." They mauled his pack at the foot of the tree while Joe stayed above watching. Eventually the bears walked off about 100 feet, then looked back and returned to circle the tree a few more times. They eventually lost interest in Joe and walked off for good. He watched them from his precarious perch, and when they were completely out of sight, he climbed down from the tree, "took off across the hills," and made it a policy to take a rifle with him after that. Even with all his years of experience with wildlife, this incident with the bears made such a deep impression on Joe that he remembered it for the rest of his life and recounted it in an interview with Hazel Lindberg when he was 84 years old.

Pre-stampede era food for prospectors was very unreliable. Being a good hunter helped immensely, but there were necessary basics that weren't always available. When staple foods were available, they were usually low quality. One account said that the flour was moldy, the rice lumpy, the fruit green, the beans full of rocks, and the bacon came in yard-long slabs and was all yellow.[4] Poor diet with a lack of fresh vegetables meant that many miners became ill. Scurvy and tuberculosis were the worst of the diseases but miners also suffered from respiratory ailments and intestinal infections that were sometimes deadly. Joe knew that he had to cache enough food and fuel to stay warm and fed for the winter while he continued the work of being a miner.

Remembering that time as not very rewarding, making just enough to get by, Joe said, "I sunk some holes to bedrock and found enough to justify opening up the ground and putting in drains. Stayed there a couple of years, finding different places to work, but it was just what you'd call grub-stake ground, and not very rich."[5] Joe and many other miners took their quest for gold beyond panning in the creeks. The classic image of placer mining is of a miner squatting down at the edge of a creek, holding a pan with some sand and water in it. Placer mining is the process of separating heavily eroded minerals like gold from sand or gravel, and one of the attractions of the method is that no heavy machinery or complicated equipment is necessary. Theoretically, a prospector could make $1 million with just a pan and the patience to do the slow, arduous work.

Chapter 5. Rocking on the Bars

Although the basics were relatively simple, the work involved in keeping a claim was more difficult than most would-be prospectors anticipated. There were early guidebooks and details of Canadian mining law published in newspapers as far away as San Francisco, and most of the hopeful prospectors were likely to have read and thought about what they would do when they arrived in the goldfields. To stake a claim, the prospector had to mark each of the four corners of the area, usually done with cut stakes from a nearby tree. Identifying information was written and attached to the stake and traditionally covered with a tin can. Each prospector had to possess a miner's certificate and was allowed to stake one claim in any given mining district. Although the laws were modified later to suit conditions, a claim ran 500 feet along the creek and "from rim to rim."[6] The creek claims were given a number based on the first claim made on the creek, which was called "discovery claim," referred to as above (upstream) or below (downstream) discovery claim. After the creek claims had all been staked, people took chances on bench claims, which were on the hillsides parallel to the creeks. In order to keep any claim, the prospector had to do assessment work, which involved development to show the value of the claim. If the assessment work wasn't done by the end of the year, the ground was again available for staking. This requirement caused many people to lose their claims.

Joe had been working at prospecting and mining for more than a year, and he knew that his chances for success were much better if he did more than swirl the water, gravel and sand around, spilling out the water to leave gold nuggets in the bottom of the pan. The process most often used was to work with the pan to test the surface, then use a pick and shovel to dig holes to a point just above bedrock, where placer gold tends to collect. Once they hit bedrock, the miners would dig a horizontal tunnel to follow the richest ground. This procedure is called drift mining, with the horizontal tunnel called the drift. The digging was usually done in the winter so that the frozen ground would not cave in on the miners. They couldn't dig the hard-frozen ground, so they would build fires to melt the ice, then dig with a pick and shovel, drawing the earth, gravel, and gold up from the hole in a bucket and dumping it in a pile on the ground. In spring and summer, a defrosting pile of gold-laced gravel, called pay dirt, could be processed with water.

In the spring of 1893, Jerry Baker, "an old fellow up there"[7] (Baker was about 50 years old at the time), proposed that they go to the newly-discovered Circle Diggings on Birch Creek. They used the same boat that Joe's party had built in 1891 to get to Circle City. Once on shore, they hiked the trail for 60 miles to the Birch Creek, which is a tributary of the Tanana River. The Tanana is a nearly-600-mile-long tributary of the Yukon River that emerges into the Tanana Valley, a lowland marsh region. The attitudes of the miners at Birch Creek was quite different than at Fortymile. There was an altruism prominent at Fortymile that stayed with Joe Quigley for the rest of his days, but the Birch Creek area prospectors were different. There was very little hospitality or friendliness and the overall mood was gloomy.[8]

Quigley and Baker were on foot, with all of their worldly possessions on their backs, and they continued searching for the right place to dig. They looked the country over and "found it all staked."[9] Baker concluded that the area was not worth working on and, at one point, broke out laughing. Joe wondered what was funny and Baker explained, "It just strikes me as funny. Here's a couple of guys with picks and shovels and without money to buy a meal, starting out to look for a million dollar mine."[10] It was one of those moments when they laughed to ward off doubt and fear.

Joe continued to work for other miners in the area for wages, and he also hunted moose for the rest of his living, selling the meat to market in Circle City for 75 cents a pound. He had developed an efficient method to get the job done in a day. "I took a Peterborough canoe and could shoot and bring in a moose a day.[11] I'd bring them in when I thought that they were about out of meat. I'd dress and quarter the animal and pack it to the canoe and take it in to Circle." This was more difficult than Joe made it sound. An individual Alaskan moose can weigh well over 1000 pounds and provide up to 600 pounds of meat. Moose have very acute senses of smell, hearing, and eyesight to spot predators, so floating quietly down the river in a canoe was a good way to hunt them. Joe could almost soundlessly glide around a bend, see a bull moose eating willows on a gravel bar or walking on a riverside trail, and have the canoe ready to transport the meat right where he shot and quartered the animal.

As more people came to Alaska to find gold, food shortages made starvation a looming concern. Big game fed many people, the demand for meat was high, and hunting for market was a profitable way to fill the stomachs of the ever-increasing population. Game could also be used in trade for other food. By the time the gold rush was in full swing, staples were so scarce that hunters had to trade an entire mountain sheep for a sack of flour.[12] As the population increased, market hunting became a conservation problem, but at this time there was plenty of game.

The way of life for prospectors in the Fortymile area was described as "a community of hermits whose one common bond was their mutual isolation…. They were nomads all, stirred by an uncontrollable wanderlust." These nomad gold seekers were "men whose natures craved the widest possible freedom of action; yet each was disciplined by a code of comradeship whose unwritten rules were strict as any law."[13] Each individual accepted the eccentricities of the others, and each lived in a "murky, airless cabin whose windowpanes were made from un-tanned deer hide, white cotton canvas or a row of empty pickle jars chinked with moss." Their cutlery was made from pieces of tin and their furniture from tree stumps.

Chapter 5. Rocking on the Bars

Joe Quigley was well suited to life in the wilderness. He was able to endure the isolation, strong and skilled enough to stay alive, and he had a deep appreciation for nature. Later, when Joe was a middle-aged man, looking back to the early days along the Fortymile River before the big gold stampede, he said, "Most of the men who were in that country have long since passed on. There were not many, but I think they were the finest group of men who ever got together in one community. Our neighbors were few and we were scattered over a large country, especially during the mining season. But tough as things were at the time, I think we all enjoyed it. Always looking for a million-dollar mine, and never showing disappointment when we didn't find it."[14] As an old man, in his 80s, he remembered these times and the people he met as some of the best of his life.

Intently focused on his prospecting and mining work, Joe still found time for a little diversion and leisure. If there was something entertaining going on while he was in town registering a claim or buying supplies, he would take it in. There were two towns in the area, Fortymile City and Circle City, and he spent time in both. Fortymile City was a small frontier settlement located at the junction of the Fortymile and Yukon rivers in Canadian territory and was a supply and launch point for prospectors who had worked their way into Alaska and up the Fortymile River.

The firm of McQuesten, Harper and Mayo established a trading post/store at Fortymile in 1887.[15] McQuesten was a very important figure in the Far North and had several nicknames including "Father of the Yukon" and "Yukon Jack" from earlier days when he founded Fort Reliance. McQuesten, François Mercier, and Francis Barnfield founded the fort in 1874 for the Alaska Commercial Company to serve as a trading post. Fort Reliance was located on the east bank of the Yukon River, about eight miles downstream of Dawson City, and it was a major landmark for traders. The Fortymile River, Sixtymile River, and Seventymile River were named for their distance from Fort Reliance.[16]

Credit at McQuesten, Harper and Mayo's store was unlimited, and a prospector could continue looking for gold even when destitute. Everything not on credit was paid for in gold dust. With no formal law enforcement, Fortymile residents lived in what one writer described as a "curious mixture of communism and anarchy."[17] The settlement was in Canadian territory but was more of an American town, getting supplies from the United States without customs payments and sending mail out with United States postage stamps.

Circle City sprang up to fill the needs of the Birch Creek prospectors. Most of these men were grubstaked by long-time Yukon River trader and Alaska Commercial Company agent Leroy "Jack" McQuesten, of McQuesten, Harper and Mayo, who began to build a two-story log store and warehouse as soon as he realized the area's potential. McQuesten had backing from

The McQuesten and Co. building and some of the citizens of Circle City, Alaska, circa 1895. Many of the residents of the mining town are present in this photograph. Leroy Napoleon "Jack" McQuesten is in the front row, second from left. The mining company's office is also the post office, and the building at the far right of the photograph is a restaurant. Joe Quigley was in the Circle City area at the time but does not appear in the photograph (photographer unknown. Charles E. Bunell Collection 1895UAF-1958-1026-766 Archives University of Alaska, Fairbanks).

trader John Healy, who brought in Chicago investors Jack and Michael Cudahy and Portus Weare. This group formed the North American Transportation and Trading Company with headquarters on the Circle City riverfront. McQuesten was known as a likeable man who got many miners started on their quest by offering a grubstake for a percentage of their strike.

The population of Circle quickly rose to 700 and there was commerce, with steamboats stopping at the town regularly. The land itself was swampy and known for its mosquitoes. Circle was a drab town and not a place for families or the civic life. There were no taxes, courthouse, post office, church, schools or hotel. There was no doctor, lawyer or priest, and the law used was the "Miner's Code" which allowed a group of miners to decide punishments for wrongdoers. Concepts of right and wrong were not based on rules, but on the moral compass of each individual.[18]

Food, supplies and cabins were left unlocked and mines were bought and sold with verbal contracts.[19] Theft was an extremely serious offense. When one man stole from a cache, his fellow miners sentenced him to hang. When no one could be found to do the hanging, the sentence was changed to expulsion from the community, with the offender ordered to live by himself

Chapter 5. Rocking on the Bars

12 miles out of town until the annual steamboat arrived. The miners took up a collection, bought him the bare necessities for survival, said good-bye and never saw or spoke to him again.[20] Personal, less serious offenses between people resulted in long feuds. It was not common to hear open quarreling, but intense hatreds developed between people who had been spending too many long nights in close quarters. Bitter feuds would end with the parties not speaking to each other or dividing all jointly owned possessions and moving elsewhere.

Debts and expenditures in these towns were usually settled with gold dust rather than cash, and miners were known for their wild spending habits. They were also known for letting off steam and being destructive, going on "sprees" from saloon to saloon, drinking excessively, buying booze and cigars for everyone in the place, and playing drunken games like throwing cordwood at each other across a room. When the spree was over, the man who started it would hand his poke of gold dust to the saloonkeeper and ask him to take the damages out of it.[21] Luckily, whether by family training, hard experience, or his inborn sense of self-preservation, Joe Quigley was not a particularly extravagant spender. He saved his money and invested it in his own business, having an eye for the long term and the big picture.

In addition to the wild antics of the miners, there were more organized forms of entertainment. Saloons had a bar, a gaming room, a dance hall, and stage entertainment. The bars and gambling would run 24 hours a day except Sundays. The dance hall would run from eight in the evening until early the next morning. The actual dancing didn't start until after midnight, with the stage dramas and vaudeville being presented first. John and Carrie Mulligan were entrepreneurial entertainers, producing vaudeville and burlesque that included satire based on suggestions from the audience.[22] There were singers and musicians like tenor Wilson Mizner or the Rag Time Kid from Chicago, and there were also actors who would perform serious dramas and plays of the day.

Dance hall girls were a part of the entertainment and there were two distinct types. The onstage performers would wear revealing costumes and then would change into fashionable gowns after the show to sell drinks. The other type of dance hall girls were women in normal Victorian era dress on the dance floor, dancing with miners who would clomp around in their hats and high boots for a dollar a dance. The women got a salary and also got to keep a percentage on the drinks they sold. Prostitution was separate from the entertainment business, and although it was tolerated, it was not condoned. The Royal Canadian Mounted Police regulated prostitution and tried to maintain control of the spread of disease. Lives of both prostitutes and dance hall girls have been portrayed as colorful, wild and fun-loving, but the reality of their lives was often sad or tragic.[23]

One of Joe Quigley's fond memories of the early days was of seeing "the Snow family and their entertainments, in both Circle and Fortymile."[24] George Thornton Snow and his wife Anna had been performers traveling through the gold camps of California. After the couple had children, they became a family troupe and went to Alaska to entertain the miners there. The Snow Family became one of the most well-known acts in the Far North. George, Anna, and their two children, Crystal Brilliant and Montgomery, had crossed the Chilkoot in 1894, dragging a three-octave organ with them. The family was its own production crew, touring the boom towns and mining camps, with Anna making the costumes, and all four of the Snows performing songs, dances and jokes. When George would go off prospecting, Anna and the children would entertain the miners. Beginning at ages three and five, the children would sing for the miners who would throw gold nuggets in appreciation.[25]

George Snow opened an opera house in Fortymile City, bringing legitimate theater to the Far North. The opera house also served as the meeting place where a group of men including George Snow started the fraternal organization the Yukon Order of Pioneers on December 1, 1894. There were 68 men present who signed the charter and Jack McQuesten became the first president of the organization. The group was formed as protection for the early miners, with the motto "Do Unto Others as You Would be Done by."[26] At the time, a man was required to have been in the Far North for ten years to be allowed to join. An initiation fee, password, and good moral conduct were required, and each member promised to help every other member if the need arose and to always spread the news of a fresh gold discovery. Although he was in the area when it started, Joe hadn't fulfilled the residency requirement and so could not be a charter member. He joined the group later, when the residency requirement changed and he had been in the area a few years longer. Joe took his pledge seriously and believed in the values that the organization espoused. He maintained friendships with other YOOP members for the rest of his life.

Chapter 6

Eldorado

Joe Quigley and Jerry Baker poled their boat up a few creeks and went trapping, each in separate areas, exploring the rolling, wooded hills. They caught beaver, mink, marten and ermine. The prices they could get made it a minimally profitable enterprise, but their main focus was on prospecting, and they continued working in this area until 1897. The creeks they were prospecting were all tributaries of the clear-running Klondike River, which is a major tributary of the muddy Yukon River.

In the meantime, the great Klondike stampede was beginning. There had always been an emphasis on the distinction between the new, naïve Cheechakos and the experienced, respected Sourdoughs and the old-timers who had been prospecting in the Far North for many years. At this point, Joe considered himself a Sourdough, even though he was only 27 years old. The great Klondike stampede brought an estimated 100,000 prospectors to the Klondike region and a large percentage of them were ignorant of what it took to survive or succeed in the Far North. This huge influx of Cheechakos made the Sourdoughs especially skeptical of rumors about the next big strike.

The first prospectors to stake the Klondike were old-timers, though, and an important figure in the stampede was Californian George Carmack, also known as "Lyin' George" (for his exaggerated claims). Carmack moved to Alaska in 1885, marrying a Tagish First Nation woman in 1887. Carmack was not popular with the other miners. Joe Quigley remembered meeting Carmack. "Summer 1896 George Carmack came down to 40-Mile to record his strike on Rabbit Creek [later called Bonanza] and boast of the fabulous gold he had seen, but the old-time experienced miners, myself included, didn't take much stock in his extravagant claims. Some of the Cheechakos went up to the Klondike, but we kept on as usual."[1] Carmack was originally credited with registering Discovery Claim, the discovery of gold that set off the Klondike Gold Rush. Historians now tend give credit for Discovery Claim to Carmack's brother-in-law, Tagish Native Skookum Jim Mason, and most recently Jim's sister (Carmack's wife) Shaaw Tlaa (Kate Carmack) has been given credit by some.

Although he was resistant at first, the stories of the Klondike strikes kept making their way to Joe, and in early 1897 he and Jerry Baker went over the ice up the Yukon River "and found everything staked."[2] At this time they each found another partner. Baker got in with a partner who had some good property, and Joe met another partner, Thomas Cook, who declared Joe in with him.

Joe and his new partner, Cook, "sunk holes on #35, in the [Eldorado] creek bed proper, thawing with good fires."[3] Because the ground was frozen, the miners used fires to make it possible to dig in the winter. The cold air would sink down the shaft keeping the ground frozen, making it unnecessary to build support for the shaft. The work with Cook paid off when they sold the claim in the winter of 1897 for $10,000 each (equivalent to about $285,000 each in 2018). Joe recollected the windfall: "My first real money after six years at hard labor in the North. Tom Cook took his $10,000.00 and went Outside, as his health was failing … made his last remaining three years comfortable."[4] Many of the prospectors planned to make a fortune and then move back to the States, and some did just that. Others, including Joe Quigley, felt they could do better and weren't finished seeking adventure.

Eldorado was originally called "Bonanza's Pup." Pup was a miner's term

Map of the Alaskan goldfields, adapted from one drawn in 1897, during the Klondike gold rush, six years after Joe Quigley went to the area to prospect for gold. Thousands of prospectors left their former lives to work in the gold fields, hoping for a sudden change of fortune (map by the author).

for the small tributaries that branched off of the streams. The name was changed to Eldorado after the Spanish term El Dorado, used to describe a mythical tribal chief who covered himself in gold dust. It was said that almost every claim on Eldorado, from number one to number 40, was worth at least half a million, some worth three times that amount.[5] Number 35 did make quite a bit of money for Joe Quigley and Thomas Cook, but their claim was on the creek and the richest part was above the water, up on the benches. In mining, the benches are the higher slopes above the narrow valley created by the stream and require different mining methods.

Boom towns were born and died based on rumors of the next big strike. The success of the Eldorado claims led to the big stampede, which led to the establishment of Dawson City. Dawson was named for Canadian government geologist George Mercer Dawson and was the heart of the Klondike Gold Rush. As it was Canadian, there was law in Dawson, with the North-West Mounted Police and courts of justice. Fortymile City was technically Canadian too but was a border town run primarily by American miners who held their meetings in the saloon. By 1897 the population in Dawson was more than 1000 and by 1898 had grown to more than 30,000. The town came to be known as "the Paris of the North" and was the largest city west of Winnipeg and north of Seattle. Instant millionaires looked for ways to spend their new-found wealth in Dawson and there were plenty of ways for them to do it. The best food, drink and clothing was available at exorbitant prices. Dance and gambling halls, bars, brothels, restaurants and supply stores all made fortunes "mining the miner." From 1896 to 1899, $29 million in gold was pulled from the ground around Dawson City. In 1899 the rush to Nome happened and much of the population of Dawson moved on with new hopes for sudden riches.[6]

In spite of the wealth and sometimes frenzied activity, life could get very lonely and seem meaningless. There was not only a shortage of available women in the Far North, but there were almost no children, and the miners treated any child they saw as something special, indulging them and giving them treats.[7] Author Edith Tyrell, in her memoirs of Dawson, tells of a miner who became angry with Tyrell's husband for some unknown reason, and when pressed to explain, he replied, "You walked by my cabin today: you had a little child by the hand, and you didn't come in. It's years since I've heard a child speak or felt a little hand in mine." When the man grasped the little girl's hand, tears rolled down his cheeks, and he left her a prize nugget as a gift.[8] The gold rush brought chaos, lawlessness, and con-artists, but it also brought more women and children, and any settlement that had more than a few children managed to provide a school. Children continued to be celebrated and cherished, and in 1900 one of the main attractions in the Fourth of July parade in Nome was the decorated carriage of the first white child born there.

Group portrait of 54 members of the Yukon Order of Pioneers posing in front of the Dawson Lodge No. 1 on Second Avenue between Princess Street and Harper Street. The YOOP was a fraternal organization formed in 1894 as protection for early miners. 1. Captain Constantine NWMP, 2. Mrs. Constantine, 3. "Billy" Lloyd, 4. Jack Devine, 5. Gilbert Dionne, 6. "Missouri Bill" Abe Gordon, 7. "Shorty" Kuttinger, 8. "Sheep Creek" Kuttinger, 9. Steve Record, 10. Jack Horn, 11. Paul Denhart, 12. John Nelson, 13. "Black Joe" Thompson, 14. Hank Somers, 15. Jimmy Treasure, 16. Benny Treasure, 17. Joe Quigley, 18. Jack Sheedy, 19. Frank Buteau, 20. John Erickson, 21. Eddie Lewin, 22. Chris Sonnickson, 23. Peter Nelson, 24. William Castle, 25. Jack Donovan, 26. Joe Cooper, 27. Al Stites, 28. Bill Dinker, 29. Unknown, 30. Henry Anderson, 31. Joe Johansen, 32. Pete Wilson, 33. "Old Man" Franklin, 34. Harry Smith, 35. Captain Morgan, 36. Frank Lawson, 37. Frank Carroll, 38. John Nelson, 39. Andrew Nordstrom, 40. Hank Scales, 41. Jimmy Kerry, 42. John Lind, 43. Skiff Mitchell, 44. Zeke Ogilvie, 45. Ed Lowry, 46. Cash Hampshire, 47. August Lindgaard, 48. John Bourke, 50. Joe Lame, 51. Charlie Anderson, 52. Billy Dryden, 53. Charles S. Levante, 54. Albert "Hooch" Fortier, 55. John Lee, 56. Harry Berryman (photographer Eric A. Hegg. Alaska and Polar Regions Collections, Elmer E. Rasmuson Library, University of Alaska, Fairbanks, UAF-1970-0058-00254).

Chapter 6. Eldorado

Joe Quigley appears in the Yukon Order of Pioneers official group photograph taken by Eric Hegg in Dawson City in 1897. He was 28 years old and had done well. He wasn't an instant millionaire, but his persistence and strength paid off enough for him to feel like he was on the right path. Plenty of honest, hard-working people failed in Alaska, and plenty of scoundrels became rich. The old rules of success were not in effect in this time and place, but sometimes good guys did okay and Joe was one of them. Joe's modest nature combined with his vision and optimism inspired him to work harder than most people, prepare for the worst while hoping for the best, see the humor in rough situations, and maintain a humble demeanor. Joe saved the money he made from #35, focused on his goals and didn't stop until he reached them, yet remained remarkably adaptable.

Eighteen ninety-seven was a big year for Joe. In addition to hitting a sizable gold strike and joining the YOOP, he discovered a creek that was officially named after him (now called Quigley Gulch). Bob Beam, John Krishy and Joe Quigley had taken on the task of blazing a new trail across the Willow Flats, bordering the Klondike River. Breaking trail in a group involves switching the lead hiker every so often because it is a Herculean task that involves stepping into virgin territory and clearing the way for those behind. Joe was the lead hiker when he saw a small creek that entered the Klondike about a mile below Bear Creek. They each located a claim there and noticed that "two or three other outfits" had followed them in and staked claims as well. Joe stayed at the location while the others went to record their ground with Captain Constantine. Constantine asked, "What Creek?" The men answered, "No name yet." The next question from Constantine was "Who located it?" When the men answered, "Quigley," Constantine replied, "Well, we'll call it Quigley Creek," and so it became Quigley Creek on the maps.[9]

Captain Charles Constantine of the North-West Mounted Police was a familiar authority figure to all the Sourdoughs. Originally from England, he had a military career in the Canadian militia and then joined the NWMP in 1885, becoming the first Mountie to serve in the Yukon district in 1894.[10] He was known for being gruff and incorruptible and he put an end to the miners' meetings that had been the method of administering rough justice up until that point. Constantine tempered justice with common sense and in his role as gold commissioner decided the names of the rivers.[11] He had forecast that a gold rush was imminent and knew the need for a police force to regulate the chaos. Believing that it was unethical for him to make gold claims himself, he left the Yukon in 1898 a highly respected man. As a parting gift the old-timers presented Constantine with a silver plate containing $200,000 worth of selected nuggets.[12]

Bob Beam, John Krishy and Joe Quigley sunk holes on their claims on the newly-named Quigley Creek but didn't find any gold. Krishy and Quigley went on to prospect around Hunker Creek and other nearby creeks. After more than a year of prospecting in the area, news of the 1899 Nome strike reached them. The Nome Gold Rush had begun when Eric Lindblom, John Brynteston and Jafet Lindberg met in Circle City and went to Alaska's West Coast to prospect, striking along Anvil Creek in the fall of 1898. Anvil City had a population of 10,000 by the end of 1899 and its name was changed to Nome. When latecomers showed up to find the area was all staked, they set up tents on the beach and discovered that there was gold on the beach. The beaches could be reached easily by ship. This location had the advantage of being accessible without any difficult climbing or hauling of equipment for miles, and it was called a "poor man's paradise."[13] The population of Nome grew to 20,000. Almost overnight it was a city with 100 saloons, dozens of stores, restaurants and hotels which were in tents or quickly constructed wooden buildings. Hundreds, including many Dawson miners, were going to Nome, but Quigley and Krishy decided not to go with the stampede.

Although joining the stampede to Nome didn't call to Joe Quigley, the lure of new discovery did. He had "always wanted to strike a million dollar mine"[14] himself and perhaps he also wanted to get away from the chaos of the stampede and the boom towns, so Joe decided to go off on a trip of his own. Before the trip, Joe went to stay at Tanacross with his friend Charlie Overheiser, who was carrying the mail from Tanacross to Copper Center. Mail carriers were heroes in Alaska. They were contract workers who went out in all weather, in an environment that is sometimes 60 degrees below zero, with high winds and driving snow, to bring the mail to even the most remote places. Most of the people who were in Alaska were starving for news from home. The lives of the mail carriers were driven by punctuality in spite of their working conditions, and they brought the people something that was valued beyond gold.[15]

Joe built himself a new boat, packed it with a quarter ton of provisions, and went up the Tanana River, toward the headwaters, because he believed it was unknown territory for prospectors up to that time. He was aware of how much of a gamble his search was and felt ready for a new challenge. He poled the boat up the Tanana and up the Nabesna River as far as he could go "till I ran out of water … it ends quick up there, at the foot of a glacier … you end up looking up at the glacier."[16] The Nabesna River is a glacially-fed, 73-mile-long tributary of the Tanana River that flows north out of the Wrangell–St. Elias Mountains. This trip made Joe Quigley among the first non-indigenous people to explore the Tanana all the way to its headwaters. He spent the summer panning in the creeks in the area but didn't find his million- dollar mine. He did find a little gold, "but nothing worthwhile."[17] Joe returned to stay with Charlie Overheiser again that winter and part of the next summer, spending his time prospecting and making river trips.

Chapter 6. Eldorado

The gold rush had changed things permanently. By 1898 the earlier, simple lifestyle of the old-timers who were dependent on small amounts of gold or a few furs to make a living was being replaced by the development of new frontiers and diverse values. It was the dawn of a new century, and knowledge of the environment and new work methods allowed better utilization of resources. Technology made things a bit easier and life became a little more complicated and a little more hectic. On June 6, 1900, President William McKinley signed a measure into law "making further provisions for a civil government for Alaska."[18] Outside forces were putting an end to a way of life that Joe Quigley had mastered, and he knew that soon he would have to make changes himself. Joe loved his early days in the Yukon and Alaska, and he enjoyed the arduous, simple life and his community of kindred spirits. He was 29 years old and at a crossroads in his life. He could have gone on to a steadier career, invested his Eldorado money in a new business in Alaska, or moved back to the States, but he didn't. Joe found a way to continue doing what he loved: prospecting and mining, looking for a million-dollar mine.

CHAPTER 7

Fairbanks

In August of 1901, E. T. Barnette and his wife Isabelle were cruising up the Chena River on the sternwheel river boat the *Lavelle Young* looking for a place to set up business in the Tanana River area when the water became too shallow for the boat to continue. They tried to maneuver the shallow Chena Slough (now called the Chena River) to get around the shallows of the Tanana River, but went aground. Captain Charles Adams refused to go further, and Barnette decided that he would set up Barnette's Cache right where they were. The Barnettes set up their business and home in what they thought would be a temporary location but would later become downtown Fairbanks. The next summer, on July 22, 1902, Italian prospector Felix Pedro (Felice Pedroni) made a big strike in the area and told Barnette about it.

Barnette saw this as an opportunity to draw business to his trading post and sent Japanese adventurer Jujiro Wada with a dog team to Dawson to spread the word of the strike. Wada arrived in Dawson in January 1903, bringing the news of the next big strike. The newspaper picked up the story, announcing "Rich Strike Made in the Tanana,"[1] and included a portrait of Wada and a map of the strike drawn by Wada. The newspaper described the area as "a district that may be destined to be known as a gold producer equal to the Klondike or Nome" and went on to vouch for Wada's reliability. By February 1903 hundreds of stampeders were leaving Dawson headed for what was later to be called Fairbanks. Prospectors who had failed in Dawson and were in debt found it a particularly attractive destination because they could cross the border into the United States Territory of Alaska and escape their Canadian debts.[2]

Miners arrived in Barnette's Cache only to find that Wada's reports had been exaggerated, prices for supplies were exorbitant, and most of the claims were already staked. Barnette had staked ten claims himself and 25 for his friends and relatives through powers of attorney, leaving very little for new influx of miners.[3] Even more impoverished because of Barnette's greed, the prospectors were furious that they had been misled, and a mob of miners threatened both Barnette and Wada with violence. This experience caused

Chapter 7. Fairbanks

Wada to leave for Nome. Although the amount of gold in the area had been exaggerated by Barnette, and he had engaged in predatory pricing, the stampede transformed the town, the unscrupulous Barnette prospered, and he became the first mayor of Fairbanks.

Barnette was soon to encounter Judge James Wickersham, who changed the town permanently. Law enforcement in the Yukon was carried out by the North-West Mounted Police, but this was the Territory of Alaska and there was no local police force. The new United States federal law divided the massive Territory of Alaska into three judicial districts with a judge for each district presiding over general jurisdiction in civil, criminal, equity and admiralty cases.[4] Wickersham was appointed to the Third Judicial District by President McKinley. The third district covered more than half of Alaska and centered on the interior. This is where Wickersham helped guide Alaska's transition from orphan outpost to full territorial status in 1912.[5] He had arrived in Nome in 1901 to deal with the lawlessness and corruption that had grown exponentially in Alaska since the gold rush began, and like many of the men and women who came to Alaska during that time, he was a remarkable person. He was born in Illinois in 1857, and although he only had an eighth-grade education, he passed the bar exam to become an attorney in 1880. He presided over many important cases in Alaska and kept personal diaries, often expressing himself in plain, earthy language. As there were only three judges in an otherwise ungoverned territory, Wickersham was one of the three most powerful government men in Alaska at the time. Through his tenacity and hard work, he earned the respect of many, left an indelible mark on Alaska, and helped shape the city of Fairbanks.

Wickersham was responsible for the town of Fairbanks being named after Charles W. Fairbanks of Indiana. The Tanana Valley gold strike stampede had caused the population to swell in 1902 as prospectors filled the area surrounding Barnette's Cache. The judge struck a bargain with Barnette that if he would rename the townsite Fairbanks, after the senior senator from Indiana, he would move the district headquarters from Eagle to Barnette's Cache. In 1903 Wickersham's headquarters were moved to Fairbanks,[6] and on a clear day the Great Mountain, Denali (McKinley at the time), was visible from his office.

Because of his success in 1897, Joe Quigley still had enough money in the bank to be relaxed about his next move. In the spring of 1903 when Joe "drifted down the Tanana and went to Fairbanks," the town was "just a few cabins and buildings and tents in the trees."[7] By autumn of that year Fairbanks had a population of 1200 people with more than 500 homes.[8] A man named Blackburn took a lease on a Fairbanks creek claim with Joe, and they "took out a dump … that didn't amount to much."[9] A dump is the dirt, gravel and other material that is dug out and piled on the ground to be sifted for minerals later. Joe became ill while in Fairbanks, contracting typhoid fever, and was nursed back to health by boom town cook and folk medicine practitioner Fannie Sedlacek McKenzie.[10] Typhoid was a common disease in the mining camps and was sometimes fatal. The disease is caused by bacteria and thrived in the camps because they were built on flat, boggy tundra with little drainage, and the tents were too close to each other with little ventilation. Many of the miners boiled their drinking water and this did limit the disease some, but it appeared in camp after camp and was the most common serious illness for miners.[11]

After organizing his court and Fairbanks' civil offices in the spring of 1903, Judge Wickersham had some time to fill before court convened in the fall. He believed that "the most interesting thing on the horizon was the massive dome that dominates the valleys of the Tanana, the Yukon, and the Kuskokwim," the Great Mountain.[12] Wickersham referred to the mountain as Mount McKinley, as some had done since 1896. Naming the mountain McKinley had always been controversial. It was officially named Mount McKinley in 1917, years after President McKinley, who had never visited Alaska, was assassinated in 1901, but many Alaskans refused to refer to it by any other than the traditional name Denali, and the state of Alaska requested in 1975 that the mountain officially be recognized as Denali.[13]

Judge Wickersham loved mountain climbing and having a view of the tallest mountain in North America made his next move obvious. The 45-year-old judge was going to be the first white man to attempt the climb to the summit. He chose three long-time close companions, Charley Webb, Morton I. Stevens and George A. Jeffery, to make the 20,320-foot climb with him and added 26-year-old Canadian John McLeod to complete the five-person team. McLeod was an especially valuable addition because of his communication skills; he spoke several Alaska Native dialects.[14] On May 6, 1903, more than 100 citizens of Fairbanks accompanied the party on the *Isabelle*, with "flags flying and the dance hall band," heading for Chena. Wickersham privately thought that the real purpose of the Fairbanks send-off party was to let it be known that the Mount McKinley expedition was from Fairbanks, not from Chena.[15] From Chena, the steamboat *Tanana Chief* took the climbing party and all of their supplies, including a poling boat and two donkeys named Mark and Hannah. On May 17 they passed an Alaska Native village at the mouth of the Nenana. Heavy ice was piled high on the bars and riverbanks, and when they reached the mouth of the Kantishna they found it running still full of heavy winter ice. Finding an abandoned boat, they spent the time waiting for the Kantishna river ice to run out, cleaning and caulking the 16-foot-long, clinker-built steamboat, which they named *Mudlark*. Steamboat propulsion systems at the time used boilers to produce steam. Boilers usually ran on coal, but wood could be used if necessary, and Wickersham's party used wood to get the boat moving.

Chapter 7. Fairbanks

The team encountered a few white trappers in the area and also met Tena Indians in their spring hunting camps along the river. Wickersham's party spent the night of May 19 in the camp of Athabascan moose hunter Nachereah. When the Natives asked if the purpose of the expedition was for gold, Wickersham explained that they were going "merely to see the top, to be the first men to reach the summit."[16] The response was laughter from the Natives, with the translator telling Wickersham, "He says you are a fool." The Tena people shared their fresh meat and their knowledge of the landscape, pointing out the easiest route for the men and mules to the base of Mount McKinley, via Chitsia Creek, to the lower slopes of the Kantishna Hills, avoiding the swamps and deep creeks, and through the gap created by Moose Creek and Wonder Lake.

On May 23, Wickersham met with the blind shaman Koonah, a tall man about 50 years of age, at Tuktawgana, the spring and summer camp. Koonah told him of Yako, the Tena's origin hero who had magically created the Denali mountain range. Yako had fathered the Tena people in the ancient past. Yako's magic formed the sacred ground of the Denali from giant sea waves sent to destroy him by Totson the Raven Chief. During a later struggle, Tebay the White Sheep Chief had climbed to his Chitsia Mountain lookout to direct the enemies of Yako to his village on the banks of the Yukon. There, the treacherous warriors from the southern sea were vanquished by Yako and his children so the Tena could live in peace.[17]

A few days later Wickersham's party made it as far as the mouth of the Bearpaw River to a Telida Indian camp where they met Chief Shesoie and his band of hunters. The Alaska Natives gave Wickersham's party detailed instructions on the best way to get to the glaciers that descend from the mountain's summit, suggesting that the poling boat be cached and that the party hike across the foothills. The party had some troubles along the way, including dropping their only axe into the water and spending hours repeatedly diving into the water to find it. After recovering the axe, they continued on foot, with the mules. The party camped along the way, marveling at the view of the Kantishna Drainage and keeping their focus on the white-peaked "Great Mountain."

They members of the expedition found that "the Great Mountain is glaciated from summit to base."[18] When the climbing party made it to a height of 10,000 feet to Peter's Glacier, they were disheartened to find that the glacier did not connect with the high ridge that they wanted to reach. They had come to a 14,000-foot-high vertical wall that was impossible to climb. That vertical wall is now known as Wickersham Wall. The party headed back toward Fairbanks, by raft, boat and steamboat, having mapped the approaches to the mountain. Although the expedition did not achieve its mission to scale the mountain, it did sample the creeks for gold along the way, found a little in

Chitsia Creek, and filed four claims when they returned from the trip in July of 1903. It didn't take long for the news to get out.[19]

In the fall of 1904 Joe Quigley's old friend from back in Dawson, Jack Horn, came to Fairbanks from Nome with a team of seven or eight dogs. Horn's prospecting in Nome had not gone well, and he didn't have money to feed his dogs. Joe had been working on what he described as a "claim that didn't amount to much" in Fairbanks and had been ill, but now he was feeling stronger.[20] Seeing his old friend and fellow Yukon Order of Pioneers member Jack Horn was heartening. As Joe described it, "I had plenty of grub cached for the winter, with no dogs. So, we partnered up." Prospectors tended to partner up for safety and to pool resources, sometimes even signing contracts that they would not abandon one another and would help the other in case of injury or accident. Their agreements also spelled out the terms of dividing what they found. Since mining partnerships came and went often in the Far North, these agreements made splitting and moving on to the next claim more congenial when the time came.

Joe and Horn heard Judge Wickersham lecture on his attempt to climb Mount McKinley, and they were inspired by the Wickersham party's gold discovery. As Joe recalled, "He told us about some of his men being able to pan out gold using just a shovel for a pan and said 'We found gold and believe there is more.'" The thought of going to an un-prospected area appealed to Joe and he started making plans to investigate the area. Joe recruited Horn for the trip, saying that "no one had ever prospected the Kantishna and suggested we get ready and make the trip up there."[21] Pooling resources with an old friend to embark on a new venture was the very thing that Joe had been waiting for.

CHAPTER 8

Kantishna

The Kantishna region is bordered on the south by the crest of the Alaska Range, on the north by the Tanana River, on the east by the Nenana River, and on the west by the lower Kantishna River.[1] In 1902 Alfred Brooks led a United States Geological Survey party of seven people and went into the area with a 20-horse pack train. Brooks described the Great Mountain known as McKinley at the time: "Climbing the bluff above camp, I overlooked part of the valley, spread before me like a broad amphitheater, its sides formed by the slopes of the mountain and its spurs. Here and there glistened in the sun the white surfaces of glaciers which found their way down from the peaks above. The great mountain rose 17,000 feet above our camp, apparently almost sheer from the flat valley floor. Its dome-shaped summit and upper slopes were white with snow, relieved here and there by black areas which marked cliffs too steep for the snow to lie upon."[2] Brooks' poetic description of the unspoiled beauty and majesty of the region predated Judge Wickersham's climb by a year and created a picture in the mind's eye that still inspires prospective adventurers.

Before Brooks had written about the Great Mountain there had already been some interest in the Kantishna region. Frank Densmore's prospecting party came to the area in 1889, crossing from the Tanana River to the Kuskokwim River by way of Croschket and Lake Minchumina. They found no encouraging signs of profit there and chose not to stay. Several years later, in 1896, another prospector, W.A. Dickey, saw the mountain from the Susitna River, estimated its elevation as 20,000 feet, and named it Mount McKinley after the United States president. Two years afterward, in 1898, George Eldridge and Robert Muldrow of the USGS confirmed Dickey's guess.[3] The region was so remote and difficult to access that it wasn't until after Fairbanks was established, 150 miles away in 1903, that prospectors became seriously interested in the area.

Wickersham's 1903 attempt to scale the mountain and his subsequent lectures on the trip caught the attention of miners in Fairbanks. Joe Quigley was ready for a new venture and fortunately still had most of his money from the sale of #35 in the bank at Dawson. Joe hadn't squandered his money like so many of the prospectors did. Living frugally while saving what he could had become routine since he left home at age 15, and he now had enough faith in the Kantishna area to invest his hard-earned reserves and forge ahead.

Former prize fighter Jack Horn had a hungry dog team and no food for them or money to buy it with. Feeding sled dogs is no small mission; they were known to gobble everything in sight including leather gloves, boots, soap, and the resin that was sprinkled on dance-hall floors.[4] Joe had food stored up for the winter and nearly $10,000 in the bank ($285,000 in 2018) but no dogs. After hearing Judge Wickersham's stories about seeing gold in Kantishna, Jack Horn and Joe Quigley were eager to explore the previously unmined territory together.

Dogs were a precious commodity. These "ravenous but indispensable creatures" were a prominent part of life in the Far North and could make difficult undertakings less difficult or impossible tasks possible.[5] As Judge Wickersham wrote in 1903, "He who gives time to the study of the history of Alaska learns that the dog, next to man, has been the most important factor in its past and present development."[6] Like most of the things that miners needed or wanted, dogs were hard to get and came at a high price. Notable gold rush journalist Tappan Adney said in 1897, "Dogs are expensive. None suitable can be had here at any price."[7] Just as depicted in Jack London's *Call of the Wild*, there was a shortage of good working dogs in Alaska, so dogs on the streets of Seattle or San Francisco were potential involuntary recruits, with thieves selling the stolen dogs to the highest bidder. Gold rush era photographs of dog sleds and mushers often show dogs that were not Malamutes or Huskies. The traditional breeds were not available, so any good, strong, reliable dogs were being sold to work in Alaska and all sorts of breeds were crossed with local village dogs.[8] The larger mixed breed dogs were better for heavy freighting, but for every other purpose the smaller native dogs were faster, would work on less food than the large mixed breed dogs, and were generally superior for the job.

Dog mushing has a very long history. Archaeological evidence of dog harnesses and other specialized equipment for dog traction, dating from between 1000 and 1600, was found in Thule[9] sites in Canada and it is possible that mushing was invented there. There are references to the use of sled dogs in the Siberian subarctic in Arabian literature of the tenth century and in the writings of Marco Polo in the 13th century.[10] Nineteenth and early 20th century dog sleds in Alaska were very different from the normal toboggans that most outsiders were accustomed to. A typical dog sled was about seven feet long, 16 inches wide, and six inches high, with an upturned bow and four longitudinal pine slats on ash wood cross frames. The sleds usually had ash runners clad in two-inch-wide steel.[11] Mushing is a specialized skill that takes hard work and patience to learn. Joe Quigley certainly had previous exposure to mushing and came to be known as good dog-musher, but there is no evidence that he had taken on the responsibility of owning his own dog team before his time in Kantishna.[12]

Quigley and Horn left on their journey in mid-winter when everything was frozen and traveling the rivers by dog sled was the best method of transportation. The capabilities and strength of a sled dog can mean the difference between life and death, and the two of them trusted the dog team. They left Fairbanks in sub-zero temperatures, with the team pulling a sled and small trailer. Mushers at that time did not ride the runners of the sled. They would often run alongside the sled with the dogs, especially if the ground was uneven, so as not to overburden the dogs with more weight. When two mushers were working together, they would take turns with one riding the weegee board, handling the gee pole and steering the sled, and the other running alongside.[13]

As Joe remembered it, "We loaded the outfit on a sled and small trailer and started out late February, 1905 from Fairbanks, following the Tanana to Nenana and then cutting across country to the Toklat River and followed the Toklat and cut across to the headwaters of the Kantishna, as we had figured that the lower Kantishna was too flat and sluggish to carry gold."[14] They had to cut their own trail, which is extremely labor intensive work and the trip to Kantishna by dog sled would have taken more than a week.[15] Optimism about their new destination helped the men keep the energy levels they would need for exploring uncharted territory in the bitter cold.

Mushers use the rivers as their main thoroughfares, and although it seems that in temperatures cold enough to freeze water that is thrown into the air before it hits the ground, the rivers would become smooth, glass-like highways, but they are not. In the smaller rivers and streams, deep pools alternate with swift shallows. The stream freezes solid to the bottom, but then the underground sources of the water continue to push upward, increasing the pressure under the ice until it pushes the ice into mounds and eventually breaks through, spreading along the frozen surface. At times the water gushes out, rising three or four feet above the surface of the ice. Sometimes many miles at a stretch along the river will be covered with a succession of the overflows, ranging from two inches to a foot in height. Some are running water, some are partially frozen, and some become "glare" ice.[16] The surface is continually changing with layers of ice. The overflow water is very dangerous because getting one's feet wet will quickly bring frostbite.

Sled dogs' feet are as important as the musher's feet. When a dog comes out of the water into the snow, the snow collects and freezes between the toes. If the ice is not removed, it will quickly cause the paws to hurt and make the dog unable to run well, so the musher will stop and clean the ice and snow from each dog's foot all along the line. This task involves cleaning 16 toes per dog, with bare hands, every time the team gets into an overflow. Having bare hands in below freezing temperatures is dangerous and could result in losing fingers due to frostbite. The dogs will clean their feet themselves if they are given time, but there are short daylight hours in winter, and it is faster for the musher to clean the dogs' feet.[17]

Joe Quigley and Jack Horn began prospecting on Flume Creek and Moose Creek. The two men saw some traps set out and left a note on one of them, which prompted the trappers to find Quigley and Horn. When trappers Joe Benson and Gus Benbenneck were questioned, they said, "Not a very good-looking country … too much gravel." With further questioning the trappers told the prospectors that "lots of rim bedrock shows." This news encouraged Quigley and Horn to do some panning in the area.[18]

They saw enough gold to encourage them to keep looking. There was gold almost everywhere they checked, but large quantities didn't appear anywhere. The men located on Glacier, Caribou, Moose, and Eureka creeks, naming the creeks and making rough sketch maps of the creeks and the area, and locating claims for themselves and for their friends. Both Quigley and Horn were Yukon Order of Pioneers members and one of the tenets of that organization was to tell other miner members where new potential gold strikes were. Joe took this seriously and was excited to include his friends in the new territory.

A sketch map is drawn from observation rather than exact measurements and notes any prominent land features with the intention of helping the prospector find his way back to the areas he explored. These initial sketch maps could be valuable to gold seekers who came along later, and occasionally an old hand drawn map would circulate for years. Joe had been drawing sketch maps of the areas he explored since his arrival in the Far North, and from time to time when he was finished with a map, he would give it to someone who could use it.

According to Grant Pearson, Joe had drawn a map, back in the Klondike in the mid–1890s, of an area with fairly good prospects, but he had taken a lease on another claim so he gave the map to a group of men in Dawson who were looking for a new area to prospect. He never saw any of those prospectors again. More than 20 years later when Joe was in Fairbanks, a man approached him to ask for a grubstake. The prospector's justification for the loan was a story about a lost mine that had yielded a fortune before the owner went to the States and died. The man's account continued with the original miner on his way back to the States, having given a map of the place to the him, leaving him with everything he needed to strike a fortune, if only he had the grubstake. Joe said that he would have a look at the map, and that if it looked promising for placer mining, he would consider the grubstake propo-

Chapter 8. Kantishna

sition. Imagine Joe's surprise when he inspected the map and recognized it as the one that he had drawn years before and given away in Dawson! Of course, the question of the grubstake was dropped at that point.[19] Whether this was something that actually happened to Joe or if it is simply an apocryphal story that became associated with him, it illustrates his tendency to quietly consider a situation, giving each person the benefit of the doubt, but ultimately being a very hard man to deceive. On many occasions Joe's slow and steady approach afforded him having the last laugh.

In the spring, when the water thawed enough for boats to get through, Quigley and Horn built a boat for themselves and the dogs and headed down the Kantishna to the Tanana, where they caught a steamer, taking the dogs and all of their gear to Fairbanks.[20] Steamboats like the *Tanana Chief* and *White Seal* traveled along the Tanana and Kantishna rivers to the point where water levels grew too shallow for the heavy boats to continue. Passage on a steamer cost $40 per person and freight cost $50 a ton.

They stopped in for a drink while they were in town, and the samples of coarse gold that Horn and Quigley had with them sparked immediate excitement in the hearts of saloon patrons. Rumors about the next big strike started to spread immediately. The exhilaration of hearing about the next big thing kept prospectors going, and the Kantishna discoveries stirred their blood. Jack Horn was being toasted as "the Father of Kantishna" as Joe Quigley made his way to the recorder's office. Joe filed his original discovery claim on Caribou Creek, along with the claims of Jack Horn and about a dozen others, on July 10, 1905.[21]

Around the same time that Quigley and Horn were staking claims in Kantishna, Joe Dalton and his partner Joe Stiles found gold while prospecting on the southwest side of the Kantishna hills. Two days after Joe Quigley had registered his group of Kantishna claims in Fairbanks, Dalton and Stiles filed their Friday Creek and Eureka Creek claims.

Quigley and Horn were anxious to get to work on their new claims. After they recorded their Kantishna claims in Fairbanks and told friends of the locations, they bought supplies and started packing. Joe recounted the story later, "loaded up on provisions, and got a small boat with outboard motor [kicker] and went back up the Kantishna that same Summer, spearheading a large group of friends and prospectors to our new strike." The excitement of new discovery kept everyone in good spirits. Joe loved being able to bring good news to the other miners and it felt great to be leading them to what felt like sure success.

By July 15, 1905, the Kantishna area was suddenly crawling with prospectors, most of them arriving by boat.[22] The activity looked like progress to Joe Quigley, and he described the scene in a later interview, "Everyone was staking claims and building cabins and starting to dig holes. We were busy too, digging holes and prospecting on the benches and some of the creeks." Estimates of how many made the trek during the stampede ranged from a conservative guess of several hundred to wildly exaggerated tales of a few thousand. The buzz about gold in Kantishna was so strong in Fairbanks that by mid–August two of the six members of the Fairbanks City Council had left for the Kantishna and a third was on his way.[23]

The creeks were full of hopeful prospectors with pans and rockers. Placer mining involves digging with picks, shovels and other hand tools through dirt and gravel, creating tunnels. Placer mining stops when the miner hits bedrock. Underground mining that goes below solid bedrock is called quartz, or hard rock, mining. Sluicing, using the power of water, motion and gravity is used to extract the minerals from other material. A sluice box is built with one or more troughs, or runs, with cross bars called riffles on the bottom. As the water passes over these riffles, little whirlpools are created behind each riffle, and the heavier gold particles are able to fall to the bottom. Lighter particles are washed over the top of the riffles and out the end of the sluice box.[24] A rocking motion will create the movement needed to create the whirlpools, and the work is often done on gravel bars in the creeks, so the miners are said to be "rocking on the bars" when they are placer mining. The miners were very busy rocking on the bars in the Kantishna area that summer.

Activity in Kantishna was so high that on August 24, Harry Karstens and Charlie McGonagall, both mail carriers, announced plans to carry freight and passengers to the area on an overland winter express route. Karstens and McGonagall had come to the Kantishna in late autumn and staked a few claims, but most of the richest ground was already claimed and the camps were short of supplies. Food was selling at outrageously inflated prices, and to these two experienced miners, the writing was on the wall. They saw an opportunity, blazed a winter trail, and promoted their freight business. Karstens arranged for a post office and a set fee of 25 cents per letter (a first-class postage stamp in the States was .02 in 1905). He also set up a small library at each post office, bringing in books and periodicals from Fairbanks. Although it seemed like a good idea, to fill a need in the expanding mining community, the business didn't go as well as they planned. Karstens later wrote that he started in the winter with a dog team and $100,000 and ended in the spring with "five hundred dollars and a lot of knowledge." The knowledge that Karstens acquired that winter would serve him well later.[25]

By late summer and early fall the Kantishna district was a hotbed of activity. Everyone was staking claims and building cabins and starting to dig. Practically every creek that heads into the Kantishna Hills was staked from source to mouth and there was also interest in the benches and ridges. Within a few weeks a number of towns were built, including Glacier on Bearpaw River, Diamond at the mouth of Moose Creek, and Roosevelt (sometimes called Square Deal) on the Kantishna River. At each place log cabins, stores, hotels, and saloons were erected.

In remote districts like Kantishna, one person was usually designated to take the claim notices to the recorder's office in Fairbanks. Joe Quigley, with his long strides, could make the 150-mile walk in four or five days and was often the person to take the filings to the office.[26] The torrent of mining activity warranted a new official mining district, so the hike to Fairbanks wouldn't be necessary. Soon, the Kantishna Mining District was authorized, and Judge Wickersham appointed Lee Van Slyke as the U.S. commissioner for the new district with headquarters at McKinley. Van Slyke arrived September 1905, at the peak of the stampede, but by the time Van Slyke arrived, the short-lived boom town McKinley had been abandoned in favor of the new community, Roosevelt.[27]

There were enough successful prospectors in Kantishna to get the Fairbanks press excited. Joe Dalton and Simon Stiles had significant success with their claims. They brought in their brothers to work with them on their Eureka and Friday Creek claims and by the end of the 1906 mining season they brought in flakes and nuggets worth $86,000.[28] Their Discovery claim yielded two large nuggets, one weighing 11 ounces and the other weighing 43 ounces. The larger of the two was called the "Queen of Eureka" and was put on display in a Fairbanks jewelry store.

The trappers Benbenneck and Benson, who had originally given Quigley and Horn the lowdown on the area, claimed #14 above discovery, which developed into one of the richest placer gold claims in the district. The pair showed up in Fairbanks with large nuggets and $10,000 in gold dust. Some prospectors weren't so open about their finds. Jim Chronister and Billy Abramsky tried to keep their riches a secret, but word got out, and a newspaper report stated, "The pokes they brought in with them would choke an elephant."[29] A gold poke was a caribou skin bag about ten inches long and three or four inches in diameter and used to carry gold dust. Since much trading was done with gold dust instead of cash, the miners would carry pokes with them.

Headlines like this one encouraged prospectors to head for Kantishna in hopes of joining the ranks of the lucky few.

Chapter 9

Joe and Fannie

Relationships between men and women at the turn of the 20th century were influenced by the stringent definitions of masculine and feminine. During the years that Joe Quigley was growing from a boy to a man, the societal definitions of a good man were fairly restrictive and clear cut. There were two distinct ideals of middle-class masculinity. One was of a "virtuous," sober, God-fearing man who worked for a large company for a steady salary. It came about because the Industrial Revolution had changed the economic structure to the point where men could not readily prove themselves and be successful in the ways that they had before. Critics of the "virtuous masculinity" claimed that modern life made men weak, as they preferred the second type of ideal, "vigorous masculinity." It was epitomized by Theodore Roosevelt's influence and called for constant physical activity, competition, and manly self-assertion.[1] These extremes of the ideal man brought about a time when men and women, even married couples, lived in separate spheres, essentially only coming together for breakfast and dinner.[2]

In contrast, the ideal woman was a remnant of Victorian era values and left very little room for the reality of survival in a rapidly changing culture. She was "the Angel of the House," a term that came from a popular poem by Coventry Patmore published in 1854. She was expected to be devoted and submissive to her husband. Ideally, she was meek, charming, graceful, self-sacrificing, powerless and pure.[3] Single women who were sexually active were considered impure and thought of as "fallen women." In response to these outdated ideals, there was an emerging feminism that suggested equal treatment of women and a broader idea of what a good woman could or should be, including well-educated and independent.[4] These were the ideals of a small minority, however, and women still had limited rights regarding property and power.

Having been on the road since he was a teenager, with no family life, and working at jobs that were completely dominated by men, Joe Quigley probably had very few substantial relationships with women other than as a son or brother before heading toward Alaska. Once in the Far North, there were not many opportunities to meet women for a potentially serious relationship. The dynamic between men and women was somewhat different in gold rush era Alaska and the Yukon, but the ingrained expectations were always there. Joe had a childhood example of how women fit in to daily life from the constant presence of older sisters and his mother helping to run the family farm. Joe's sister, Emma, ran a business with her husband, as did other women at the time, but in general, women were marginalized and relegated to homemaking and child rearing.

White women in Alaska during Joe's time there were often entrepreneurial or working at jobs that served the large population of miners in some way, but they were in the minority. In 1890, the year before Joe came to the Far North, the non-indigenous population of Alaska had eight males for every female.[5] Some white men had been known to use alcohol to take sexual advantage of Native women and were often disrespectful and bigoted, so although some miners married indigenous women, most Alaska Natives chose to distance themselves from the mining camps, for good reason. In non-native culture, societal disapproval of white men taking Native wives grew as the white population increased.[6] Socially acceptable romantic and domestic relationships between men and women were difficult to establish.

By the turn of the 20th century when Joe and Fannie became a couple, there were more women, but they were still in the minority (more than two men for every woman).[7] Many of the women arriving were wives and daughters of the men who had already been working in Alaska, and these women created a more traditional domestic life and social structure. The traditional home life was not Joe's world. He was an independent, work-obsessed prospector and miner who was self-reliant and often isolated. He had been in the Far North since he was 21 years old and had developed his ideas about responsibility in a partnership between adults from his gold claim partnerships with other miners.

Arriving to the Kantishna mining camp during the fall of 1905 was Fannie McKenzie, later to be Fannie Quigley.[8] Fannie was tiny, barely five feet tall, a tough-talking, hard-drinking, feisty woman with an entrepreneurial spirit and capacity for hard work. She had worked her way west from Nebraska at the age of 27 as a cook in railroad construction camps. When she wasn't running her own traveling food service, she worked in roadhouses and was known for her cooking and her brassy charm. She was at home in the mining camps and had earned the nickname "Fannie the Hike."[9] Some said that the nickname was a reference to her stint as a dance hall girl when she would "hike up her skirts," but the moniker was more likely bestowed upon her because she had been hiking from camp to camp, hauling her tent and cooking equipment, to set up her "Meals for Sale" post. Upon her arrival in the Kantishna area she set up her traveling restaurant business again.

Joe Quigley and Fannie McKenzie's relationship was confusing to people.[10] Some didn't realize that Joe and Fannie were a couple when they were, and some thought that they were married when they weren't. There is no record of exactly when they became a couple. Some accounts say that Fannie and Joe met in Fairbanks at the mining camp in 1904, when Joe caught typhoid fever and Fannie nursed him through it.[11] Another holds that that they met years earlier, in Dawson, where Fannie was a neighbor of Joe Quigley's Kantishna mining camp partner, Jack Horn.[12] It is very likely that they were at least aware of each other's existence during the Dawson years.

Whether Fannie and Joe were acquainted as early as 1900 is not certain, but Fannie married Canadian Angus McKenzie on October 1 of that year. During their short-lived marriage, Fannie and Angus operated a roadhouse together on Hunker Creek, but the combination of alcohol and their bad tempers was volatile.[13] By December 1901 their domestic violence made it to the newspaper and included the information that Angus had given Fannie "an eye," causing her to have him arrested for assault and drunk and disorderly conduct.[14] Angus told the court that Fannie was also drunk at the time, and the case ended with them paying the $30 fine together and being released. Their marriage only lasted another year. By 1903 Fannie walked out on Angus and forged on to become one of the most well-known characters in Alaska.

Even though both Joe and Fannie were extremely hard-working, skilled, creative, and resilient, they were opposites in many ways. Joe was an imposing figure at 6'4", all bone and muscle, with sharp features and a quiet, gentle manner.[15] Fannie was a tiny dynamo who always used her "outdoor voice," told exaggerated stories and peppered her speech with curses that were considered unprintable by the writers of the day.[16] She was practical enough to wear men's clothing when she was working in the Alaska wilderness, but she also would wear dresses sometimes. Fannie was often seen as a colorful character who had a tough-love approach to those she liked, and she was an entertaining conversationalist. Because of her propensity for being loud and forceful, some found her intimidating or off-putting. Joe, who was much more casual and easy-going than Fannie, was among those who were charmed by her. He found her to be a lively companion and hard-working partner.

Fannie's parents were immigrants and she was raised in an isolated Czech farming community in Nebraska. She had a childhood of deprivation, with her mother passing away when Fannie was only five years old. Fannie was quite bright, but given very little education, and she learned English as a second language. She was charismatic, with a quick wit, but she was nearly illiterate and was resistant to the more refined social graces. Societal constraints associated with traditional femininity did not appeal to Fannie, and she eschewed the middle-class lifestyle that had been developing in the Far North as "respectable" women made their way to the area as wives of successful men or coming to work in the towns as nurses or teachers.[17]

Chapter 9. Joe and Fannie

Joe grew up on a farm in a long-established pioneer family of community leaders. He was comfortable with a broad range of society, articulate and impressively adaptable. He was generally known by other miners and his friends as a man of vision, persistence and reserve, and he was respected for his honesty and reliability.[18] In addition to remarkable physical endurance Joe had an insatiable intellectual curiosity, loved to read, and was always eager to learn something new. He spent his days working on his claims, prospecting, and collecting rocks and minerals. His evenings were spent studying the samples he collected. Joe was described as gentle, handy with everything, and easy-going.[19] Although he worked tirelessly and enjoyed the solitude of prospecting, he did take some time for leisure, valued his friends, and enjoyed a shot of whiskey and a good laugh.

Joe had grown up in rural western Pennsylvania where hunting was part of life and wild game was a staple of the family diet. Even young children were taught to hunt, and game meat was plentiful. Joe taught Fannie to hunt, which was essential for the subsistence lifestyle they lived in isolated Kantishna. She told her sister in a letter that she had never killed anything before she came to Kantishna.[20] Fannie was a good student and became a renowned hunter and trapper. She was a woman who could hunt for meat and butcher it, grow vegetables, and make a gourmet meal from her harvest. These skills were a source of pride for her, and Joe was proud of her abilities as well.

According to Fannie, their agreement was that Joe worked the mines and she "did all the rest."[21] That was not a completely accurate statement, but Fannie had a tendency to exaggerate facts for the sake of effect and usually made herself out to be the hero of every story. Joe was inclined to underplay his own achievements and didn't seem to mind letting others take credit for his work.[22] He did handle both the labor and the business side of the mining operation while Fannie focused on the domestic scene. The domestic scene was much more complicated and labor intensive than an average household in that time period would be, and the business of being an independent miner required infinitely more labor, dedication, skill and adaptability than the average job. Joe Quigley was inclined to be generous with partners and respectful of women as individuals in a time when men in his position were not required or pressured to be. He treated Fannie as an equal partner in business, putting her name on numerous mining claims.

Before she met Joe, Fannie made what appears to be her first claim on Clear Creek back in 1900, but it was canceled for nonrepresentation after she failed to do the required assessment work. She was not an experienced miner, but like almost everyone in the Far North at the time, she was interested in profiting from mining. Fannie's luck changed when she met Joe Quigley. Her first claim in Kantishna was on January 1, 1907, and witnessed by Joe.[23] Because of her entrepreneurial background feeding miners, Fannie was already familiar with the miner's way of life. Joe shared his knowledge of prospecting and mining with Fannie, but she was not much of a hands-on miner. After filing a claim, miners were required to do at least $100 worth of assessment work each year. Plenty of people owned mines and paid others to do the work, and although Fannie had never been able to afford that luxury before, she and Joe struck an agreement. Joe did the work for his own mines and for Fannie's as well. The trade-off was that Fannie kept them both well fed and did do much of everything else that it took to make a reasonably comfortable life in the cabins that Joe built for them. Later, both Joe and Fannie would refer to the other in the press as their "pardner,"[24] and they were genuinely partners in business and in living off the land in the remote foothills of the Great Mountain.

By 1906, when Joe and Fannie were living together in Kantishna, he was 37 years old and she was 35. Joe, having left his parent's home at age 15, had been on his own for most of his life and had been in the Far North prospecting, mining, hunting, trapping and independently making his way in the challenging conditions for 15 years. He had already proved that he could survive and prosper without a wife. Fannie was strong, had an adventurous spirit, and had been surviving as a woman in the man's world of gold-rush era Alaska for several years. These two were not idealistic teenagers, hoping for a romantic dream life. They were adults in the prime of their lives, working both independently and together to build something.

Joe Quigley and Fannie McKenzie with four of their dogs in Kantishna. Both were excellent mushers and each had their own dog team (Alaska and Polar Regions Collections, Elmer E. Rasmuson Library, University of Alaska, Fairbanks, UAF-1980-0046-00244).

Chapter 10

Hard Rock

The first winter in the Kantishna Mining District was harsh and a genuine threat to life and limb. The pioneers were living and working in a secluded place that had a dream-like beauty and unimaginable riches, but it could also be a frozen, deadly hell that had no fast way in or out. In the winter, Kantishna miners would get around by hiking, sometimes wearing snowshoes, or use a dog sled. Hudson Stuck wrote that the old-timers had a saying that "traveling at 50 degrees below is all right, as long as it's all right." As long as humans and dogs could keep in "constant brisk motion," had a good trail with convenient stopping places, and nothing went wrong, a person could travel by dog sled in the extreme cold in much the same way as he did during any other time.[1] If anything went wrong, there could be serious trouble or death. The smallest thing could cause a traveler to need to stop, and no amount of clothing could keep a person warm while standing still in those temperatures.

Joe learned to be an excellent dog musher. Even in temperatures 50 degrees below zero, blizzards and white-out conditions, he could handle the sled and the dog team. Mushing, like skiing, requires balancing body weight and leaning with the turns. It also requires that the driver keep a grip on the controls of the sled and be ready when the dogs take off—they are powerful animals who like to hit the ground running. Driving a sled that is weighed down with supplies and provisions requires extra care, and the dogs are sensitive to the driver's skills and needs, but the driver must remember to be aware of any problems a dog might be having. Mushing is one of the many specialized skills that Joe needed to make it through the harsh winters.

The weather in Alaska was, in fact, harsher in Joe Quigley's time than it is in the present time. There are still cold snaps in the interior of Alaska that reach minus 50 Fahrenheit, but because of climate change, there has been measurable change, and the weather has gotten warmer since the turn of the 20th century. Current-day cold snaps occur with less frequency and for shorter periods of time than they did historically.[2] According to NASA, 46 gigatons of ice from Alaskan glaciers was lost on average each year from 2003 to 2010.³ Since then glaciers have been melting at an even more alarming rate, changing the landscape of Alaska and endangering wildlife and humans.

Many miners and prospectors lost fingers and toes due to frostbite and died from the extreme weather. Joseph Brochu of Moose Creek wandered, lost in a snowstorm, for four days before being found with such severe frostbite damage that both of his feet had to be amputated. Some died in the wilderness and weren't found until much later. One man died while prospecting during the winter, and when his decomposing body was found in the spring, he was buried there but never identified. Experienced miner and pioneer John W. Johnson's dog led people to his master's body, which was near a six-foot hole he had scooped into bedrock on Caribou Creek. He was buried in the hole the next day and the dog stood guard over Johnson for at least a month.⁴

Many were still optimistic in spite of the physical toll taken on the miners, and in the spring of 1906 the people in Kantishna put in a large order in Fairbanks for food and supplies. Shopping took an extraordinary amount of organization and planning because it was normally done only once a year. The supplies were shipped to Diamond City, which was the head of navigation, the farthest point above the mouth of the river that could be navigated. The head of navigation could change depending on the seasonal water level and the size of the boat. After freeze-up, the goods would be transported the rest of the way by dog sled to the people who ordered them.

The initial excitement of working a new mining district was wearing off as it became apparent that the richness of the area was inconsistent. The amount of work required to make any profit combined with tough conditions, the extreme remoteness of the area, and a general air of disappointment was too much for most. Mining activity continued throughout the summer and into the fall for the most successful of the miners, but the frenzied activity in Kantishna was short-lived. By the winter of 1906 the population had dwindled to only the most tenacious die-hard miners. Roosevelt, Glacier, and Diamond City were almost completely deserted. There were no rich bars or claims on the creeks, just grub stake claims.⁵ Some miners had relocated to Roosevelt because a good dry trail extended 13 miles to the mines from Roosevelt, whereas the trail from McKinley was a wet one, requiring quite a bit of wading in water to the knees and waist.⁶ Glacier remained as winter quarters for a number of miners.⁷

Commissioner Van Slyke left Roosevelt in August 1906, reporting to Judge Wickersham that only 20 men were left in the district and that the towns were abandoned. In actuality, 60 to 70 miners were still working their claims in the district.⁸ Van Slyke exaggerated the number in his report because he was unhappy and wanted very much to leave his assigned location. Federally-appointed commissioners were the only official authority over a vast area and were responsible for many tasks. They were not paid a fixed

Chapter 10. Hard Rock

Musher Joe Quigley in a traditional parka with a sled and a five-dog team. In the winter, dog teams were the best method of transportation available in remote Kantishna and could carry very heavy loads for hundreds of miles (National Park Service DENA 3511).

salary but were paid based on the fees they charged for each transaction. In addition to recording mining claims, Van Slyke was serving as the official for everything from receiving mail to investigating deaths, and as the population dwindled, he was unhappily making very little money in the Kantishna mining district.

Jack Horn stayed in Kantishna for about three years before moving to Fairbanks to make his home. He had already been in the Far North for many years and had some success. In 1897 he was listed as a passenger on one of the "Klondike Treasure Ships," the steamer *Portland*, traveling from Alaska and the Yukon to Seattle.[9] The *Portland* was operated by the North American Trading & Transportation Company and arrived in Seattle on July 17, 1897. Of the 68 passengers on board, 40 of them were miners, and the ship carried about $1 million in gold. The passengers had deposited a total of $177,500 in small amounts with the ship's purser. Horn is listed as a former prize fighter from Tacoma and had deposited $6,000. Eight years later he was short on cash in Fairbanks and partnering up with Joe Quigley. When Horn left Kantishna, he took up a good farming spot near Fairbanks and raised and sold vegetables. Fresh foods like milk, eggs, fruit, and vegetables were scarce and precious, going for exorbitant prices. The extremely short summers made growing produce difficult, so the rule of supply and demand could make the owner of such a business very successful. By 1939 Horn was running a sawmill on his "attractive homestead."[10] When he cashed out and left Alaska, Horn made $12,000 from the sale of the produce business. He lived out his retirement in California until his death.[11]

Although he did find a two-ounce nugget lying near some exposed bedrock and then later found some more nuggets in the same place, Joe Quigley's original placer claim never yielded a fortune. Years later he talked about the transition from placer mining to quartz mining: "I kept my eyes open for real possibilities, the while making grub-money. Finally, I found some float—good sized pieces of quartz with gold in them." He traced the float to a rounded hill about a mile from Wonder Lake between Eureka and Friday creeks and traced the veins as well as he could from surface outcroppings and indications. He staked the claims as he made the discoveries and had them recorded.[12] As was his way, Joe didn't show his disappointment when the placer mining in Kantishna was modest but saw it as a cue to take a different approach. Throughout his life Joe used his setbacks as tools for growth, continued to take risks and followed the detours in his path to success. He believed that the real profit to be had in the area would come from lode mining and put his focus on that. He continued to do placer mining to pay for the daily necessities of life and for the explosives for his quartz mining while looking to the quartz mining for a bigger payoff.

Identifying the gold-veined quartz float, Joe worked from the bottom of the hill toward the top, digging in various spots as he went up. The higher he went up the hill, the deeper the holes. Gold is intruded in solution through faults in the rocks and then solidifies in the faults in veins. Joe was able to trace which way the veins dipped and found four different veins in this hill. Quarts claims were 1500 feet by 600 feet, and a person was allowed to make as many claims as he did the assessment work for. Joe worked along mineralized quartz vein systems that cut metamorphic schist. Once he decided to develop a mine, he would build a tunnel by drilling a pattern of horizontal holes each about six feet in length at the mine face, fill each hole with explosives, and set the charges off, shattering up to 50 tons of rock. This process is sometimes referred to as the "blasting cycle."[13] After all the powder smoke had left the underground workings, Joe would return underground and clean out and transport the shattered rock fragments to surface locations, storing gold- and silver-bearing quartz ore at one site and the waste schist in another site. This back-breaking process was done repeatedly to extend the tunnel.

Joe Quigley was not the only prospector in the area who believed that hard rock mining was the way to go. Others made discoveries in the Glenn Creek area from 1907 to 1909. The emphasis in the Kantishna camp was shifting from gold to other minerals, including silver and antimony. Tom Lloyd and Billy Taylor chartered a ship to bring in hard rock mining equipment in late 1906, and although an early freeze-up postponed Lloyd and Taylor's plans until the next year, they agreed with Joe that the real profit was in the mineral-bearing hills.

The first lode mining in 1905 was of antimony rather than gold. Joe Quigley shipped 12 tons of stibnite ore from the Last Chance mine on Cari-

Chapter 10. Hard Rock

bou Creek, taking advantage of high prices offered during the Russo-Japanese war. Stibnite is the most important source for the metalloid antimony, which was in great demand for artillery uses.[14] Joe also found gold, silver, and other mineral veins along Mineral Ridge, later renamed Quigley Ridge.[15] Joe and Fannie had gold claims in Kantishna with partners that included Judge James Wickersham and Billy Taylor. It appears that Wickersham did not make any money from his Kantishna claims between 1905 and 1908 and told Taylor to avoid hiring help or otherwise contracting debts because "some of the people interested with us have a bad case of cold feet, and refuse to raise more money at this time for prospecting."[16] Wickersham did have enough supplies on hand for the partners to do some prospecting and assessment work through 1908.

Kantishna was one of the last gold rushes in Alaska. It came as personal mining was dying out and corporate-style mining was growing. The fact that the high-paying areas were all deep in the ground required huge capital investment, large equipment and large crews. Joe had been looking for a million-dollar mine since before the big gold rush, and once he made it to Kantishna, he dedicated himself to the location. He was invested to the point where he would have to sell out to corporate interests in order to make the amount of profit he was looking for. Large mining companies would not invest until the development work was done to prove the worth of the mines. Development work involved the back-breaking labor of hand digging tunnels and ditches using a pick and shovel to intersect and follow the mineralized veins.[17] Joe Quigley spent most of his life digging those tunnels.

By coming to Kantishna and getting involved in hard rock mining, Joe had shifted his lifestyle from the arduous but fairly unrestricted life of an itinerant prospector to the more stable, sometimes tedious life of staying in one place, preparing his discoveries for sale to the highest bidder. Fannie was also living a more settled life now, after years of her freewheeling life as "Fannie the Hike." She had established a domestic routine that helped the two of them live off the land while Joe searched for wealth underground. They managed a subsistence lifestyle, and as was his lifetime habit, Joe saved some money along the way. The lifestyle made sense for a long-term plan, but was very taxing, and a big strike was the only thing that would afford them a chance to change to an easier way of life. Each day presented them with an endless round of back-breaking chores. Hard work was not optional; it was the only way to stay alive.

In some ways the life they were living was the same as Joe had always lived. Prospecting, mining in relative isolation, and taking breaks to go to town for supplies or business had been part of Joe's routine from the time he arrived in the Far North. He could measure his progress by how many feet of tunnel he dug or how many ounces of gold he found. For Fannie, though, the routine they'd created could be tedious beyond her tolerance. She was a social person, accustomed to working in roadhouses or meal tents where there was always some news, gossip, or conversation going on. She now lived miles from her nearest neighbor and spent most days alone while Joe worked in the mines. The dogs kept her company, but human companionship was often in short supply.

Joe continued to do placer mining in the summers and invest whatever he made beyond "grub-money" into his hard rock mining in the winter. Some miners would spend the winter holed up in their cabins, almost hibernating like bears, just surviving until spring, but Joe continued to work during the winter months, using fire and dynamite to hand dig tunnels. He was prospecting on the ridge between Eureka and Friday creeks, now known as Quigley Ridge, climbing and digging on the steep slopes tirelessly as Fannie continued to hunt, trap, preserve, and prepare food, feeding anyone who came through the remote area.

The small mining community in Kantishna developed a symbiotic relationship with the adventurers who came through to conquer the Great Mountain and the scientists who came to study it. The miners served as hosts and guides, while the mountaineers and field scientists brought news of the outside world to the miners. Joe and Fannie were the most well-known couple, and sometimes the only couple, there. Between the two of them they could provide nourishment and comfort, entertaining stories, and genuine knowledge of the remote area and survival skills in the wilderness. They became the hosts to almost everyone who passed through. The visitors, in addition to doing the work they came to accomplish and providing a refreshing break in routine for the isolated miners, would write about their personal experiences with the miners, which gave a contemporary view of the mining community and the people in it.[18]

Chapter 11

"An accurate observer of nature"

Joe Quigley knew the foothills of Denali intimately. He and his miner cohorts spent years walking through the forests, tundra, and hills, prospecting, hunting and simply exploring. It is a hiking tradition to build cairns along trails and to mark the corners of mining claims. Joe and his friends built many cairns, sometimes as a group and sometimes individually. There is a large cairn with a pointed capstone on Wickersham Dome, near Quigley Ridge, and it has been speculated that Joe built this particular cairn by himself.[1] Cairn building is an ancient tradition that crosses many cultures, but when looking at photographs of Joe and the Wickersham Dome cairn, his Irish and Scottish ancestry and their centuries of cairn building comes to mind.

Joe's expertise regarding the foothills made him useful to scientists and explorers. One person who took a particular interest in Joe's knowledge and skills was Charles Sheldon. Sheldon began the tradition of wildlife research and conservation in the area and is sometimes referred to as "the Father of Denali National Park."[2] Sheldon met Joe Quigley and Fannie McKenzie in 1907 when his boat ran into low water and he and his guide Harry Karstens were forced to stop and pack Sheldon's goods more than 20 miles to the head of Glacier Creek, where they spent the night at Joe and Fannie's place. Sheldon noted in his diary how much he enjoyed their company and said, "Quigley was one of those rare honest chivalrous men, found here and there in Alaska, who combined successful individual mining with the traits of a true hunter and an accurate observer of Nature."[3] He compared Fannie's wilderness survival skills to those of Alaska Native women. Joe and Fannie enjoyed Sheldon's company as well, and the three of them stayed in touch with one another after the visit.

Sheldon came from a Vermont family involved in marble quarrying and manufacturing. He attended prestigious schools and graduated from Yale in 1890, the same year that his family business collapsed. After college, he be-

Joe Quigley at a cairn on Wickersham Dome, which was located close to Quigley Ridge, circa 1912, when the pointed capstone was still in place. Some say that Joe built this monument alone, but generally cairn building was a group project (National Park Service DENA 3512).

Chapter 11. "An accurate observer of nature" 75

came involved in the railroad business and invested in one of the richest silver and lead mines in Mexico, becoming financially secure enough to retire at age 35. His self-made wealth enabled Sheldon to follow his passion as a conservationist with a particular interest in mountain sheep.[4] Sheldon's work in the Denali region resulted in the identification of 23 different mammals and 32 species of birds. His diary was the earliest study of natural habitat in Denali and was published as a book in 1930.

A few months after Sheldon's visit to their cabin, on February 15, 1908, Joe and Fannie and three of their dogs arrived at Sheldon's cabin to get a load of sheep meat and stayed for a two-week hunting excursion. The days were mild for an Alaskan February, with a stiff south wind. Sheldon, his guide Harry Karstens, Joe, and Fannie went out for sheep three times over a period of five days, and Joe went out alone once. Karstens and Joe Quigley had known each other from earlier times prospecting in the Dawson area and maintained their friendship over the years. Although the hunters all saw and stalked sheep that day, none were killed. They did kill and eat some grouse.[5]

A week later, Charles Sheldon and Fannie McKenzie went hunting alone. Sheldon referred to her as "Mrs. Quigley" even though she and Joe weren't married yet. Fannie had never killed anything before she moved to Kantishna and had been learning to hunt from Joe, who was an exceptionally skilled hunter. She was now getting pointers from Charles Sheldon, who was very well known for his exemplary hunting skills as well as his scientific studies of Dall sheep. Fannie was learning from the best and was a good student. On the day they went out alone, Sheldon and Fannie kept track of a band of sheep by watching a raven that kept flying and circling over the sheep. Ravens are effective hunters and sometimes use cooperative techniques for hunting game that is too large for one bird to kill. They are known to eat carrion and would certainly enjoy the opportunity to dine on the leftovers from the hunt. On this day, though, Fannie's rifle misfired twice and then she missed again when a band of 34 sheep were running from the gunshots. Joe Quigley was off hunting sheep by himself that day and also came back empty handed.[6]

A blizzard kept everyone indoors February 26–28 with the exception of Sheldon, who went for a few short excursions into the woods to observe birds and said that "snow so filled the air that I could not see in any direction."[7] Unfortunately, there is no description in Sheldon's diary of the how the four people passed the time for three days inside of a 12-by-14-foot cabin, but it seems likely that they shared stories of their experiences in the wilderness. Sheldon's only notes about the time were that Joe and Fannie were delightful guests and that he greatly enjoyed their visit.

Once the snow and wind stopped raging, Harry Karstens, Joe and Fannie went up the river with a dog team to hunt for sheep to feed the dogs, who were completely out of food, while Sheldon went up Cabin Creek for rams. At the end of the day, the Quigley party came back with two ewes and a yearling ram, and Sheldon came back with two rams. The next day, March 1, everyone went out separately looking for sheep to hunt but didn't get anything. Joe and Fannie went home to Glacier Creek early the next morning.[8]

During their long conversations, Joe Quigley told Charles Sheldon about an unusual experience he had with a lynx. Spending so much time around wild animals, Joe understood their normal behavior and also had a few experiences when animals did not behave in the usual way. Sheldon found this story fascinating and recounted it in his diary, prefaced with the opinion that they story was "as unusual as it is reliable."[9] Early one morning while checking trap lines near Glacier Creek, Joe saw fresh lynx tracks. Canada lynx weigh between 20 and 40 pounds and generally hunt at night. They are very skilled hunters with exceptional hearing and eyesight, and their preferred diet is snowshoe hare. Lynx normally avoid humans but will attack a human if they feel threatened.

When Joe returned to the same area later in the day, he saw a female lynx near where the tracks had been. Typical felines, lynx are stalk-and-ambush hunters,[10] and this one had decided to stalk Joe. She was crouching about 15 feet away, facing the trail. As Joe passed, the unmoving lynx watched him. Knowing that he was being stalked, Joe continued down the trail for a short distance and cut a willow club and then started back, staying on the trail, until he was opposite the lynx. As Joe turned slowly to approach, the lynx began to growl ominously and rose up as Joe came nearer. When Joe was within six feet of the lynx, he raised the club, and the cat sprang into some low willows and ran, circling, to a spot 200 or 300 feet down the creek behind him. As it ran, Joe threw the club at the lynx but missed. Continuing to walk and picking the club back up, Joe noticed that the lynx was about eight feet straight up the bank, which was too steep for a man to climb, so he decided to get nearer and then run quickly down the ice to gain enough momentum to jump high enough to reach it with the club. As he jumped upward with the club held ready to strike, the lynx sprang at him, which allowed Joe to strike the lynx on the head, mid-air, stunning it. Joe was luckier than the lynx that day and was probably quite surprised by the incident. The lynx skull became part of the collection of the U.S. Biological Survey in Washington, D.C., as one of Joe's contributions of specimens for government studies.

Joe Quigley was known, as Charles Sheldon had remarked, as "an accurate observer of nature" and was a consultant to geologists and conservationists the entire time that he lived in the Kantishna region. After Alfred Brooks' study of the area that began in 1902, the USGS sent Stephen R. Capps, who spent many seasons in Kantishna and became friends with Joe Quigley. Capps reported on mining activity and was instrumental in the movement to establish Mount McKinley National Park. In 1917 Capps wrote an article

Chapter 11. "An accurate observer of nature"

for *National Geographic*, reporting that large numbers of game animals were being taken by market hunters, which supported Charles Sheldon's studies. The various studies led to Mount McKinley National Park being created as a two-million-acre wildlife preserve.[11] After nearly a decade of dedicated work, Sheldon, Harry Karstens and others persuaded Congress to create Mount McKinley National Park in 1917. McKinley (now Denali) was the world's first national park established to conserve wildlife.[12]

After Sheldon left the area, Joe continued to send him reports on the animals that he and Fannie hunted. He would list and measure each one, sending the statistics and detailed descriptions. In a January 1909 letter to Sheldon, Joe sent the measurements of two rams that included the spread of their horns at the top, at the base following the hair line and "square around at base" as well as the length of the horns and the number of inches "around the outside of the turn." He also mentions "the glasses" several times and describes the exact locations where each animal was found. He tells Sheldon that he is "thankful for the glasses," which seem to have been a gift from Sheldon. Joe became known for using field glasses, and some photos of him show a binocular case hanging from his shoulder. He talks about the animals that they got for meat for the winter and the foxes that they caught to sell. Fannie was quite the trapper, and Joe told Sheldon that she got a marten and 11 weasels (ermine) to sell. He mentions various types of mice including one that "seems to be a little different" and says that he will be sending the specimen to Sheldon. Joe told Sheldon of his observations of animals that they weren't hunting or trapping as well, mentioning porcupine, wolf, a bear, and the mating habits of the sheep. He also mentioned in his letter to Sheldon that the white owls (snowy owls) seemed to be scarce that year and attributed it to fewer mice than normal.[13]

Joe expressed the expectation of being in that part of the country for another year "unless I sell, or something unexpected happens." He also talked about how much he enjoyed watching animal behavior through the field glasses and described how he watched a fox near the Toklat catching mice for more than an hour, explaining how the fox would "make holes where the mice come up through the snow, till it showed up, and then pounce on it like a cat." In a reference to something that Sheldon had done for him in the past, Joe said, "Please let me know what would most interest you, or if there is anything I can get or do for you here, as I would be thankful for an opportunity to do something for you, that you would appreciate, the same as I do what you have already done for me."[14]

Getting national park status for the area did not immediately curtail the threats to the animals living there, and scientists continued to do studies in the park. In the early 1920s Dr. Olaus Murie of the U.S. Biological Survey arrived to study caribou. Dr. Murie's brother Adolph Murie joined him in

1922, researching mammals, birds and ecology. Dr. Olaus Murie was married to Margaret "Mardy" Thomas, who had grown up in Fairbanks, and Adolph Murie married Mardy's half-sister Louise Gillette.[15] Both couples worked together on wildlife conservation and ecology issues, and their life's work greatly influenced wildlife management policies and wilderness conservation in Alaska. Adolph Murie has been called "Denali's Wilderness Conscience" and his work and association with the park continued until the early 1970s.[16]

The first 20 years of research on large mammals concentrated on caribou, Dall sheep, and wolves. In 1926 research done by scientists George Wright and Joseph Dixon examined the dynamics between the various animals in the park, recording 86 species of birds and 25 different mammals, and created the first comprehensive ecologically based survey of the park.[17] Their extensive research collections and field notes resulted in a book, *Birds and Mammals of Mount McKinley National Park, Alaska* (1938).

In 1928 park rangers Grant Pearson and Fritz Nyberg responded to a big die-off of the Dall sheep by capturing some and trying to save them. Joe Quigley sent a photo of the two rangers feeding a lamb to his nephew Lloyd Quigley in Vancouver, Washington. On the back he had written, "Two of McKinley Park Rangers, friends of mine feeding a young mountain lamb." The Dall sheep are suited to their life on the steep slopes and use the rocks and crags to elude predators. The rams and ewes live in segregated groups except for mating season in late November and early December. The rams have massive curling horns and fight each other by butting heads to establish which males will get to reproduce. The ewes have smaller horns and protect themselves and their lambs by going off to the most unapproachable cliffs available to them. Ewes are able to reproduce at about age three and give birth to one lamb a year, usually in May or June. It was Adolf Murie's studies of the wolf-sheep relationship that later helped push wildlife conservation efforts from predator elimination to habitat conservation, when he determined that Dall sheep numbers were declining because of severe late winter weather, rather than predation, and that predators played an important part in a healthy ecosystem.

Trapping and market hunting was taking a toll on the wildlife in the area. There was also a big horned sheep die-off due to weather in 1928 and again in 1932. Efforts to save the Dall sheep included rangers feeding lambs. Market hunting in Kantishna escalated radically from the times when Joe would kill one moose at a time and sell the meat at Fortymile. Market hunting had been illegal since just after the turn of the century but continued illegally well into the 1920s. Miners were allowed to kill rams in the park for their own use and for dog food. Market hunters destroyed herds of mountain sheep by killing with no regard for the continuation of the herd. These mercenary hunters took as many animals as they could to sell the meat and fur, with their

Chapter 11. "An accurate observer of nature"

only concern about the animals' life being how to end it more efficiently to increase profits.

Alaska is caribou country and they were periodically abundant in Kantishna. Caribou are very large deer, with the males weighing up to 600 pounds, and were a staple in the miners' diets. Their hides and antlers were also very useful. You can see caribou antlers attached above cabin doors in old photographs from the area. One Kantishna camp miner, John Anderson, made chairs from moose and caribou antlers with seats made from the hides.[18] Male caribou shed their antlers in November or December, after mating. Female caribou keep their antlers until birthing or after giving birth in June.

Caribou are similar to reindeer in that both are migratory and highly adapted to cold weather, with specialized coats and hooves. They are considered the same species, but caribou are somewhat larger and are native to North America, whereas reindeer are native to Scandinavia and Russia. Reindeer are one of the oldest domesticated species in the world, but caribou are wild. Caribou make the longest overland trek of all animals worldwide, and because they are so wide ranging, they face many challenges to their survival in the wild.[19] They are particularly vulnerable to the effects of climate change and habitat loss. In the early days, subsistence hunters and the small number of miners in the area did not interrupt migratory movements of the caribou. As time and technology brought more people with new hunting methods, the caribou were threatened. Development of roads, current era sport hunters arriving by aircraft, and climate change all endanger the migratory patterns and the lives of the caribou herds.[20]

The first study of plants in the park took place in 1927 when botanists Inez Mexia and Frances Payne of the University of California collected wildflowers and shrubs. Another major research project concerning vegetation was done in 1930 when the University of Wyoming's Dr. Aven Nelson and Ruth Ashton Nelson collected and classified hundreds of different plants for the Museum of London and the Smithsonian Institution.[21] Other scientific investigations in Denali included a study of cosmic radiation at high altitudes, U.S. Army tests of cold weather equipment, and studies of glacier movement. All of the early nature studies there contributed to our understanding of ecology, and the park continues to be a source of valuable information for conservationists.

Chapter 12

Community

Kantishna was a very remote, isolated community. In Joe Quigley's time, the lack of transportation was a problem for the business of mining and for the daily lives of the miners. Joe was able to withstand the rigors of life in such a remote place because he was innately suited for that life. He was physically strong with plenty of stamina and he had an iron will and an ability to stay focused to the point of obsession. These traits got him through his early years in the Far North, where he learned the specialized skills needed for the life of a miner under the tutelage of the old-timers he met. By the time he was settled in Kantishna he was a Sourdough himself and generously shared what he learned with anyone who could benefit from it. A friend would later recall, "He would go out of his way to do you a favor, and he wouldn't hesitate to tell you something that would make it easier for you. He knew all the tricks to get by out in the wilderness."[1] Joe had a tolerance for, and even a need for, solitude, and yet loved his friends and truly appreciated a good laugh or a kind gesture and offered both to the people around him whenever he could. In the Kantishna mining camp each person was at once a rugged individualist and dependent on his neighbors, even though the nearest neighbor was likely to be ten miles away. The citizens of the Kantishna Mining District were also tied to the Fairbanks community as Fairbanks was tied to the Kantishna miners.

Fairbanks had grown quite a bit in the few years since Joe and his cohorts began working in Kantishna. Like all boom towns, Fairbanks was made up of people who had decided to stay in a place in spite of the extreme climate to conquer the physical challenge of getting gold out of the earth. The closest other town was at least eight days' travel by sleigh or ten days' travel by steamer.[2] Isolation was a constant problem in Alaska at that time and any source of news became especially important. The first newspaper in Alaska was a weekly called the *Alaska Times*, based in Sitka and begun in 1869.[3] The *Fairbanks Daily News*, which would become the *News-Miner*, began operations in 1903. In those times before telecommunications, the newspaper covered the mining activities in Kantishna from the mining camp's inception and reported on Joe Quigley's activities regularly.

Fairbanks was situated on the banks of the Chena Slough, which was an offshoot of the Tanana River. The water was shallow but navigable most of the time, and the first street of the Fairbanks mining camp followed the curve of the river, with each street after it following that curve. Along Front Street a long row of businesses in wooden false-fronted buildings were painted white, green, and a ruddy ochre trimmed in red.[4] On the opposite bank of the slough were warehouses on piles where the ships would dock. There were more business buildings on Second Street and some on Third, with the buildings becoming progressively smaller down to two-story homes and then low one-story log houses as the town fanned out and away from the water.

Twenty-three saloons were on Front Street. Genteel ladies did not walk on Front Street but turned down and walked on Second. The red-light district was known as "the Row." This area was established, along with the saloons, before families began moving to Fairbanks. Once wives and children were living there, a high, solid board fence with gates in it was built across Fourth where it left Cushman, and another one across Fourth where it emerged on

(Left to right) Pete Buchholz, William McPhee and James Wickersham with a moose, ca. 1914-1915. The moose was a pet of Buchholz, who had a harness for it and would walk it around Fairbanks. This led to a regulation restricting hoofed animals from using the sidewalks of Fairbanks (*Fairbanks Daily News-Miner*, 11 April 1940). McPhee was an early pioneer who owned saloons in Fortymile, Dawson, and Fairbanks, and he was one of the sponsors of the Sourdough Expedition. Judge James Wickersham was one of the most powerful men in Alaska, and during his attempt to climb Mount McKinley, he found gold in the Kantishna region in 1903 (photographer unknown. Lulu Fairbanks Collection, Elmer E. Rasmuson Library, University of Alaska, Fairbanks, UAF-1968-69-1945).

Barnette, two blocks down. Immediately behind the Row, on Fifth, Sixth and Seventh, were the houses of the elite who made every effort for their dwellings to look like middle class homes back east. Eventually a large courthouse was built on Second and Cushman, and soon two banks were established as well as drugstores and grocery stores and doctor, lawyer and dentist offices.[5]

The Pioneers of Alaska fraternal organization Igloo #4, Fairbanks, Alaska, was begun in 1909 and Joe Quigley was a charter member. The organization was "formed in the early Territorial days to meet the civic and social needs of the growing population."[6] At that time there was a notable lack of both territorial and local government and an absence of a viable court system. The affairs of the people and their community were handled by themselves, often through miners' meetings. Organizations like the Pioneers of Alaska provided practical help—food, shelter, medical, and other assistance—while also promoting civic order in the form of government, courts, and education. They met social needs t by hosting church services and school activities, putting on dances, dinners, holiday celebrations, and providing gathering places for conversation for those who spent most of their time in the awe-inspiring but lonely Alaska bush.[7]

On his application to the POA Joe Quigley lists his permanent address as Kantishna, Alaska, and on the line that asks, "If married, state to whom," he wrote Fannie Quigley. This certainly shows the nature of their relationship, if it was not an accurate legal description. Fannie was still using the name McKenzie at the time, and she would not be legally married to Joe for nine more years. Under names of living relatives, he wrote R. O. Quigley, Butler, Pennsylvania. This had to have been his older brother since their father, R. O. Quigley, Sr., died in 1907. Joe's mother had passed away in 1900, and although he had quite a few other living brothers and sisters on the West Coast and in Pennsylvania, he didn't list any of them. His occupation is listed as miner and his emergency contacts are listed as Fannie Quigley and R. O. Quigley. Fannie was his partner in every sense of the word. The Pioneers of Alaska Igloo #4 met the first and third Monday of each month at Eagle Hall in Fairbanks, and Joe was active in the group.[8]

Community life in Fairbanks was enhanced by the various clubs and organizations. The mission of the Pioneers of Alaska was similar to the Yukon Order of Pioneers, which Joe had joined back in his early days in the Far North. The basic humanitarian ideal resonated with his own philosophies, and it seems reasonable to think that he gravitated toward group associations for both idealistic and practical reasons. He had a sense of responsibility for the community and also knew that belonging to a group boosted his business contacts.

Fraternal orders were everywhere in America, with total membership in the millions. The Pioneers of Alaska was one of the lodges unique to the

North. Another was the Arctic Brotherhood Lodge, which was quite posh, and it seemed that their events were designed to show how much luxury could be laid over the wilderness. As more families moved there, Fairbanks society became more organized.[9] By 1911, centers of social activity in Fair-

The 1909 Charter for the Pioneers of Alaska Fairbanks Igloo #4. The list of charter members of the Fairbanks chapter includes Joe Quigley and many of the other miners in the Kantishna Mining District. Fairbanks was the largest city in Alaska in 1909 and was at the peak of its gold production (Elmer E. Rasmuson Library, University of Alaska Fairbanks, UAF-1989-0166-00453_neg glass).

banks included Presbyterian and Episcopal churches, a ladies' aid guild, a women's civic club, sewing clubs, lodges of Freemasons (which Joe joined in 1921) and the appendant body the Order of the Eastern Star, Eagles and Lady Eagles, and Moose and Lady Moose clubs. The men's groups were explicitly organized around the principle of masculine identity and excluded women.[10] The effect was to strengthen solidarity among men. The associated women's groups, such as the Order of the Eastern Star, the Lady Eagles, and the Lady Moose, were essentially ladies' axillary groups and were originally formed to ensure that women supported or at least tolerated the men's groups. Fannie didn't join any of these ladies' groups. In 1912 the Pioneers of Alaska extended membership rights to women and Fannie was inducted into the Pioneer Women of Alaska on February 19, 1916.[11]

In 1910, ten years before the passage of the 19th Amendment, several states had given women the right to vote, but equal rights were still only the ideal of a minority. Couples who lived together without the benefit of marriage continued to be looked down on by the general public. Cohabitation not only besmirched a woman's reputation, it was also illegal. When official forms needed to be filled out this issue became something that couldn't be ignored, and cohabiting couples asked themselves if they should lie and say they were married, with the woman using the man's last name as a cover for their unmarried status. Joe had already listed "Fannie Quigley" as his wife on the Pioneers of Alaska application and clearly saw her as his wife, yet she was legally still Fannie McKenzie.

When census taker Ernest J. Foster filled out the rolls for Kantishna area for the 1910 census, Joe and Fannie were living on Glacier Creek. Joseph B. Quigley is listed as the head of household, a self-employed gold miner, single, 40 years old, owning the home outright, born in Pennsylvania, with parents born in Pennsylvania. Fannie was listed as "Fanny McKensey [sic]," servant (!), married for nine years, 38 years old, not a homeowner or renter, born in Nebraska, with parents born in Germany. Fannie was not a pretentious person and didn't generally hide the fact that she and Joe were not married, but social pressure made others call her "Mrs. Quigley" before it was true. Listing her a "servant" on the census was another inaccuracy used by an outside source to make her situation look socially acceptable. The fact was that Joe and Fannie weren't married yet because Fannie was still legally married to Angus McKenzie. Women's social standing was very much defined by the men they were with. Living with but not being married to Joe meant that Fannie's official status was employee or servant. Even in the Alaska bush, leftover Victorian social standards influenced community values.

Although the miners were socially tied to Fairbanks and other towns, the Athabascan people who were living in Kantishna when the miners arrived were geographically closer. The interior of Alaska had been Athabascan country for centuries and the Native people knew how to sustain a subsistence lifestyle without decimating the supply of wildlife, fish and vegetation. Many of the stampeders were not "accurate observers of nature," as Charles Sheldon had described Joe Quigley. When the large group of miners arrived, most of them were careless and destructive, indiscriminately killing wildlife for food and clearing swaths of forest to make lumber and build cabins. They netted fish by the thousands for dog food and rerouted and muddied the creeks, which negatively affected the fish. Miners also burned the vegetation off their claims, which sometimes caused out-of-control wildfires. Some of the stampeders were racist, and some were sometimes violent, treating the indigenous people with disdain.[12] When the stampede happened, the population grew in an unnatural way, burdening the natural resources.

Chapter 13

The Great Mountain

There was only one landform that Joe Quigley would refer to as "The Mountain"; all the rest were "hills" or "humps."[1] The Great Mountain called McKinley (now Denali) garnered respect from the citizens of Kantishna and attracted adventurers from all over the world. He loved the Great Mountain and met many of the people who tried to conquer it. Joe and Fannie's home was a launching place where adventurers who had their sights set on Mount McKinley went to be nourished and encouraged on their way up or greeted and replenished when they came back down. Joe and Fannie were friends with both the successful and unsuccessful mountaineers and were sometimes the first people outside of the climbing party to hear the firsthand stories of the climb.

Old friends of Joe and Fannie's concocted a plan that led to one of the most unusual and controversial efforts to reach the top of the mountain. The Sourdough Expedition in 1910 was a group of four miners, Tom Lloyd, Billy Taylor, Pete Anderson, and Charlie McGonagall. All were miners with some experience under their belts, and so the group was dubbed the Sourdoughs. Three of the four of them, Taylor, Anderson, and McGonagall, shared mining claims with Joe and Fannie. Alaska miners had a certain sense of humor that often resulted in practical jokes, and one such joke turned into a climb to the peak of the tallest mountain in North America. As Tom Lloyd told it, "About two weeks prior to the Pioneers' Order being organized here [Fairbanks, November 1909] Bill McPhee and me were talking one day of the possibility of getting to the summit of Mount McKinley, and I said that I thought that if anyone could make the climb, there were several pioneers of my acquaintance who could."[2] Lloyd was a former sheriff from Utah who had been mining for years in the Kantishna district and was in the Washington Saloon in Fairbanks having a conversation with saloon owner Bill McPhee. McPhee had been in the Far North since 1888 and was a founding member of the Yukon Order of Pioneers. It was in McPhee's old Fortymile saloon, back in 1896, that George Carmack first announced the gold findings that started the massive Klondike Gold Rush of 1897. He had certainly heard more than his fair share of miners' boasts over the years and didn't hesitate to express his skepticism.

Chapter 13. The Great Mountain

At the time of Lloyd and McPhee's conversation in the summer of 1909, there was a big debate in the news about the legitimacy of Dr. Frederick Cook's claim to have reached the North Pole in April of 1908. Frederick Albert Cook was a physician and explorer who was noted for his claims to have reached the summit of Mount McKinley in 1906. In 1909, after reviewing his records, the University of Copenhagen ruled Cook's North Pole claim unproven. Alaskans had always been skeptical about Cook's claim to have climbed Mt. McKinley, and the new shadow cast on Cook's North Pole adventure was enough to make him a complete laughingstock among the miners. McPhee, Lloyd, and other Sourdoughs saw Cook as typical of the city men, with their fancy equipment and special clothing, who garnered dramatic headlines for doing what the old-timers could do as a matter of course.

During the exchange between Lloyd and McPhee, McPhee said that he didn't think any living man could make the ascent, but Lloyd told McPhee that he and a friend had been on and around Mount McKinley more than anyone else had and that he believed the two of them could climb it. McPhee challenged him, saying that the middle-aged and paunchy Lloyd was too old to do it, causing Lloyd to respond that if he couldn't do it, he could find men who would.[3] The conversation escalated into a challenge for Lloyd, with an offer of $500 from McPhee for expenses, if Lloyd would make the trip himself. Two other local businessmen put up $500 each and Lloyd accepted the challenge.

Lloyd chose other Kantishna miners as his traveling companions, knowing that they were tough, accustomed to the weather and terrain, and shared that certain tenacity that is necessary to be a subsistence miner. Only one of the men, William "Billy" Taylor, born on March 15, 1883, in Ontario, Canada, was under the age of 40. Taylor was a big man, 27 years old, easy-going, and "strong as a horse."[4] He spent his 28th birthday on the glacier during the climb to the peak of Mount McKinley. Charles McGonagall was a was a former mail carrier and musher who had come north in 1896 and at one time had spent 34 consecutive days outdoors when the temperature never rose above minus 50 degrees Fahrenheit.[5] Pete "the Swede" Anderson and Billy Taylor were described by Hudson Stuck as "two of the strongest men in all the North." Anderson and Taylor worked particularly well together, with Taylor describing Anderson as "a big husky Swede" and a "hell of a good fellow on the trail."[6] The Sourdough party all had exceptional wilderness survival skills and, with the exception of Lloyd, were extraordinarily strong men and able to travel tirelessly.

Thinking that with a strong telescope a flag might be visible from Fairbanks, Lloyd, Taylor, Anderson, and McGonagall agreed that they should take a 14-foot-tall spruce flagpole with them on the climb and plant it on the peak when they made it up there. They were outfitted in Fairbanks in the same manner as any mushers, and they wore their normal winter clothes. Prospectors always travel light and, as was the custom, their equipment was minimal. It's been said repeatedly that they didn't even take a rope with them. They took rations of caribou meat, bacon and beans, flour, dried fruit, hot chocolate, coffee and doughnuts. The climb was a matter of endurance. Lloyd ended up waiting at Willow Camp in the foothills, and only Taylor and Anderson took the pole to what they thought was the summit but turned out to be an outcropping a few hundred feet below the summit. McGonagall said that he stopped short of the summit because it wasn't his turn to carry the pole. They took a few photographs with a five-dollar Brownie camera to show that they made the climb, but the low-quality pictures weren't very useful.

The Sourdoughs were typical prospector/pioneers in their attitudes and personalities. These men performed presumably impossible feats, where they risked their lives repeatedly and then downplayed the achievement. With the exception of Lloyd, who was so anxious to have bragging rights that he lied about the details of the trip to make himself look like a hero, they had a hatred of publicity and did things "for their own peculiar reasons."[7] Because their normal way of going about things was based on an intense desire to only prove themselves to themselves and to their small group of friends in the North, they didn't conduct their journey to the highest point in North America with scientific precision or press release-ready organization. The simply set out with the intention of getting to the top. After their three-month-long trek, only Tom Lloyd went to Fairbanks to "close the incident." Taylor, Anderson, and McGonagall all went back to Kantishna to work their mines, doing business as usual, seeing the walk up the mountain as a novel interruption to their quest for gold.

There was some general confusion and disbelief regarding Lloyd's account of the Sourdough climb. At first Lloyd exaggerated the story, saying that they climbed both peaks, when in fact they had only climbed the north summit. It was also reported that all four of them made it to the top, when only two actually went all the way up. Because of these inaccuracies some people were as skeptical of the Sourdoughs as the Sourdoughs had been of Frederick Cook. Ultimately it was proved that Cook was a fraud, but the Sourdoughs were vindicated a few years later when the Karstens–Stuck expedition returned from their successful climb and reported that they spotted the Sourdoughs' flagpole on the peak.

More organized than the Sourdough Expedition was Belmore Browne's third attempt to conquer Mount McKinley. Historically, Browne is more well known for his scenic paintings of Alaska and the Canadian Rockies than he is for his mountain climbing. He studied at the New York School of Art and the Académie Julian in Paris, and his work is included in the collection of the Renwick Gallery at the Smithsonian American Art Museum.[8] In addition to being a fine artist, Browne was an avid outdoorsman and made several attempts to climb Mount McKinley.

Browne's first failed attempt to reach the peak was in 1906 and was organized by Herschel Parker, an adjunct professor of physics at Columbia University, and Dr. Frederick Cook, before the validity of his trips to the Arctic and Antarctic regions had been questioned. The trip was financed by Professor Parker and an unnamed wild game hunter from the east who was unable to make the trip.[9] Professor Parker and Belmore Brown's second attempt was in 1910, the same year as the Sourdough Expedition. They approached the southern face of the mountain with the principal motivation of "duplicating Dr. Cook's photographs and settling once and for all time his Polar claim."[10] The second attempt also failed to reach the peak. Not easily dissuaded, Parker and Browne began planning their third attempt immediately and decided that the next time they would approach the north face rather than the south.

On their third attempt in 1912, Browne and Parker came very close but could not complete the mission because of harsh weather. This failed attempt was especially heartbreaking, as they came within 150 feet of the summit be-

The Parker-Browne expedition party visits with Joe and Fannie before their third attempt to reach the peak of Mount McKinley in 1912. Belmore Browne, who became more well known for his paintings than for his mountaineering, was highly impressed with Joe and Fannie's lifestyle. Fannie McKenzie, standing in the doorway, is flanked by Browne on the left and Joe Quigley on the right. Herschel Parker stands to the right of Joe. The expedition included international photo journalist and documentary filmmaker Merl LaVoy as the official photographer (photograph by Merl LaVoy, Elmer E. Rasmuson Library, University of Alaska, Fairbanks, UAF-1981-0208-p394).

fore having to admit defeat.[11] The entire party stopped in to visit Fannie and Joe, and Browne was quite taken with their lifestyle.

As described by Browne, Joe and Fannie's home was "spacious and clean, well-lighted and cheerful. Books and magazines bespoke lively intellectual interests. A flourishing garden, with flowers and vegetables, fed soul and stomach. Their permafrost cellar kept meat frozen, and their cooler kept vegetables fresh." Browne compared the meals Fannie cooked to Roman feasts, with meats, breads, vegetables, jellies, pies, and a wild rhubarb sauce that Browne said beat any tame rhubarb he had eaten. They drank ice-cold potato beer that Fannie had brewed at home.[12] Browne's detailed and romantic view of the Quigley cabin does create a wonderful picture of how Joe and Fannie lived. Their walk-in refrigerator/freezer system was actually one of Joe's tunnels dug into the permafrost, with insulation in a section to keep it from freezing. The first self-contained refrigerator for home use wasn't introduced by Frigidaire until 1923, and home freezers that could hold anything larger than an ice tray didn't come into use until 1940. Joe and Fannie were very skilled and ahead of their time in their ability to preserve food. Using their cooling system, along with their large thriving garden and their superb hunting skills, they kept themselves and many other people well fed for years.

In April 1912, the same year as the Browne–Parker attempt, Joe Quigley wrote to his friend Charles Sheldon, telling him that things were essentially the same as when Sheldon was there a few years earlier. Joe wrote that "the boys are mining a little in summer and either trapping or prospecting in the winter" and "[I] have been too busy running a tunnel to tap a ledge and am in over 100 ft. now, but expect to tap the ledge in a few feet more." Joe reported to Sheldon that this had been the finest winter he had ever seen since his arrival in the north, with "no cold weather and very little snow."[13] He elaborated on "no cold weather" by explaining that it hadn't gotten any colder that minus 40 degrees Fahrenheit, and that was only for a day or two. Illustrating the idea that one man's ceiling is another man's floor, reports of the same temperatures made it to Alaska newspapers when Pennsylvania and New York also reached minus 40 degrees Fahrenheit that winter. Unprecedented weather reached the entire eastern seaboard, and Atlanta, Georgia, received four inches of snow.[14] Joe added that Fannie was busy putting up (preserving) moose nose jelly and had harvested a large crop of vegetables during the summer of 1911, including 1500 pounds of potatoes. A postscript to the letter explained that a small bouquet of native flowers was enclosed, from Fannie to Mrs. Sheldon.[15]

Charles Sheldon and Joe Quigley's mutual friend, Harry Karstens, had tried his hand at several businesses since they were all together on the hunting trip in 1908 and was now back in the foothills of Denali in 1913 as the guide and climbing leader for the first complete official ascent of Mount McKinley. Coming to Dawson City at the age of 19 in 1897, Henry Peter

"Harry" Karstens mined on the Seventymile Creek, very close to where Jack London held a claim at the time. Karstens and London likely crossed paths at Henderson Creek and it is said that London, who later became a beloved author of novels about the Far North, at least partially based his main character in *Burning Daylight* on Karstens.[16] In addition to being a prospector and miner, Karstens worked as a packer hauling stampeders' heavy packs over the Chilkoot Pass and later became a contract mail carrier using a dog team to deliver mail in the Far North. This position put Karstens among the ranks of the most stalwart, rugged, dependable and respected people in the North, braving the most extreme conditions imaginable and gaining the highest respect from the citizenry. Eight years after arriving in the Far North, Karstens started an overland winter express service business with fellow mail carrier Charlie McGonagall (a member of the Sourdough Expedition), hauling freight and passengers from Fairbanks to Kantishna. In 1908 Harry Karstens is listed on some Kantishna district group mining claims with Joe Quigley and Fannie McKenzie, along with W. H. Taylor, Charles McGonagall, Thomas Lloyd, James Sedlacek, and U. J. Paxton.[17] By 1913 Karstens and Joe Quigley had been acquainted for at least 15 years.

Karstens' experience made him the perfect guide for 50-year-old Archdeacon Hudson Stuck. British-born Stuck had emigrated to the United States at the age of 20 in 1885, working as both a cowboy and a schoolteacher in Texas. In 1889 he studied theology in Sewanee, Tennessee, at the University of the South, becoming an Episcopal priest in 1892 and serving congregations in Texas until his move to Alaska in 1904. Stuck served under Missionary Bishop Peter Trimble Rowe and with Reverend Charles E. Betticher, Jr., founded numerous missions in the Tanana Valley over the next decade.[18] Stuck had a long-held dream of climbing Mount McKinley, which he, like many Alaskans, called Denali. He felt that making the climb on the Episcopal church's 25th Alaska anniversary would gain public awareness and donations for the church's work on behalf of the Alaska Natives.[19] Stuck was referred to as the Archdeacon of the Yukon and viewed the climb as God's work. He relied heavily on his younger, sturdier companions, and in the preface to his book *The Ascent of Denali* expressed gratitude to "Mr. Harry P. Karstens, strong, competent, and resourceful. The real leader of the expedition in the face of difficulty and danger."[20]

Karstens and Stuck made the ascent with theology student Robert Tatum and 20-year-old Alaska Native Walter Harper, the first to reach the summit. Walter Harper had youth, strength, exceptional skills, and a notable family that tied him to Alaska history. Walter's father Arthur Harper came to the United States from Ireland in 1850 and spent his life following gold stampedes.[21] Heading north and prospecting alone on the Tanana River, Arthur Harper later joined a trading concern with Jack McQuesten and Alfred Mayo.

There were very few white people in the area at the time, but Harper won the respect of local Natives. McQuesten, Mayo and Harper opened several trading posts as each new rush began and are credited with opening the Far North to prospectors. Arthur Harper's wife was a respected Koyukon woman, Seyn-dahn, or Jennie Albert, and Walter Harper was the youngest of their seven children. Walter's parents separated, and he was raised by his mother in the traditional Athabascan way. He was 16 when he attended school at St. Mark's Episcopal Mission for the first time, learning to speak, read and write English. Archdeacon Stuck made note of Walter Harper's skills and employed him, along with several other Alaska Native youths, in his traveling ministry. Harper was an exemplary interpreter, guide and musher. As the archdeacon's assistant, Harper had discussed climbing the mountain with Stuck many times. The party also included two teenage Gwich'inn students from the mission school, John Fredson and Esaias George, picked for their outstanding dog handling and mushing skills.[22]

The party endured difficulties along the way. An accidental fire destroyed a sack containing wool socks, many pairs of gloves and mittens, and fur garments including Karstens' fur parka. The fire also destroyed three silk tents, shovels, an axe, dog food, and 30 rolls of film. Precious rations were destroyed, leaving them with no sugar, powdered milk, baking powder, pilot bread, or dried fruit. Luckily their supply of pemmican, sausage, milk chocolate, and some other essentials were not lost in the fire. When they examined the remains of the site, they determined that the fire was caused by either Karstens or Stuck carelessly dropping a match when lighting their pipes.[23] A month after the fire, on June 7, 1913, at 1:30 p.m., the summit was reached. Tatum planted a flag that he had made from handkerchiefs, and Stuck ensured they put up a six-foot-tall cross. The party stayed on the summit for an hour and a half in extreme conditions before heading back.

In May 1913, while the Karstens–Stuck party was on the mountain, Fannie wrote to Charles Sheldon, telling him that they had just had an earthquake that night. The earthquake must have been a small one, because there was no report of it by the climbing party. She then explained that a party was currently climbing Mt. McKinley, remarking that she would not want to be in their place because there are so many earthquakes, which could create snow slides, and reminisced about an earthquake the previous year that had three days of aftershocks. She reported that they had been having fine weather so far on their expedition, but that they hadn't stopped in to see her on their way to climb the mountain.

On their way back down the mountain, the Karstens–Stuck expedition stopped in Glacier Creek at the Quigleys' where they were welcomed and entertained by Joe and Fannie. While they were there, Charlie McGonagall came for a visit and Karstens had the pleasure of delivering the news to his

Chapter 13. The Great Mountain

old friend that the Sourdough's flagpole was seen on the summit of the Great Mountain.[24] Karstens later became the first superintendent of Mount McKinley National Park in 1921 and remained in that position until 1928, but between the successful climb and his 1921 appointment, had some difficulties.

There was no controversy about the Karstens–Stuck party reaching the peak of the Great Mountain on this expedition, but there was some objection to the post-climb publicity and profits made. When the diaries of the various men in the party were examined it appeared that the archdeacon, who was physically frail in comparison to the other members of the party, exaggerated his own importance and hardship in the expedition. Karstens had long wanted to make the climb with Charles Sheldon, whom he respected as an exemplary outdoorsman, and was bitter when the headlines covering the first successful, official climb to the summit of the Great Mountain praised Hudson Stuck almost as if he had carried the expedition by himself.

Karstens was impoverished because he had missed the lucrative spring freighting season while making the climb. Stuck seemed to be oblivious to the financial sacrifice that Karstens had made and was undermining Karstens' chances at capitalizing on the successful climb by announcing to the press that Karstens had no expectation of profit. Karstens wrote to his friend Sheldon, "I had a nice little sum of money. Now I am broke and in debt, working my head off the get even so I can go on the new stampede at the head of the Tanana." In August, in response to enquiries from Sheldon, Karstens wrote a long letter describing the climb and expressing his feelings about having led the expedition for Stuck: "Why shouldn't I have a man with me, one worthy of the ascent and not an absolute parasite and liar?" Further explaining his frustration, he wrote, "We were equal partners. He was to finance the expedition and it was not to cost me a cent. I was to furnish the experience."[25] Headlines worldwide shouted about the "Stuck Expedition" and only one small town newspaper, the *Ruby Record Citizen*, referred to it as the "Karstens–Stuck Expedition."

Hudson Stuck did try to redress the oversight when, in an interview for the *New York Sun*, he said, "It could be more properly called the Stuck-Karstens expedition.... Some of the papers referred to Mr. Karstens as my guide, which wasn't fair to him. He is entitled to just as much credit as I am."[26] The press had already taken their stance, though. Stuck signed a lucrative book deal and went on a lecture tour, lobbying for the church. In the end, it was Stuck and the Episcopal church that gained the greatest profit from the expedition.

The two men who did the most to ensure the success of the climb, Walter Harper and Harry Karstens, were not given honors proportional to their contribution. Walter Harper was a handsome and appealing young man with a "sweetness of temper and an amiability that attracted people to him."[27] His sister Margaret described him as "having scads of personality," adding that "girls were crazy about him."[28] After becoming the first man to officially set foot on the top of North America's highest mountain at the age of 20, it seemed that he had a bright future ahead of him.

Harper continued his education and got accepted to medical school. Five years after the climb, on September 1, 1918, Harper married a nurse, Frances Wells. Harper and Wells met when Harper was recovering from typhoid fever, a few years earlier. Archdeacon Stuck officiated the wedding at the Fort Yukon chapel, which had been decorated with autumn leaves. Harper and his new bride booked the last boat of the season to the States and were headed to Philadelphia where he was to attend medical school. Their plan was for Harper to return to the Far North as a doctor to "care for the Indian people of the Yukon."[29] He also had plans to climb "Denali's wife," Mount Foraker, the second highest peak in the Alaska range. The new Mr. and Mrs. Walter Harper boarded the SS *Princess Sophia* on October 22, 1918. In the night, the ship hit Vanderbilt Reef in Lynn Canal. A storm was raging, and 38 hours after hitting the reef, the ship foundered and all aboard were lost. Walter Harper was 25 years old at the time of his death. He and Frances were buried together in Juneau.

CHAPTER 14

Struggle

The miners lived on hope and hard work, and Joe Quigley was a prime example of that. He and the other miners were the barometer by which people judged the way fortune was headed. The newspapers in Fairbanks and other small towns reported on the progress of Kantishna with gossipy attention to the miners' activities because, for the towns, "the miners were life."[1] Miners and the businesses that catered to their needs were a huge part of the economy in those days, and the Kantishna area appeared to have so much potential that almost any activity there seemed to be print-worthy. Newspaper articles carried headlines that seemed trivial, such as "Friday Creek Mining Man Comes Out for Dental Attendance," but in fact it was important to the people to know that there was a dentist to go to because at various times there had been none available.[2] Kantishna was so remote that "Gasoline Boat Owner Intends to Take Supplies to Quigley" was a hopeful headline and showed progress.[3] "Kantishna Looks Good to Expert"[4] and "Quigley Has Been Notified as to Result of Expert's Tests"[5] were published to assure the public that things were going in the right direction. Joe, having invested body and soul into the area, felt compelled to continue on his quest to mine the valuable minerals in his beloved Alaska hills. He understood that being a source for the press had an effect on the fate of his community, and so he was usually prepared with a factual, yet positive statement for journalists.

Sometimes things became dire enough that it was difficult for even the optimistic Joe Quigley to paint a rosy picture. Nineteen fourteen was a rough year in the Kantishna area. In March Joe and Fannie arrived in Fairbanks, reporting to the press that many of the Alaska Natives in the Kantishna area were at the point of starvation and that at least 20 children would perish very soon unless they received assistance immediately. One of the reasons for the starvation was that the Natives' dogs were dying of distemper and so they were unable to visit their usual places to hunt for food. Tom Savage, a Kantishna prospector, had loaned three dogs to Natives to carry a man with a broken leg to Nenana, but two of the three dogs died on the road, making it very difficult to deliver the patient. Traditionally the Far North had a culture of sharing. The Natives already knew, and the white population learned, that sharing was necessary for survival. Because of that necessity, relations between whites and Natives were not as tense as in the States.

District prospectors had been sharing their supplies with the indigenous people during the emergency but were at the point where they too were running short. The Quigleys stated that the miners "would not be able to keep the Indians alive until warm weather."[6] They also told the reporter that the Nenana mission would not send supplies to the Natives when requested to do so. The St. Marks Mission and Tortella School had been established in Nenana in 1907 by Archdeacon Hudson Stuck and Reverend Charles Betticher, Jr., with the purpose of serving native children of the region, but in this instance, they did not offer aid. The federal officials had not been notified of the situation at the time of the report, but the article stated that something would be done that day.

A little more than a year after the distemper outbreak, on July 5 and 6, 1915, Native leaders from the Tenana River attended a meeting with government officials in Fairbanks to discuss their concerns about white prospectors and settlers intruding on their hunting grounds. By this time Judge James Wickersham had become the Alaska Territory's delegate to the United States Congress, and he encouraged them to consider one of two legal options: Native allotments or reservations.[7] Alaska Natives had watched the dramatic impact that the prospectors and settlers had on their world over the previous years and were now engaging in a public dialogue about the government's responsibilities to Native people that went back to the Treaty of Cession in 1867.

At one time Natives had guided and rescued military explorers. Military detachments governed the Territory of Alaska from 1867 until the Organic Act of 1884 was passed so that the U.S. could establish civil government and prospectors could receive titles to the lands where they discovered gold.[8] By the beginning of the 20th century, Alaska had become "a white man's country."[9] "Now, the Tenana Chiefs were articulately describing how both options presented by Judge Wickersham were incompatible with their hunting and fishing life, which called for unrestricted access to hunting, fishing and trapping areas. The Natives also called for medical assistance, and education in the form of industrial schools. They expressed a desire to be informed about events affecting their lives and livelihood. The Tenana Chiefs were seeking a relationship with the government and the means to attain rights, opportunities and control of their affairs, in the new realities they were facing."

The Kantishna mining community was not immune to crime, tragedy and loss. Friends of Joe and Fannie's died from exposure, drowning, freezing, mining accidents, violence, suicide, and disease.[10] Sometimes the long winters and harsh conditions drove people to madness. People in the community tried to help each other with the problem of isolation by visiting one another's cabins, but poverty and deprivation were also problems. Slim Carlson, a trapper who lived alone, once received a visit from Joe Quigley who brought some coffee for Carlson as a treat. When the two men sat down in Carlson's cabin for a meal of game meat, Carlson refused the coffee, saying that he couldn't afford coffee or tea "and do not want to partake because I would be unhappy for not having it."[11] Instead of using the coffee, Carlson made tea from a wild plant called Hudson Bay Tea, or Labrador Tea, that grows wild in damp conifer forests. Carlson was born in Sweden and emigrated to the United States as a child, coming to Alaska in 1914 for railroad work. He was known for getting along well with the Natives in the area and lived off the land alone until his death in 1975.[12]

As the population dwindled, each loss of a fellow pioneer cut deeper. A few months after Joe and Fannie went to the newspaper with a plea to help their Alaska Native neighbors in 1914, personal loss struck them. Their friend Billy Lloyd was the ex-officio recorder and everyone trusted him. As a matter of course, they would walk over to Lloyd's office on Glen Creek to register a claim or transaction. Joe knew Billy from the early days, and they are pictured together in the 1897 Yukon Order of Pioneers group photograph. Billy was the composer of a popular miner's song called "Are You Rockin' Every Day?" The song was the anthem of the Order of Pioneers of the Yukon and the Order of Alaska Pioneers and was sung in saloons from the Klondike to Nome.[13] Billy had come down with "stomach trouble," and Fannie, known for her knowledge of folk remedies, tried to help him. His problem was beyond anything Fannie could do for him and Billy Lloyd died in Tom Lloyd's cabin on June14, 1914.[14]

Although World War I began in July of 1914, the United States did not declare war on Germany until 1917. Alaska was still a territory, and the impact of the war on Alaska was somewhat different than in the States. The general feeling of its residents was that the Alaska Territory was treated as an abused colony of the United States.[15] The territorial government had limited powers, leaving the citizens of Alaska at the mercy of the out-of-touch bureaucracy in Washington, D.C. Fairbanks was further away both in physical distance and culture from Washington than Washington was from Paris, France. Alaskans, particularly subsistence miners like Joe Quigley, were exclusively dependent on the natural resources that their environment offered. With hard work and ingenuity, they were able to derive sustenance and the cash income needed for imported necessities. Yet these resources and the land itself were controlled by distant administrators. At the same time that Alaska Natives were feeling the uninvited changes and encroachment of a foreign culture, the pioneers felt that outside forces were constricting their freedom of action.

In addition to the environment being harsh, and the government bearing down on them, the threat of disease hovered over the people of Alaska. In 1918 there was a worldwide flu epidemic. Nearly 200,000 Americans died.

Five hundred million people fell ill worldwide and 3 to 5 percent of the world's population died in only 15 months, making it the second deadliest pandemic in human history.[16] The pandemic took a while to make its way to the Far North, but the flu hit Alaska hard, wiping out 3000 people in the territory between 1918 and 1919. By April 1920 the disease came to Fairbanks and Nenana, and patients filled the government hospital. By May 3, patients were also crowding the railroad dormitories and Cooney and Southern hotels. Fairbanks and Nenana are only 55 miles apart, and the epidemic spread in both towns simultaneously. When a call went out for volunteers for nursing duty,[17] Fannie volunteered at the Alaska Railroad Hospital in Nenana. Eighty-two percent of the influenza deaths in Alaska were Alaska Natives, and the disease decimated their population.[18] Per capita, more people died in Alaska of the Spanish flu than anywhere else in the world other than Samoa.[19]

Over the years, the shifting conditions of the Alaska Native people, due to interruption of their traditional lifestyle, called for radical adaptive changes. Native culture was always based in change and movement, but the acceleration of those changes brought by the white population, including several waves of devastating disease, wreaked havoc on Alaska Natives. As their numbers dwindled, bands and families regrouped and consolidated. Seasonal camps that had been strong now only consisted of one or two families. Nearby cemeteries held entire family trees, with only a few living representatives from each family.[20] For the survivors, the influx of gold miners, explorers and other travelers brought temporary economic opportunity, with the Natives rendering services in transport, accommodations, and provision of meat. Growing dependence on the cash economy weakened the traditional Native culture. Unsuccessful white miners turned to hunting and trapping for cash as well, creating competition for the local game. Eventually, the Native domestic scene changed as the family structure shifted from nomadic to one where the family stayed home in a village while the hunter-trapper roamed.

Throughout the years, in good times and bad, Joe kept digging tunnels, and Fannie kept cooking. When he could afford it, Joe hired Native men to help him dig. Joe was ten years into the Kantishna venture and still going full steam ahead. In 1915, he filed claims named "Martha Q" (after his older sister Martha), the White Hawk and the Keystone (his home state, Pennsylvania, is known as "the Keystone State"), all on Quigley Ridge, and then, in 1916, he filed on the Pittsburgh Lode in the same area.[21] It seems that Joe never forgot where he was from, even though he hadn't been back to Pennsylvania in 30 years. Maybe the series of memorial names for his mines was a sign of homesickness or, more than that, a comforting reminder of the past because he was feeling the threat to a way of life that was rapidly becoming extinct.

Chapter 15

Postwar Resurgence

The Quigley garden was a continuing source of inspiration for everyone who knew of it. While studying Mt. McKinley in 1916, USGS geologist Stephen Reid Capps stayed with Joe and Fannie and took special interest in their garden. They did not have the only garden in the area but theirs was remarkable. In a 1913 letter to Charles Sheldon, Fannie had written, "Every man in this camp has a garden," but Fannie had an impressive green thumb and her garden stood out above the others for both the quality and quantity of vegetables it produced.[1] The garden was a source of pride for Fannie and Joe would refer to it as "Fannie's garden."[2] The high latitude, causing extreme hours of darkness and light, along with the extreme temperatures and high altitude made growing food an entirely different business than it was in more moderate climates. There were wild blueberries and wild rhubarb growing in the area, and Fannie was expert at working with the wild plants as well as with the plants she cultivated. Capps' field notebook mentions cauliflower, cabbages, radishes, onions, potatoes, rhubarb, rutabagas, cucumbers, tomatoes, corn, oats, blueberries, strawberries and flowers.[3] This bounty, along with the cold storage methods used at the Quigley compound, kept the couple and a steady stream of visitors fed and healthy over the years. In a place and time where many starved or fell ill due to malnutrition, this made a major impression on anyone who experienced it.

Malnutrition can come from not eating enough food or from a severely unbalanced diet. Both of these happened in the Far North as food shortages were prevalent during the early years of the gold rush. Natives perished in droves when salmon runs failed. Cheechakos would arrive and sometimes die because of their lack of survival skills, but in the Kantishna camps, the experienced miners could hunt the plentiful wild game and survive on a very meat-heavy diet. Rather than starving from lack of food, they were more likely to suffer from symptoms of vitamin deficiency. One of the diseases that plagued northern miners was scurvy, which is caused by a lack of vitamin C. Although the disease is rare now, it was a serious threat in late 19th- and early 20th-century Alaska. Scurvy can cause anemia, edema, gum disease, loss of

Joe and Fannie in their garden. The short growing season can be fewer than 70 days, and each day can have up to 20 hours of sunlight. Soil was carried up the hill by hand for the raised beds. The garden produced a wide variety of vegetables that the Quigleys would preserve in various ways, including their cold storage tunnels (Alaska and Polar Regions Collections, Elmer E. Rasmuson Library, University of Alaska, Fairbanks, UAF-1983-0149-01867).

Joe with his rhubarb harvest while a dog rests in front of the Quigley cabin. The flowers growing behind stacked stone walls around the foundation of the cabin were inspiration for some of Fannie's embroidered pictures (Alaska and Polar Regions Collections, Elmer E. Rasmuson Library, University of Alaska, Fairbanks, UAF-1980-0046-00566).

Chapter 15. Postwar Resurgence

teeth, shortness of breath and severe pain, and it can eventually bring convulsions and even death. Early symptoms of malnutrition, such as extreme tiredness, can be disguised as the effects of overwork, so a miner could become very ill or even die without realizing what the underlying cause was. Considering how essential good nutrition was to survival, and how difficult it was to achieve, it is no wonder that Fannie's garden and cooking were considered nearly miraculous by some.

Toward the end of World War, I, in 1917, mining in Alaska had a resurgence, and things were looking up for Joe and Fannie. World War I brought about an increased demand for copper as well as a boom in the salmon industry when the military purchased salmon from Alaska canneries to feed the troops. The Alaska Territorial Legislation signed a resolution that was similar to most state legislatures, supporting the declaration of war, and enacted legislation on seditious acts during wartime with violations punishable by a fine or imprisonment or both. The Third Territorial Legislature also created the Alaska College of Agriculture and School of Mines, which later became the University of Alaska, Fairbanks.

In Kantishna, Joe leased the Little Annie Claim on Quigley Ridge and began work on the Red Top Claim above Moose Creek. Edgar Brooker and Mace Farrar worked the Alpha Claim on Eldorado Creek. Two hydraulic outfits came in as well. Kantishna Hydraulic Mining Company worked the gravel on Moose Creek and Mount McKinley Gold Placer Company worked Caribou Creek.[4] Joe had already been doing hard rock mining for years, with his biggest obstacle to profit the transportation of tons of ore to the smelter. For years, he and the other area miners were transporting the rocks by horse or sled to the Kantishna River, where the ore could be loaded onto large barges. Steamboats could then push down the Tanana and Yukon rivers to St. Michael for trans-shipment by ocean-going vessels to the smelter in Tacoma, Washington. The cost of this transportation process was so high that only the richest ore could be shipped. The rest was left in the ground until transportation costs were reduced.[5] So even though there were plenty of precious metals in the ground, the quality of the ore had to be extremely high to be worth processing.

Finding a more efficient way of getting the ore to market required a bigger operation than individual subsistence miners could provide. Joe was consistently trying to secure interest from investors and working to get better transportation to the area to make more profitable mining possible. The miners in the Kantishna district were an especially energetic and optimistic group. Ignoring the logic of trends and general conditions, they held a vision of a bountiful future that depended on the development of transportation. Books, petitions and tracts appeared from the hopeful pioneers of Alaska to the powers that be in the United States Congress, clamoring for a federally funded transportation system consisting of the railroad, roads and trails.[6]

At the same time that the miners were appealing for better transportation, there was a push to make the area an official national park and preserve. A worldwide national park movement had begun in 1872 when Congress established Yellowstone National Park in the territories of Montana and Wyoming "as a public park or pleasuring-ground for the benefit and enjoyment of the people" and placed it under exclusive control of the secretary of the interior. The National Park Service was begun in 1916 when president Woodrow Wilson signed an act creating a new federal bureau in the Department of the Interior responsible for protecting the parks and monuments that were established at the time as well as those established in the future.[7]

Charles Sheldon first conceived of the idea of preserving the Denali region as a national park in 1906. Now, more than a decade later, he was still working to make it happen. Sheldon was a personal friend of President Theodore Roosevelt and a member of the Boone and Crockett Club. The Boone and Crockett Club is an American nonprofit organization founded in 1887 by Theodore Roosevelt that advocates fair chase hunting in support of habitat conservation. The club is North America's oldest wildlife and habitat conservation organization and was very influential. Key members included anthropologist George Bird Grinnell, Civil War general William Tecumseh Sherman, forester and politician Gifford Pinchot, and other wealthy and prominent men.[8] Making use of his significant contacts, Sheldon presented the plan to his fellow members of the Boone and Crockett Club. They decided that the political climate at the time was unfavorable for Congressional action and that the best hope of success rested on the approval and support from the Alaskans themselves. Sheldon believed that the first step was to secure the approval and cooperation of the delegate who represented Alaska in Congress. In October 1915, he took up the matter with Dr. E. W. Nelson of the Biological Survey at Washington, D.C., and with George Bird Grinnell, with the purpose of introducing a suitable bill in the coming session of Congress. The matter was then taken to the Game Committee of the Boone and Crockett Club, and after a thorough discussion, it received the committee's full endorsement.

On December 3, 1915, the plan was presented to James Wickersham, now Alaska's delegate in the U.S. House of Representatives, and after some deliberation Wickersham gave his approval. The plan then went to the Executive Committee of the Boone and Crockett Club where it was unanimously accepted on December 15, 1915. The next step was to present it to Stephen Mather, Assistant Secretary of the Interior, in Washington, D.C. He immediately approved it. The bill was introduced in April 1916 by Delegate Wickersham in the House and by Senator Key Pittman of Nevada in the Senate. After much lobbying, the bill was passed on February 19, 1917, and on February 26, 1917, 11 years from its conception, the bill was signed in legislation by President Woodrow Wilson, thereby creating Mount McKinley National Park.

Chapter 15. Postwar Resurgence

The mood was evolving in the Kantishna mining camp. New attention was coming in from investors, and for Joe there was a personal shift toward legitimization, assessment and expansion. On February 2, 1918, a year after their community had been officially declared a national park, Joseph Buffington Quigley and Frances "Fannie" Sedlacek McKenzie were officially married. They had been living together for more than a decade. Joe was 48 years old and Fannie was 46; it was Joe's first marriage, Fannie's second. Although their marriage license was signed by Commissioner Van Orsdel,[9] Edgar Brooker, Jr., claimed that his father Edgar Brooker officiated. It was said that Brooker didn't have a Bible handy for the ceremony but did have a Montgomery Ward catalogue and used it in place of the traditional Christian Bible.[10] Whether true or not, the story shows a non-traditional attitude toward the marriage. There aren't any photographs documenting Joe and Fannie's wedding, and there are no reliable accounts of the ceremony, but the marriage certificate proves that they were legally married at last.

The fact that Joe and Fannie had been living together for more than a decade and that they were both in their late 40s prompts one to question why they bothered to marry at this late date. There were probably multiple reasons. Although there were many couples in Alaska who lived together without the benefits of legal marriage, "illicit cohabitation" was against the law and that law was occasionally enforced.[11] Getting married may have been

Nestled in the foothills of the highest mountain in North America, the Friday Creek compound on Quigley Hill included several cabins that Joe Quigley built, including guest quarters (Alaska and Polar Regions Collections, Elmer E. Rasmuson Library, University of Alaska, Fairbanks, UAF-1980-0046-00253).

part of some internal drive Joe and Fannie had to live an above-board life. No record was found of Fannie divorcing her first husband Angus McKenzie, so it is possible that McKenzie died by this date, making it easier for Fannie to legitimize her domestic partnership with Joe Quigley. In addition, and perhaps more important, there was the question of business and financial security for Fannie. By this time the Quigley mines were becoming more attractive to outside investors. A legal marriage would cement Joe and Fannie's business partnership, ensuring Fannie's inheritance if Joe was to die before her. In spite of their personal differences, Joe respected Fannie as a partner and had a desire to make sure she was taken care of.

After Joe and Fannie tied the knot, they moved to the Friday Creek cabin. The Friday Creek camp was luxurious by miners' standards. Joe built them a larger than average cabin to live in and several other cabins for guests and other uses. The compound was high on Quigley Ridge with a breathtaking view. They were one of the few married couples in the area and had come to a meeting of the minds on what a partnership means, giving each space to develop as individuals. They were two people who maintained their

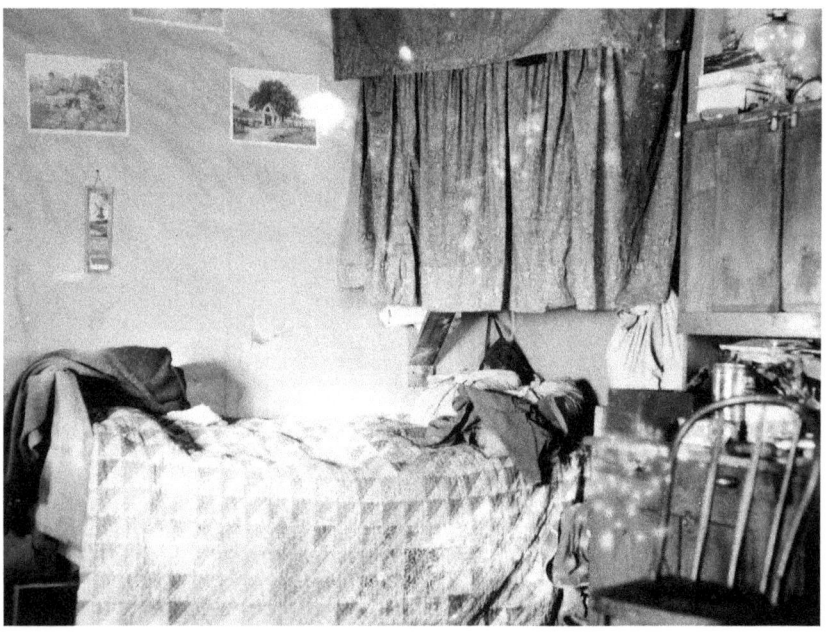

The interior of Joe and Fannie's cabin showing a handmade quilt and bed, decorative pictures, and a calendar on the wall. An oil lamp and books that Joe used to study mineralogy are on top of the handmade cabinet (Alaska and Polar Regions Collections, Elmer E. Rasmuson Library, University of Alaska, Fairbanks, UAF-1980-0046-00266).

Chapter 15. Postwar Resurgence

The interior of Joe and Fannie's cabin showing their large wood burning stove. During the winter there would be as few as four hours of daylight in a 24-hour period and the temperatures were often minus 50 degrees Fahrenheit and lower (Alaska and Polar Regions Collections, Elmer E. Rasmuson Library, University of Alaska, UAF-1980-0046-00267).

independence from the expectations of the mundane world by living off the land in the interior of Alaska. Joe had found somewhat of a balance between the "strenuous life" of rugged masculinity and his intellectual and creative interests, with some of the comforts of the more refined world outside.[12] He kept his compulsion to travel satisfied with frequent trips to Fairbanks and other Alaska towns, staying active in the fraternal orders he belonged to, and making business contacts. He was a very adaptable man who maneuvered through society fairly easily when necessary and was able to communicate effectively with a broad range of people.

Fitting in with regular society was more difficult for Fannie than it was for Joe for a number of reasons. Even in the Far North women had many unwritten rules about what constituted acceptable behavior, and Fannie didn't have a background that prepared her to fit in with polite society. She wore men's clothing, cursed even more than the average male miner, and drank heavily. Her brief forays into the social structure of the women in Fairbanks were sometimes awkward. She aggressively stated her opinion frequently and told stories about herself that were varied in their truthfulness or accuracy but illustrated her disinterest in being considered traditionally feminine or lady-like. She was aware that she was different but was either uninterested in fitting in or unable to adjust herself enough to be part of the regular social structure.

In her relationship with Joe, Fannie's adventurous spirit and drive to prove herself as an exemplary hunter, craftsperson, cook, and gardener were not thwarted. Joe's expectations of her seemed to be based as much in traditional mining partnerships as in traditional marriage partnerships, and he treated her as an equal partner. In their subsistence lifestyle in the wilderness she had found her niche and was not very comfortable anywhere else. She had achieved stability and level of security that she had not been given in her childhood and that she had not been able to form as an adult until she found herself with Joe Quigley in Kantishna.

Fannie had made her own way in the world and done the best she could, but it was not a "happily ever after" story. Her soul was both soothed and aggravated by the stability she had found. Staying in one place for a long time is very different from the life that earned her the nickname "Fannie the Hike," and although her lifestyle in the wilderness with Joe was satisfying in ways that she hadn't experienced in her youth, she was isolated and often lonely. That loneliness exacerbated her alcoholism.

It seems that by the time Joe and Fannie got married, the romance between them had already waned, and they frequently bickered. They kept most of their disagreements private, but there was one issue between them that stood out above the normal domestic spats. Fannie's excessive drinking was a serious problem. That struggle was public knowledge and many people recounted their memories of spectacular quarrels between Joe and Fannie as well as stories of Fannie's outrageous behavior when she was drunk. By all accounts, Fannie was an alcoholic, and that made life more complicated and difficult for both of them.

In the beginning, it's likely that Joe thought Fannie might be content with the stability that their partnership offered and feel less of a need to be intoxicated. After a number of years, it became evident that her drinking and behavior were out of control, and to his frustration, Joe could do very little to influence Fannie's conduct or her relationship with alcohol. Her behavior became increasingly difficult for Joe to live with, but every aspect of his life was inextricably tied to hers. They were interdependent and heavily invested in the path they had chosen. Joe felt that he had no choice but to keep working toward developing the mines into something that would attract high-paying investors and continue to hold up his end of the partnership with Fannie.

Over time, Fannie would transform from the charming, nurturing woman that many people loved into an unreliable, emotionally abusive bully. Among her regular self-entertainments was to get drunk and start shooting her rifle at the chimneys in Kantishna. Typical of the mining community's tolerance of each other's eccentricities, the neighbors would hear her shooting but "figured she was a good shot" and let it slide.[13] Normally, she would joke with and tease people she liked, but when she was drunk, her teasing and jokes were cruel. She became arrogant and demanding and would belittle anyone who dared displease her. Her recounting of events slid from exaggerations to outright lies. Even her famous culinary skills were subject to her mood swings. If Fannie liked a person, she could be charming, nurturing, and kind, but if she didn't like a person, she would deliberately cook bad food for them. Denise Abby recalled, "If she didn't like you, heaven help you. I can't tell you what a bad cook she was. Often, she had had very bad food which she made worse." Pete Bagoy added, "Enough to gag you. It was awful." This habit caused some people to avoid her cooking altogether.[14]

Despite their differences, Joe and Fannie attended to the unrelenting work required for life in the Alaska bush together and kept a united image for the increasing number of people who knew of them. Joe continued to develop the mines, study, and seek the interest of investors. Fannie continued her routine hunting, trapping, gardening and cooking, and she created beautiful needlework. Belmore Browne described Fannie as "an artist with a needle." Like all folk artists, Fannie found ways to express her creativity while making useful objects as well as making some purely decorative pieces such as her embroidered depictions of flowers. Her cooking was creative as well, going beyond the normal camp food. Making a meal was an involved and well-thought-out process. In addition to having to plan the purchase of staple items like flour, butter and eggs a year in advance, she processed many of the basics herself. Fannie would kill an animal, butcher the meat, render the fat and then use that fat to bake pies from berries she picked or rhubarb she harvested, then deep freeze some of the pies for future use. Although inconsistent and moody, Fannie proved her expertise at wilderness survival skills and was a master of the outdoor life.

Joe had an engineer's penchant for precision and a leaning toward a scientific approach to mining. He was exceptionally skilled in the construction of utilitarian objects. In addition to cabin building, his mastery of carpentry gave him the ability to build both large and small things that they needed, including furniture, sheds, and boats. The blacksmithing skills he'd learned as a teenage apprentice in Nebraska enabled him to build and repair metal objects. Joe also utilized every part of the animals that he and Fannie killed, using moose skin to make his own babiche, or rawhide. He typically formed the rawhide into strips for making fastenings, animal snares, snowshoes, and other things, and he was known for making the best babiche around because it did not stretch after it was put in place. This reliability was much appreciated by those who used it.[15] Joe and Fannie's skills as craftspeople served them well and afforded them freedom from the level of consumerism that life in a city would have required.

In addition to performing the Herculean tasks required to maintain their wilderness lifestyle and develop the mines, Joe was a self-taught photographer. He loved taking pictures of wildlife and of the people who came to visit his home. He built himself a darkroom and brought photo supplies in so that he could develop and print his own photographs. Park ranger Grant Pearson stated that Joe took some of the best caribou, mountain sheep and other wild game pictures that Pearson had ever seen.[16] As Charles Sheldon had said, Joe was "an accurate observer of nature," and because of his intimate knowledge of the wilderness, he was able to use his hunting skills to capture the images of wildlife up close in their natural habitat, giving a rare glimpse of the animals that was not available to many.

Joe and Fannie were very connected to the other inhabitants of a community that stretched for miles but was sparsely populated. When they would visit people, Fannie tended to their ailments and exchanged gossip, and Joe would bring tea or coffee, staying to talk, which relieved the sense of isolation that they all felt from time to time.[17] Joe consistently volunteered to deliver the local mail, which gave him the opportunity to talk to each person as he brought their correspondence and packages. People often commented that long-legged Joe could walk impressive distances in record time, making him a natural for the job of mail delivery. In some ways, Joe and Fannie were the social center of their community. They had been there since the beginning and stayed after many others left. They helped new arrivals including park rangers get familiarized with the particulars of the area, and they knew everyone. Visitors had often heard of the Quigleys before they came to Kantishna and saw a meeting with Joe and Fannie as the highlight of their stay.

CHAPTER 16

Expansion

The role of the railroads in the settling of the American West in the late 19th century was paramount, and although building them in the Far North was more difficult than in the States, their impact was no less influential in the development of the Alaska Territory. The Alaska settlers believed that just as the railroad had brought "an empire of hardy and industrious citizens" to the desert in the west, it would also bring industry and development to the frozen north.[1] Joe Quigley and his mining cohorts in Kantishna had been constantly appealing for railroad development for years, believing that it would increase their mining profits.

Construction of the Alaska Railroad was quite different from building a railroad through the American western deserts had been. Remoteness, terrain, and climate were only some of the obstacles that a multitude of surveyors, engineers, and suppliers had to deal with. Beginning in 1915 the Alaska Engineering Commission and the Interior Department agency, which was run by U.S. Army engineers, deployed the men and material for the massive task. Laborers built bridges and laid track, and contract "station gangs" did the preliminary clearing, grading, and excavation. The crews worked toward each other from Anchorage in the south and the northern construction headquarters in Nenana. Every mode of frontier transportation was used for the work: dogs and sleds, horse-drawn double-ender sledges and wagons, pack animals, and boats. Once track was laid for a section, trains shuttled supplies for the next increment.[2]

Railroad construction brought more people and new towns sprung up along the way as camp followers progressed with the railroad. The town of Nenana was one of those towns and had quite a few newly-built businesses in 1919 when Joe and Fannie visited the hospital there for Joe to have a toe amputated.[3] It was common for miners to lose toes to frostbite and that is most likely what necessitated this visit. Nenana was 160 miles from Quigley Ridge and had expanded rapidly since 1916 when the railroad connected Nenana to Anchorage.[4] The St. Mark's Episcopal Church Mission and Tortella School had been there since 1905, and the post office was added in 1908, but railroad construction expanded the population suddenly, and it reached nearly 1000 by 1916.

The railroad reaching as far as navigational waters at Nenana meant that supplies and materials could be shipped from there. Nenana is only 55 miles from Fairbanks and the development put the two towns in competition with each other for some kinds of business. Nenana was closer to the Kantishna Mining District than Fairbanks, but Fairbanks was the largest city in the interior of Alaska and offered goods and services that Nenana did not.

Joe Quigley was a steady as they come but never stagnant. His active mind craved new information, and he was able to revise his business strategy as times changed. The motivation for all miners was, at least in part, to attain sudden, life-changing wealth, but there was more to it than that. At the age of 50 Joe Quigley had assessed his life so far and come to terms with it. The University of Alaska, Fairbanks began in 1917 as the Alaska Agricultural College and School of Mines, and Joe jumped at the chance to delve deeper into the subjects he had been studying informally for decades. Charles Bunnell was the president of the University of Alaska from 1921 to 1949, and Earnest Patty was UAF's first geology professor.[5] Joe became friends with both men and many of the other students. Going to school in middle age gave him opportunities for business networking as well as legitimizing his knowledge of prospecting and mining. When telling the story later he said, "I started digging tunnels and realizing my need for more exact knowledge of mining, I went over to the University of Alaska and took courses in mining and geology and assaying. Dr. Bunnell became my friend as did several students and assayers."[6] Some people at his age slowed down, but Joe still had the drive to move onward and upward.

Joe continued to prospect, study and dig. He had tunnels on four veins, rises into the veins, and engineers' reports on the whole operation. He had a proclivity for precision and had even been described as "a self-made scientist."[7] He purchased an assaying kit and began evaluating his own and other's finds. Learning the process of assaying saved Joe a good amount of money when he could assess his own claims. A story told by Grant Pearson about Joe's assaying experience illustrated how Joe was a man who was not easily fooled and how he used his natural skepticism and easy-going personality to settle things when there was doubt.

There was a grubstake prospector in the area known as "Grubstake Bill." He had approached several people with a small nugget that he claimed was gold, asking them to invest in his potential operation. The man eventually made his way to Joe, showing the nugget and telling the story of how he had "run it down from rock with a blowpipe outfit."[8] A blowpipe outfit was a way that assayers determined the presence of specific minerals in ore, and by saying this, Grubstake Bill was trying to assure Joe that the nugget had been

Chapter 16. Expansion

tested and was most assuredly gold. Joe asked permission to test the nugget himself, to see if it was gold, and the man acquiesced. Part of an assayer's test includes putting a small amount of the mineral in acid. Hydrochloric acid, sulphuric acid, and nitric acid were used in various assaying processes.[9] Joe dropped the nugget into a bottle of acid and it disappeared, leaving a green streak behind it which showed that it was copper, not gold. The story goes that Joe said, "That was the last of Grubstake Bill." Like some other stories about Joe and Fanny, this one sounds like it may or may not be factual, but there were many people at the time who were looking for grubstake money and Joe was doing some assaying at the time, so it may have happened.

The subtle shift in the Kantishna mining community between 1910 and 1920 is reflected in the U.S. census. The population of the entire state of Alaska was 55,536 in 1920, which was a drop of 14.5 percent from 1910. Mining had fallen into the hands of large businesses. Although the large mining operations attracted many new workers, the companies only required a set number of employees, and many individual prospectors left. Many men had gone to join the army or off to work in war-related industries during World War I. When the war ended some veterans returned, repopulating the area somewhat, but as the economy of the territory changed, so did the population.[10]

(Left to right) Joe Quigley, Joe Sway, Miss Lindstrom, Miss Ryan, and Nels Henderson stand in front of the General Store at Roosevelt. Nels Henderson was known for hauling supplies into the Kantishna with his gas-powered boat (Alaska and Polar Regions Collections, Elmer E. Rasmuson Library, University of Alaska, Fairbanks, UAF-1969-0092-00024).

In the 1910 census, none of the Kantishna residents listed were born in Alaska and only four, including Fannie, were female. All were white, with about two thirds of them born in the United States and the rest from Canada, Ireland, Scotland, Sweden and Germany. A few of the men are listed as married but did not have wives living with them. One specifically notes, "wife in U.S." Two of the men were listed as trappers and one as a carpenter, with the rest listed as miners or prospectors. With the exception of one 26-year-old, all of the 1910 population was between the ages of 31 and 54.[11] This was a typical mining community, consisting of mostly white men in their 30s and 40s who were working on their own account, mining for gold.

By 1920, Fannie Quigley was the only female in the immediate area and was now listed as a housewife rather than as a servant, as she had been in 1910. The racial makeup of the census was the same, still all whites living separately from the Alaska Natives in the area. The balance of those born in the United States, Canada and Europe was about the same as it had been.[12] Although the age range was similar to the 1910 census, the overall population was a little older, and the occupational breakdown gave a different story than it had ten years earlier. Larger companies with employees had moved in, and fewer people were listed as individual miner/prospectors. There was a cook, a guide, a teamster, five laborers, a civil engineer and an electrician listed in 1920. The rest were listed as miners or prospectors, but more than a third of the miners worked for wages, and only 15 were working on their own account or were listed as employers. The mining operations had gotten bigger, and a few die-hard prospector-miner types were still working on their own. The population still consisted primarily of men looking for gold, but there was now more of a hierarchy with large company owners and employees. Larger equipment and more technology were being used, bigger financial investments were made, and more pressure to be involved in large operations or quit was applied.

By late 1920 there was still a 100-mile gap in the railroad connection between Healy and the Susitna River crossing. This was some of the most difficult construction of the entire railroad line. This gap contains Hurricane Gulch and Riley Creek, which required steel bridges. At Moody, on the park's northeastern corner, a sliding mountain required constant stabilization and periodic grade reconstruction. The Nenana River Gorge, between Moody and Healy, included tunnels and track perched on cliffs that overlooked the turbulent waters of the glacial river.[13] In the spring of 1921 the Alaska Engineering Commission decided to close the gap in the line, with round-the-clock track laying and trestle construction. Other crews continued grading south, beyond the gorge and past the park entrance at Riley Creek. When the Nenana River froze for the year, crews used it as a highway, transporting heavy equipment through the gorge.

Chapter 16. Expansion

Joe continued to prospect and work his other claims, but from 1919 to 1921 Thomas P. Aitken leased Quigley's silver lead ore property, the Little Annie mine. Aitken was a mining entrepreneur who had emigrated to the United States from Scotland in 1894 and came to Alaska in 1897. Aitken sent a crew to Kantishna in the spring of 1919 with supplies, a complete blacksmith shop, drill steel, and horses to improve a pack trail to the mining property which was approximately 27 miles long. A scow named the *Mary* was specially built for the service and made several trips between Nenana and Roosevelt, carrying supplies to the miners. Operations were increased, and in September 1919, the large steamboat the *Shusana* was chartered and along with two gasoline boats delivered 200 tons of supplies for the winter to Roosevelt. The first load of ore was delivered on December 11, 1919, and by the spring of 1920 Aitken had delivered as much as 800 tons of the richest ore from the mine to Roosevelt. The American-Yukon Navigation Company was contracted to transport the ore from Roosevelt to St. Michael at the mouth of the Yukon River for trans-shipment to Tacoma.[14]

Even with the improved transportation methods brought in by Aitken, there were problems. Early in the season, when the water levels were high, the light draft steamer *Reliance* made two round-trip trips from the mouth of the Kantishna River to Roosevelt, but on its third trip the steamer was stopped at the mouth of the Bearpaw River by low water. The low water situation left 500 tons of ore stuck in Roosevelt until a powerboat was used to haul the ore to the Tanana in several trips. In late September 1920 the company had to stop work because low water prevented its boat from proceeding beyond the mouth of the Bearpaw River. By February 1921 Aitken decided to abandon mine operations, citing high costs, insufficient quantity of high-grade ore, and differences of opinion with Joe Quigley over the property lease agreement as the reasons. Joe said that careless mining by Aitken was the reason for the profit margin being too low.[15]

Aitken's pull-out had an impact on the community, not just on the Quigleys. When the Quigley mines gained interest from investors, it was part of what gave the people in the area hope for another boom. The Kantishna Mining District was already established back in 1905, but then, in 1919, the optimistic miners laid out a townsite on Moose Creek at the mouth of Eureka Creek and named it Kantishna. The new town was approximately 30 miles from Roosevelt. Joe and Fannie Quigley were selling townsite lots with U.S. Commissioner C. Herb Wilson handling the sales for them.[16] Commissioner Wilson was also the storekeeper for Kantishna and was looking forward to the increase of commerce and population. The entire community was let down by Aitken's withdrawal, and Joe felt the worst sting of it.

Transportation problems continued to plague Kantishna and were particularly unfortunate for freighters George Moody and James Moore that autumn. In September 1918, Moody and Moore had used their launches to haul about 25 tons of supplies for Aitken and others to Roosevelt, including a stock of supplies for the store in Kantishna. On the return voyage from that delivery, they encountered a blizzard and the river began running heavy with ice. They tried to find safety on the Bearpaw River, hoping the weather would clear, but on October 3, the river froze. Stuck in the ice, Moody and Moore were forced to leave the launches in the Bearpaw River for the winter. In five days, the men who ran the launches had to hike out of the country, spending three nights of the journey in cold weather without blankets.[17]

The Alaska Road Commission in the Department of the Army supervised construction and maintenance on territorial roads. The miners in Kantishna and their supporters in Nenana continued to lobby for improved access, and by 1921 the Alaska Road Commission suggested that the ARC and the Park Service should cooperate in the building of a road through the park to meet the needs of both the miners and tourists. The cooperative effort took 16 years.[18]

McKinley Station was opened in 1921 and Harry Karstens was appointed ranger-at-large, with a token annual salary of $10.[19] Up until that time, the park was official in name only, with no protections in place. Karstens was responsible for enforcing park boundaries and poaching regulations, which were met with vehement opposition from poachers and market hunters.[20] On Thanksgiving Day 1921, the McKinley Park Hotel opened, operated by roadhouse man Maurice Morino, serving holiday dinners that included game meat, local potatoes, and wild berries to the Riley Creek railroad trestle workers.[21]

The Alaska Railroad from Seward to Fairbanks was completed in 1923 and caused a decline in riverboat operations in the Kantishna District. By 1925 there were only 13 men mining in the Kantishna District, and in 1926 Joe Quigley was interviewed by the newspaper about the future of mining in the area, which reported, "It is his belief that mining in the Kantishna will be at more or less of a standstill until adequate transportation facilities are provided." The system in use at the time, which involved either hauling ore to Roosevelt on the Kantishna River for shipment in the summer or hauling ore to the railroad, required values to be unusually high to yield a profit. Much of the ore being shipped was silver and antimony. Joe told the reporter that in his opinion, it was practically impossible to depend upon such transportation methods for large-scale operations.[22]

Joe shipped ores to Shelby, California, to be smelted. Selected ores often ran $1000 per ton of ore shipped. Quartz mining was a very expensive operation, so he spent his summers placer mining on the bars, on the creeks, and then "blowing the money I made, on the tunnels and stopes in the winter."[23] He bought dynamite and hand drilled the rocks, using a single jack alone and a double jack on the rare occasions when he could afford help. He shoveled and wheeled the rock out on the dump, sorting ores if necessary. This method was known as "hammer and steel" drilling and took a certain dexterity. Single jacking involved an individual holding and turning the steel with one hand while hitting the steel with a small hammer held in the other hand. Ambidexterity was very helpful for the single jack driller because he could work longer by shifting the hammer from one hand to the other to distribute the work. In double jacking one or two drillers hit a drilling steel with large sledgehammers while a holder turned the steel slightly after each blow. As the hole deepened, the holder substituted longer steels in a way that did not interrupt the driller's disciplined rhythm.[24] Joe explained, "Usually one blast would bring down the whole vein for a short distance. Sometimes a small shot would keep you wheelin' for quite a while and sometimes a pretty heavy shot would yield only a couple of wheelbarrows full, depending on the faulting of the rock."[25] Joe dug hundreds (some said thousands) of feet of tunnel single handedly, in this painstaking way over a period of years. He continued to ship the richer ores, but the shipping costs were prohibitive.

As arduous as the methods Joe was using were, they were highly effective compared to the way he and other miners dug when dynamite or blasting powder wasn't available. Traditional mining employed the use of simple tools such as shovels and pickaxes. Individual prospector-miners were very resourceful and not afraid of hard work. They would endlessly pick away at the ground and rock to get to their treasure. Fannie was also very resourceful, but her focus was on alcohol rather than gold. Not only was commercially-made alcohol difficult to obtain in the remote area where she lived, but it had also become illegal when Alaska signed the "Bone Dry" law by a vote of nearly two to one in 1918.[26] Two years later, the United States began Prohibition, a constitutional ban on the production, importation, transportation, and sale of alcoholic beverages that was in effect from 1920 to 1933. Bootleggers were busy during these years, and in Alaska a series of underground tunnels were constructed so that bootleggers could conduct business without being observed by the territorial police.[27]

Fannie would pick blueberries in the summer and make blueberry wine, which she kept in a barrel in the tunnel. She had also managed to acquire enough bottles, caps, malt and other ingredients to brew beer. Glass bottles were extremely expensive and hard to come by at the time, so this took quite a bit of planning on her part. Having beer and wine readily available was different for Fannie than it was for Joe. Although he did enjoy a drink with friends, he was not inclined to excess. Unfortunately, Fannie was compelled to get drunk even when the negative impact of her drinking was obvious to everyone. This frustrated Joe greatly. He would hide his personal supply of whiskey in his tunnels, but Fannie would always find it and drink it while he was away.

By the early 1920s, just a few years after they made their marriage official, Joe and Fannie had a conflict that remained in many of their neighbors' memories. Knowing that Fannie was not able to control her drinking, Joe was not in favor of her making her own beer. He was sometimes away for weeks at a time, and she had developed a routine. Her general practice was to hide the booze and the equipment for making it just before Joe was expected to come home from prospecting or hunting. Tension had been building between the two of them, and one day he came home early from a trip to Fairbanks to find Fannie soused and the stock of bottles out in plain sight. Calm, quiet, easy-going Joe Quigley had had enough. His anger and frustration got the best of him, and he broke all of the precious glass bottles.[28] Gossip of the incident traveled quickly and soon everyone had heard about the heated argument.

The fight between Joe and Fannie made an impact on the memory of 16-year-old Edgar Brooker, Jr. Edgar had arrived with his mother when they came to visit Edgar's father, U.S. Commissioner Edgar Brooker, Sr., and stay in Kantishna for the summer of 1922. Edgar Jr. wrote of his time there and remembered the Quigleys well. He also recalled that Joe and Fannie would leave Quigley Ridge together sometimes to visit nearby towns, and at least once during the winter, they would go to the movies. Fannie would dress for the occasion by wearing a dress on top of her overalls, which did cause some notice.

Joe Burns operated a movie house in Nenana. Vic Durand was a one-man band for the theater, providing music to accompany the silent films, playing the piano with his feet, a harmonica from a neck holder, and a violin with his hands, making the entertainment complete. Fannie, with no regard for the other patrons of the theater, would sit in the audience, explaining in a loud voice, while the film was playing, what the movie was all about and what was going to happen next. According to Brooker, no one in the theater had the nerve to ask Fannie to keep quiet.[29]

One of the high points of Brooker's summer in Kantishna was a trip out to the railroad, on foot, with Joe Quigley and Pete Pemberton to catch the train to Nenana and Fairbanks. As young Edgar remembered it, the distance from the McKinley Park Station to Kantishna and Friday Gulch was about 94 miles. There was no road, and the only way people traveled the distance was on horse or by foot. They "traveled light and ate light ... the way Joe traveled." Edgar and Pete were "dragged out at the end of each day" because "Joe was a regular mountain goat" (Joe Quigley was 53 years old at the time). After a short stay in Fairbanks, Pete and Edgar headed back, leaving Joe to finish his business trip. Pete had been over the trail twice before and Edgar had been once. They realized that it was "quite an undertaking" with no road and no markers, and they felt a bit anxious without Joe Quigley's experience to guide

Chapter 16. Expansion 117

them, but they made it without getting lost and had no trouble from wild animals. They did see a lot of game, which thrilled young Edgar, and they carried a rifle for protection but never needed it.[30]

Brooker's notice of Joe as someone with the energy of a much younger man was something that others remarked on for Joe's entire life. A man in his 50s was considered fairly old at the time, but Joe Quigley displayed a vitality that contradicted his chronological age. Joe joined a curling team in Fairbanks in 1922, even though he had never played before. Curling is a game played on ice in which large, round, flat stones are slid across the surface toward a target mark. Members of a team use brooms to sweep the surface of the ice in the path of the stone to control its speed and direction. Joe and his two teammates won the championship for Fairbanks after a close call, making his first experience with the sport a celebratory one.

On Quigley Ridge, behind their cabin on the south side of Friday Creek, Joe had done his own lode work on the Red Top mine, where there was both gold- and silver-lead ore. He leased Red Top to Hawley Sterling of Fairbanks, and Red Top produced about $5,000 worth of gold between 1920 and 1924. Among the highest productive lode mines on Quigley Ridge during the 1920s were the Martha Q, Gold Dollar, and Gold Eagle, which together produced more than 1200 tons of ore worth about $300,000.00.[31]

CHAPTER 17

Celebrity

With new inroads to the remote area came more interest from outsiders who wanted to visit. Alaska was seen as America's own exotic location and people in the States wanted more stories of the Far North. This was the transition time between print journalism and electronic media.[1] Silent newsreels were distributed and would soon develop into talking newsreels. There were no radio shows yet, and dime novels were still very popular. For entertainment, people still went to vaudeville shows and read adventure stories that brought fact and fiction together in a way that sometimes made it hard to distinguish between the two. Wild West shows were still popular until about 1920, and Alaska was seen as the last frontier. In some people's minds, Joe and Fannie were the personification of that ideal.

Wild West female characters like Calamity Jane and Annie Oakley still captured the imagination of the public, even though their era was over. Because of Fannie's frontier location, being the rare female in her place and time, and her loud, colorful personality, it was easy to project a Calamity Jane–type character onto her. People tended to romanticize female characters like Fannie, and writers liked to portray her as an oddity or "colorful character" rather than as a normal woman.[2] Local lore attributed the stories of many women to Fannie.[3] Some writers presented Joe and Fannie as characters similar to those in the dime novels. Whether deliberately or inadvertently, Fannie played to the writers by telling exaggerated stories. Averse to sensationalism, Joe tended to underplay himself.

As Joe and Fannie Quigley's reputations spread, visitors made the trek to Kantishna to see how they lived. Ruth Wilson, a young widow from Omaha, Nebraska, made a trip to Fairbanks in 1919 to see her miner brother William Campbell. While there, she accepted an invitation from Fairbanks photographer Nan (Mrs. L. E.) Robertson to come along with her to Kantishna. They traveled up the Kantishna River as far as Roosevelt and then hiked 30 miles from there to Quigley Ridge. The highlight of Wilson's trip was a chance to join Joe and Fannie on their annual hunt for meat to last the winter. An article

Chapter 17. Celebrity

was published in the *Cordova Times*, with many photographs of the adventure, and reprinted in the *Alaska Dispatch*.[4]

In 1921 writer Mary Lee Davis and her husband, engineer John Allen Davis, journeyed six days by dogsled and packhorse into the Kantishna region on what is now the Denali Park Road to see Joe and Fannie.[5] In 1917, United States Mine had established a mining experiment station in Fairbanks to help prospectors determine the value and quantity of minerals, which in turn was expected to help them decide whether or not to launch full-scale mining operations. John Allen Davis was the chief mining engineer of the Fairbanks station and he was required to travel the territory to make assessments. Mary Lee Davis was a prolific writer of newspaper and journal articles and an adventurous person who went with her husband on his inspection trips. Mary Lee wrote stories of the people she met on their journeys, with many of the profiles eventually compiled into a book called *We Are Alaskans*. It included a chapter about Fannie, called "Little Witch of Denali." Mary Lee was particularly interested in women who had chosen to make Alaska their home and was proud to have joined forces with them. Mary Lee and John Davis visited the Quigleys for 11 days. John Davis and Joe Quigley scouted the area for mineral prospects while Mary shadowed Fannie as they hiked though the hills and Fannie told stories of her life in the Kantishna mining region.

Mary Lee Davis was not the only writer who was captivated by the Quigleys' lifestyle. There was a sense that the new roads and the railroad coming

(Left to right) Fannie Quigley, Joe Quigley, visitor Ruth Wilson, and Kantishna miner Joe Dalton on an Autumn moose hunt, 1919 (photograph by Nan Robertson, Alaska and Polar Regions Collections, Elmer E. Rasmuson Library, University of Alaska Fairbanks, UAF-1969-0092-00730).

through would soon ruin the old way of life. People wanted to see it before it was gone, and Fannie was particularly interesting to the curious because there were so few women who were willing to live such an isolated existence. Fannie was determinedly old-fashioned and represented a vanishing way of life to people. She seemed to enjoy the opportunity to share her knowledge of survival in the wilderness (it was, after all, what made her special) and had a tendency to embellish her stories. There is no way to know if Fannie simply exaggerated her own prowess for the sake of a good story and innocently co-opted apocryphal stories into her own personal tales, or if she lied to aggrandize herself because she wanted the attention and admiration that came with being a hero. Any blurring of the truth that came from Fannie could also have been amplified by the writers.

Excelling at traditionally male activities like hunting and trapping was a source of pride for Fannie and a source of curiosity for the public. Joe seemed to take it in stride as simply part of their partnership agreement, and he would mention in letters to family that "Fannie got a moose" or "Fannie got a fox."[6] Lois McGarvey was a writer who admired Fannie and wanted to learn some of her hunting and trapping skills. Although McGarvey gave Fannie a fictitious name, calling her "Hattie," she wrote in detail about fur trapping with Fannie.

While checking Fannie's trap lines, Fannie and Lois McGarvey came to a trap Fannie had set for lynx. As McGarvey tells it, there was a lynx caught in the trap by one toenail. The cat's pelt would bring $150 at market, so when McGarvey saw the lynx alive she raised her gun to shoot it in the head. According to McGarvey, as she approached, the cat held up one paw, with the trap dangling from the claw. She wrote, "if a lynx could weep, he was weeping."[7] She decided to yank the chain on the trap, breaking off the claw and letting the lynx go. McGarvey said she felt a "sinister presence" behind her and turned to see Fannie watching the lynx disappear. Fannie was infuriated and yelled at McGarvey, "Now, that is enough of you! I knew you was screwy, and I gave you the best part of the line. You can just go to hell back where you came from! You are a sissy, and better go into a sissy business!" McGarvey apparently saw Fannie as a villain of sorts, setting the reader up with a mental picture of a crying cat holding up a trap by its injured toe. McGarvey was also openly impressed with Fannie and wrote about the innovative cold storage tunnels that "Hattie McLain" used to store food but left Joe Quigley out of the story altogether.

The line between fact and fiction was not a sharp divide with writers then. It wasn't until the 20th century that the idea of objectivity in journalism was introduced with any seriousness, and in the early 1920s that line was still fuzzy. At a time when Freud was developing his theories of the unconscious, and painters like Picasso were experimenting with Cubism, journalists were also developing a greater recognition of human subjectivity.[8] Since the time of Teddy Roosevelt, Alaska had been presented as the ultimate proving ground for masculinity and so the Quigleys with their wilderness skills were a subject of curiosity and were used as characters who typified a lifestyle.

The types of inaccuracies purported by writers included both invented facts and exaggerations of reality. For example, in her story of Fannie, Mary Lee Davis states that Archdeacon Stuck outfitted at the Quigley cabin before the successful climb to the peak of Denali, but this was simply not true. At the time of the climb, Fannie wrote to Charles Sheldon saying specifically that the party did not stop on their way up. There's no way to know if Fannie changed her story when talking with Davis or if Davis was using journalistic license to build a picture of a heroic figure. Davis does mention "sleeping with Fannie's epic tales still ringing in my ears" and goes on to describe Joe and Fannie as a study in contrasts. Joe is depicted as long and lean, quiet, and tending toward understatement, while Fannie was "pouring out words in rich hyperbole."[9] Although there was truth to these descriptions, they were simplified and exaggerated into characterizations to satisfy readers.

At the same time that Davis and others were writing about Fannie and Joe, the film that is considered the first feature-length documentary, *Nanook of the North*, was being filmed in the Far North, in Canada. Robert Flaherty was an American explorer for mineral deposits in the Hudson Bay Territory and had spent several years prospecting in the area with the help of Native people. He had filmed one of the expeditions but then accidently destroyed the film by dropping a cigarette onto the highly flammable negative.[10] He decided to go back to the area with the specific goal of making a motion picture about the life of a Native family over the period of a year. Much of the film was staged and the family was not a real family. The Inuk man, "Nanook," was portrayed by Allakariallak, and his "wife" was not his wife at all. The film was released in 1922 with many inaccuracies. It was criticized for those inaccuracies and for the cartoonish depiction of the Inuit people, but it was very popular. The film was ultimately considered the first of its genre and is an excellent example of how the line between non-fiction and fiction were not well defined at the time.

There are a few typical Alaska miner stories, some more believable than others, that have been associated with Joe and Fannie. The people who were told the stories believed them. Edgar Brooker, Jr., remembered a silly story, told to him by Fannie Quigley, of a very crowded cabin. She and Joe hitched up a few dogs and headed out for a hunting trip on Sable Mountain. They intended to spend the night in the Igloo Creek cabin, which was used by various travelers in the area. It was customary in the Far North to leave doors unlocked, to invite travelers to stay, and to use a vacant cabin if needed. Brooker remembered staying at the cabin himself during the summer, and he knew that it was a very tiny, one-room structure with a simple stove. There were two wide bunks with poles fastening the bunks to the walls of the cabin. There were no dog houses and it was very cold that night, so Joe and Fannie brought the dogs in with them. Fannie and Joe were barely settled in, just falling asleep, when a Native couple with their dogs came by and settled in for the night, using the other bunk. Once again everyone settled down and started to drift off to sleep when a mailman who was driving a double-ender sleigh with one horse pulling it came to the cabin. They couldn't leave the horse outside in weather 40 degrees below zero, so the mailman and the horse came inside for the night. All five people, the horse and two dog teams finally got settled down in the overcrowded quarters, but not for long. As soon as everyone got to sleep, the horse nudged the stove pipe and knocked it down, startling dogs and humans alike, ending any chances of sleep for everyone.[11]

There is a controversial and often repeated story about Fannie and an animal skin that has many versions. It is clearly derived from a tall tale stretching back to the days of the buffalo hunters in the 1880s. As the story goes, Fannie was out hunting and had killed and skinned a bear or, in some versions, a moose. It was cold and getting dark, and she knew she couldn't make it home, so she wrapped herself in the wet hide and went to sleep. In some versions the hide had frozen around her and she had to cut her way out. She was not the first or last person to tell this story about themselves and the theme has appeared in various adventure stories and films. She told a version of it to Mary Lee Davis and didn't mention freezing weather or cutting herself out of the hide, but she did say that the dogs "never did get over smelling me!"[12] Opinions vary as to whether it truly happened to Fannie, but it's certain that she told the story in first person when she and Joe visited Joe's family in Pennsylvania. In that version she said that she gutted the animal (a moose) and crawled inside the carcass.

Joe was uncomfortable with the idea of being a celebrity, and in February 1930 he wrote a letter to the editor of the Lapeer County *Michigan Press* referring to the responses he and Fannie had gotten from an article published the previous May. The Michigan publisher, Harry M. Meyers, had visited the Quigleys when he came to visit his son Bill, who served as a ranger in the park for a year. The original article was on par with others that had been published and talked about the Quigley's rugged lifestyle and "the bleak country that lots of outdoorsmen would hesitate in traveling over." The article told an anecdote about how Fannie had been ready to hike 120 miles to the railroad to catch a train to go look for Joe, whom she hadn't heard from in a month, but then Joe arrived home just as she was leaving to find him. Readers were fascinated by the description of the Quigley lifestyle and the response to the article was overwhelming. The publicity resulted in quite a bit of fan mail, including letters simply addressed to "Fannie Quigley, Interior of Alaska."

Chapter 17. Celebrity

When Joe wrote the letter to the editor of the Michigan paper, the *Fairbanks Daily News-Miner* found it interesting enough to reprint it. In the letter, Joe thanked Meyers for the copies of the article that had been sent to him and went on to describe a bit about their lifestyle in his casual way, talking about hunting and the weather, and he also told Meyers, "I am afraid that both Fannie and I would hesitate before visiting Lapeer for the people there might expect to see super-human beings, and we would hate to disappoint them."[13] He tended to normalize his extraordinary lifestyle when describing it and did not want people to have exaggerated expectations of him.

Various visitors wrote about Joe and Fannie during their years in Kantishna. Journalists, scientists and engineers who were sent there for work, curiosity seekers, adventurers, and park rangers all wrote stories of Kantishna that included Joe and Fannie as highlights in their memoirs. The Quigleys managed to not only survive but thrive in an environment that many couldn't fathom living in, bringing the fantasy of wilderness living to life. Through a combination of hard work, ingenuity, bravery, and the ability to learn from their mistakes, Joe and Fannie overcame many obstacles and performed feats that were far beyond the reach of the average person. They also had the good luck to be physically strong, healthy, and disease resistant enough to live through epidemics. They were resilient and were able to work together in spite of their differences in order to reach their goals. When modern researchers dig through the various accounts of Joe and Fannie Quigley, it takes a bit of analysis and patience to sort fact from romanticized fantasy, but those sources are valuable as accounts of things that happened as well as statements on the awe with which the average person looked at the couple. Approaching the stories with even the most skeptical mind set still leaves a picture of people who led extraordinary lives.

Chapter 18

Flight

Even though Joe had chosen to live a primitive life in the Alaska bush, he was attracted to technology. His frequent trips to Fairbanks and keeping up with news from the outside helped to keep his spirits buoyant. On one of those trips in 1924 he heard a radio for the first time. It was an Atwater-Kent battery-operated table model and he enjoyed it so much that he bought it immediately and brought it back to Kantishna. At that time there was only one radio station in Alaska, but the whole mining camp got to hear the radio broadcast and the miners were mystified when it played.[1] Joe also loved to fly, and as soon as the opportunity arose, he began traveling by plane.

The mid–1920s were a time of great change for the citizens of Alaska. Living in a vast, sparsely populated place with extreme weather made transportation and communication an issue of utmost priority for everyone. The constant struggle to get adequate train transportation for the ore was an ongoing concern, but there was also the problem of getting people, mail, and everyday supplies from one place to the other. Air travel would open Alaska up and give the citizens a new freedom of movement, but it was a rare and expensive proposition. Ten years after the Wright brothers' exhibition at Kitty Hawk, North Carolina, the first plane was seen flying in Alaska. It would be more than a decade after that before regular air transportation was available.

On June 21, 1913, Captain James V. Martin arrived on the ship *Alaska* with a Martin type tractor biplane in pieces to be put together in Fairbanks.[2] The arrival caused major excitement for the town and an exhibition was scheduled for July 3, 4, and 5 in Exhibition Park. Martin's wife, Lily Irvine Martin, also a pilot, was billed as "the first woman to fly a plane in America" and would demonstrate the machine on the ground.[3] Captain Martin would fly the plane. Admission to Exhibition Park was $2.50 and the festivities included horse races, boat races, foot races, and rock drilling. According to *Fairbanks Daily News-Miner* editor W. F. Thompson, the town had more than its share of people who did not believe that a machine could fly through the air.[4] They would be proven wrong, and air travel would become a key method of transportation in Alaska.

Chapter 18. Flight

It took a while for flying to become accessible, with commercial flights becoming available with Wein Air Alaska in 1927. Before the commercial flights began, entrepreneurial bush pilots were offering flights for hire in their small planes. The use of small planes for transportation quickly became popular in Alaska and by the end of the 1920s airplanes were in common use for passengers and small quantities of freight. In the summer of 1926, when bush pilot Joe Crosson came to the Fairbanks area, he was anxious to build a customer base and knew that word of mouth was the best advertising. Joe Quigley remembered their first meeting happening when he was getting ready to go home from Fairbanks. "When Joe Crosson first came in, he was having a hard time getting customers, so he asked to fly me back. I told him the field was pretty well prepared, but never tried it before."[5] Quigley, Crosson and fellow pilot Ed Young took off for Kantishna. Quigley had prepared an airfield in anticipation of having planes land, but it had never been tested. Crosson knew that pilots and miners had very different ideas about what constituted a suitable landing strip and was known to say that miners would think they had a fine landing field when "an eagle couldn't even land there."[6] Crosson was determined to try whatever seemed even remotely possible, but arriving near Quigley Ridge, he looked over the terrain and realized that landing would be a challenge, so he set up a pattern to land on a gravel bar near Moose Creek.

The landing did not go as well as was hoped. Crosson did land and was up to the end of the "little field" when he saw that the gravel bar was too short and that the plane was going into the river. When he saw water under the wing he accelerated, hoping to fly over the river, but the plane dipped over the bank into a deep hole. It landed with the nose straight down, wrecking the props and wings and throwing Quigley's face against a strut. When they landed in the field, before Crosson accelerated, Quigley thought they had landed and had unhooked his safety belt. Both Joe Quigley and the plane sustained some damage. The tips of the propeller were bent and the crankcase was broken, leaving the pilot with no way to fly the 150 miles back to Fairbanks and no radio to call for help. Joe Quigley emerged from the plane with his face split open from eyebrow to lip and dripping with blood.

Fannie hurried down to investigate the crash landing and saw that Joe's face was torn completely open and would need stitches. Joe kept a surgical sewing kit for all his years in the Far North because miners were accustomed to performing serious first aid on a regular basis. Working in the wilderness with no doctors nearby meant that people learned to handle emergencies themselves. The first thing Fannie did was pour ice water down his nose, which was flayed open, with the flesh "laid clear back on both sides." The ice water did its job and stopped the bleeding, which meant it was time for Fannie to get the sewing kit and sew Joe Quigley's face back together.

There are many accounts of what happened next and they all seem to agree that stitching up Joe's face involved quite a lengthy and animated discussion. At first, Fannie tried to use the baseball stitch that she normally used to make moccasins. Joe knew this approach would not work well, as it would pucker the skin and cause scarring. He had a specific stitch in mind that he knew would work. It took a good bit of arguing, while he was bleeding and in pain, to convince her to sew each stitch separately, tying them off individually and going straight across the cut. The wound looked pretty horrific at the time, but in the end Joe never saw a doctor about the injury, and his face healed with barely any scar.[7] In her typical fashion, Fannie would recount the story later, portraying herself as a hero, telling how she used a moccasin stitch and it all turned out fine, thanks to her. As much as Joe would underplay his own achievements and display a casual toughness, Fannie would consistently brag about her prowess and skill and had no qualms about exaggerating.

With Joe Quigley's face repaired, they now had to address the problem of the plane. Always resourceful, the Kantishna miners got the plane out of the water by rigging a Spanish windlass, which is a process of securing a sturdy rope to something immovable like a tree and also around the object to be moved. The rope is tightened by twisting a large stick or pole through the loop that runs between the immovable object and the object to be moved. The twisting action tightens the rope, pulling the object to be moved. Once the plane was out of the water, it stayed put until Crosson returned the following week with George King, landing on a larger gravel bar a few miles away. King and Crosson spent several days repairing the broken plane and flew it back to Fairbanks.[8]

Fifty-seven-year-old Joe Quigley and 23-year-old Joe Crosson became friends after that, flew together often, and had more than one rough landing. Once, when Quigley rode with Crosson to Nenana to get the mail, the plane blew a tire as it landed. Quigley had certainly learned to keep his safety belt fastened, and Crosson was an excellent pilot. Crosson's skill circumvented any injuries or major damage to the plane during the rough landing. Resourcefulness was essential to survival in the Far North and people tended to cooperate with each other, being helpful and hospitable. So when Crosson remembered a man who used the same size tires on his truck as were on the plane, he was able to borrow a truck tire and put it on the plane. Crosson and Quigley went on their way with the mail and had a smooth take off.

Joe Crosson became an Alaskan hero. He was known as the first to land on Mount McKinley's glaciers and was celebrated on radio, in advertisements, and in comic books.[9] He helped pioneer air routes throughout Alaska and in 1929 made headlines for doing a rescue search for his friend and fellow pilot Carl Ben Eielson in Siberia during the winter. He once delivered life-saving serum to Barrow, Alaska, over an uncharted mountain range without the aid of navigational aids or communication tools. When famed aviator Wiley Post

Chapter 18. Flight

(Left to right) Lillian Crosson, Fannie Quigley and Joe Crosson in front of Crosson's plane near Moose Creek, 1926. Joe Crosson flew mercy missions in the Far North and pioneered air routes throughout Alaska. Crosson and Quigley became friends after a crash landing cut open Joe Quigley's face in 1926 (photograph by Joe Quigley, Fannie Quigley Collection, Alaska and Polar Regions Collections, Elmer E. Rasmuson Library, University of Alaska, UAF-1980-0046-00086).

and beloved actor and humorist Will Rogers perished in a plane crash in Alaska, Joe Crosson was asked to fly their bodies home. Crosson's sister Marvel was also a pioneer aviator, the first woman pilot to earn a commercial license in the Territory of Alaska, and was killed while participating in the Women's Transcontinental Air Races in 1929.[10]

After the incident with Crosson's plane and Joe Quigley's injury, the Territorial Road Commission contracted with John Anderson of Wonder Lake to construct an aviation field on a bench above Moose Creek near the mouth of Lake Creek. The new airfield enabled local miners to often take passage on planes to Moose Creek.[11]

Chapter 19

Back Home

By the early to mid-1920s Joe and Fannie had the surplus cash they needed to take a trip outside. They went to visit family in several parts of the United States, including the West Coast and Pennsylvania. Joe hadn't been to Pennsylvania since he'd left as a starry-eyed 15-year-old 40 years earlier. It is difficult to discern exactly when they went on the trip because various memoirs and stories from family members conflict. In a school paper that appears to have been written in the 1930s, one of Joe's great nephews, Bob Johnson, wrote that Joe and Fannie visited Pennsylvania in 1922. In a letter to her sister dated March 23, 1923, Fannie mentions that they had been thinking of "going out" but that Joe had decided to ship some ore instead, and she adds that she will try and get out next fall. Based on a combination of factors, including passenger listings, the best estimate is that they made the trip during the fall/winter of 1923–1924.[1]

After 40 years Joe Quigley was finally returning to see his family in Pennsylvania. His siblings were excited to see their little brother who had run away from home with big dreams so long ago. Joe was now a middle-aged man with memorable stories of life in the Far North to tell. Both of Joe's parents and several of his 13 siblings had passed away while he was in Alaska. Joe and Fannie visited with the sisters, brothers and in-laws who remained, and everyone relished their tales of life in the Far North. Although Joe had grown up on a farm in Armstrong County, some of his siblings had moved to towns in the area. Joe's sister Emmaline Quigley Fair, who'd had the general store with her husband, was now a widow and still lived in her own home in East Franklin near the old Quigley farm. Joe remembered Emma's husband John Fair from when he would go into John's general store as a child. John had passed away in 1916 at the age of 85. It may have been a hectic visit for Joe and Fannie but was a memorable one that generated family stories told to children and grandchildren about the uncle who went to Alaska and discovered gold.

Returning to Alaska, Joe was more determined than ever to sell out. He loved prospecting, but the constant hard work of mining and living off the

Joe and Fannie visiting family in Pennsylvania. In the back row, from left to right, are Hanna, widow of Benjamin Quigley, Amanda (facing right), unidentified Quigley brother behind Amanda (possibly William Huston Quigley), Joe Quigley, Fannie Quigley, unidentified man (possibly Charles Cooper). In the front row, from left to right, are Martha Quigley, unidentified woman, Emmaline Quigley Fair, Charles Grider Quigley. Several of Joe's siblings had passed away and some lived on the West Coast. Joe had not been to Pennsylvania in 40 years and there is no record of him returning again after this visit (Alaska and Polar Regions Collections, Elmer E. Rasmuson Library, University of Alaska, Fairbanks, UAF-1980-0046-00236).

land was wearing on both him and Fannie. While they were traveling, he and Fannie had also visited relatives in Oregon, and he stayed in touch with them with regular letters and expressed a desire to buy property there as an investment. At this point, Joe was especially aware of having missed out on building a family of his own, and he knew that at his age, he would not be having his own children. He maintained correspondence with his brother Lincoln and his wife Marietta and their children and grandchildren. Their son Lloyd and Lloyd's wife Zelne named their oldest son after Joe and he was thrilled. The boy was called "Little Joe." Joe very much enjoyed having a namesake and wrote a letter to him in January 1926 when the boy was a year old. The letter is written on Hotel Alaska stationery and is addressed directly to the child.

Kantishna, Alaska
January 31 1926
Mr. Lloyd Joseph Quigley

Dear Sir.
I have not had the pleasure of meeting you as yet but hope I may have that pleasure sometime in the near future. Will now introduce myself. I am Joseph Buffington Quigley,

your Great-Uncle. Not Great in any way except that it just happens through the course of events that I am one of your Great Uncles and I sure was much pleased when Grandma Quigley wrote and & informed me that Lloyd Joseph Quigley had arrived strong & healthy. Hope you can stay with us many, many years and grow up to be a fine strong manly man that not only myself, but that the world may be proud of.

I am coming to see you some of these days & hope that we may get to be great friends & that our friendship may grow stronger as we grow older.

Will now close. Wishing you all kinds of joy & happiness on this little old planet. From your affectionate Uncle J. B. Quigley

Kantishna, Alaska

P.S.
Please always remember to be kind & good, but most especially to mother.[2]

Joe sent another letter to "Little Joe," also on Hotel Alaska stationery, six months later to announce a special gift of a bear skin. The envelope was addressed to the boy, and the salutation was "Dear Nephew." Joe suggests that the boy might like to play on the bear skin or he could "give it to your mama to trim a coat with." Joe explains that he killed the bear himself some years ago and adds a postscript explaining, "Aunt Fannie did not come to Fairbanks with me, so I am making a very short stay."[3]

In a letter dated February 18, 1927, Joe congratulates Lloyd and Zelne on the birth of another son, Kenneth Quigley. Joe also writes about his friend, Mr. Turnison, saying that Turnison has "a house rented near yours, near the high school building [in Vancouver, Washington], so he will be a near neighbor of yours." Joe states that he is sending Mr. Turnison with an undisclosed amount of money for Zelne to start a bank account for Little Joe, saying "the interest will add up in time," and he tells Zelne that she can "fix it so he can draw on it when you think he is the age it will be most useful to him." Joe explains that he is sending the money to her because he feels a mother always has the best interest of the child in mind. How Joe met Mr. Turnison is not clear, but Joe wrote about him several times, saying that Turnison had rented a house in Vancouver but was called back to Alaska before he could move into the Vancouver house to testify in a case tried in Fairbanks. Joe seemed anxious to get Turnison to meet the Vancouver Quigleys and promises that he will be "sure to hunt you up" when he goes south again. Joe mentions Turnison frequently in his correspondence and clearly holds Turnison in high regard. He writes that he had never met Turnison's wife and family, but "he is well thought of in this country and I think you will all like him."[4]

Joe appears to be somewhat frustrated by having been unable to visit and explains, "I did not get out last summer to see Little Joe but hope to go out some time about next Aug. or Sept." He also seems to be feeling isolated in Alaska and imagines having his nephew visit Kantishna. "Wish we had Little Joe up here with us. Would love to teach him to hunt big game. He sure would be lots of company here for us." Joe adds some previously asked-for advice for Little Joe's upbringing, telling Zelne to encourage the boy to stand up for his own rights when playing with other children: "that is one thing a child should be encouraged to do, even if he does get a bloody nose now & then." Aware that he is a man with no experience raising children, Joe qualifies his opinion with "Of course, that is just an old codger's ideas & I might be wrong." Joe went on to ask about his brother and sister-in-law, Lincoln and Marietta, and their granddaughter, Vern's daughter and Joe's great niece, Vernetta. He refers to Vernetta living with Lincoln and Marietta, saying, "She will be a great company to for Link and Etta. Otherwise it would be lonesome for them, with both Verne & Lloyd gone." Vernetta's mother died in November 1921, when Vernetta was only nine months old. Her father, Vern, remarried and had two sons in 1925 and 1928, but Vernetta was listed in the 1930 census as living with her grandparents Lincoln and Marietta. It seems that they may have raised her.

As he did in most of his correspondence with people from outside of Alaska, Joe talks about life in Kantishna and reveals that he hopes to move to the States to settle after "next summer." He laments not having taken his brother Lincoln's advice about buying land in Washington as an investment, and he says that he is sorry he missed peach and pear season and missed going out to pick berries his family. Joe didn't realize that it would be more than a decade before he would get the opportunity and resources to make the move. He describes the winter, calling it "very nice," and saying, "Of course we have some 40 below zero, but that is to be expected here." He writes that he and Fannie have had caribou in sight of the house all winter and that they "can't starve here as long as we have a gun and ammunition." Joe mentions the garden and says that he got two boxes of fresh apples from Yakima and two cases of eggs. "We have to buy everything by the case here as it is 80 miles to the nearest grocery store & that one does not carry a very large supply."

Toward the end of the long letter, Joe apologizes for Fannie not writing back to Etta. "I have been after her for some time to answer it, but she is a very slow writer & hates to write so bad. She says she is afraid they will laugh at her poor writing. I tell her that folks are so far away that she won't be able to hear them laugh. If I thought I could write & make people laugh I would write more often, as it does anyone good to have a good laugh now & then." Although a quick learner, Fannie was practically illiterate because of lack of opportunity for an education. She did write letters occasionally, and they are child-like and sincere. Fannie had been willing to write to the highly-educated Charles Sheldon in 1913, but according to Joe's letter, she was self-conscious about writing to her sister-in-law.

Life in Kantishna continued on for Joe and Fannie, and as the park became more popular with tourists, things changed. A few more rangers were

Chapter 19. Back Home

hired, including Grant Pearson who came to Alaska in 1925 and became a park ranger at Mount McKinley National Park in 1927. He worked with Fritz Nyberg under Superintendent Harry Karstens. The population of miners was dwindling, with only the most persistent prospectors staying in the area, working their hillside claims. Pearson was not in the park for long before he met the half dozen or so miners left in Kantishna when he was sent to deliver the mail. First on his route were John and Paula Anderson, who were very hospitable. John Anderson had taken to making furniture, lamps and chandeliers out of caribou antlers, and this made a lasting impression on Pearson.[5] Since caribou shed their antlers each year, Anderson always had a plentiful supply for his craft. The Andersons were homesteaders, arriving in the Kantishna Mining District in 1918, with property on Wonder Lake. They had some mining success there and also engaged in trapping and breeding foxes for sale. The couple left Kantishna for California in 1929.[6]

Next on the trail was "Little" Johnnie Busia whose nickname reflected his 120-pound, 5'4" stature. Busia was a neighbor of both the Andersons and the Quigleys. Born in Croatia in 1891, Johnnie Busia arrived in Kantishna in 1918 to join his father who had been mining there since 1906.[7] Busia had rigged up a clever way to cross the water to his cabin, involving a seat that hung from a cable system 50 feet above the canyon. This could be a bit of a test for the uninitiated and certainly added security and privacy in a place where no one locked their doors. He was a friend of the Quigleys and sometimes a drinking buddy of Fannie's. He concocted a homemade liquor made with molasses, rice, hops and sugar called Kantishna Champagne and would offer it to friends and guests. Busia was the last miner to live in Kantishna year-round and as a consequence ended up with the job of burying the dead, both human and canine. He talked with Pearson about his role in the ritual of burials, which would vary according to how much he respected the deceased. "Last winter Joe Dalton die, I bury him. This winter Pete Nelson die, I bury Pete. I like a man; I build a box to put him in. Old Pete was a good neighbor and he got a box. Joe didn't get a box." Joe Dalton and Busia had been in a long-standing feud over some mining business that Busia felt was unfair, and Dalton was looked upon by some as a selfish man. Busia also told Pearson about burying Mr. Jim, Busia's lead dog: "When Mr. Jim died, I made a good box for him. He's buried on the knoll, back of the cabin." It was not very far to hike from Busia's to Joe and Fannie Quigley's place, where Pearson was well fed by Fannie, given a tour of the compound, and struck up a friendship with the Quigleys that would last for many years.[8]

The miners and the park rangers were friends and would play practical jokes on each other. Grant Pearson recounted a story of a time when he made a three-day trip from Copper Mountain to McKinley Park Station with Joe Quigley and two others.[9] They arrived at a shelter cabin that had recently been vacated by two women botanists who had been using it for six weeks for their studies. The small group found that the guests had left some clothes behind, including a pair of women's underwear. This brought out the juvenile side of their humor and one of the men, as a joke, secretly slipped the pair of the women's panties into the backpack of another member of the group, thinking that the surprise and embarrassment when he opened the pack and saw the unexplained women's undergarments would be hilarious.

At the end of the first day's walk back, the miner opened his pack, saw the panties, responded as expected, and everyone had a laugh. The prank became a running joke when that miner feigned getting rid of the panties but instead surreptitiously slipped them into Joe's pack. The next night when they were unpacking for the evening, hilarity ensued when the panties appeared among Joe's things. Joe said, "This'll be the end of that stuff!" and disappeared out the door, presumably to dispose of the panties. The third night, the group was at the ranger's cabin at park headquarters, the park clerk's wife came over to greet them and Pearson told her that he had some letters that had been sent in by one of the prospectors to be mailed. He proceeded to dump the contents of his pack on the floor to find the letters. Pearson was extremely surprised and embarrassed when the panties spilled out on the floor with the mail. Joe tried to keep his composure, simply shook his head with a bemused grin and said, "Now, who the dickens would pack a pair of ladies panties around like that! Is that your good luck charm?" Pearson was sure that it was Joe who put the panties in his pack.

By the mid–1920s there were plenty of tourists coming through Mount McKinley National Park, and they were interested in the Quigley compound and lifestyle. Joe was a well-known and respected miner and prospector, but he did not have the flamboyant personality that Fannie did, and he did not like to be presented as extraordinary, even though he was. His interests were in getting his mines sold or leased for a good price and moving to the States for at least part of each year. This process involved developing the mines and curating relationships that led to investors. He was often not home for weeks at a time. When tourists came through, Joe was likely to be working in the mines, off hunting or prospecting, or away in Fairbanks, leaving Fannie to greet most visitors.

Fannie was candid with visitors and did not hide the fact that she liked to drink. Once, Father Fitzgerald, a missionary, and his pilot made an unplanned landing to avoid a storm and ended up having Fannie cook then a meal at the Quigley cabin. Fannie served a caribou stew, but Father Fitzgerald carefully picked the meat out of the stew and put it on the side of the plate. Fannie exploded at him. "What the hell's the matter, don't you like what I do to caribou?" Fitzgerald replied, "You know today is Friday, Mrs. Quigley, I don't eat meat." "I see," said Fannie as she went into the kitchen, returning

Chapter 19. Back Home

with a bowl of lettuce. "Here. Eat rabbit food. Rabbits are religious every day of the week." The good-natured clergyman took it well and offered to pay for his stay, which of course Fannie refused. Wanting to express his appreciation for her hospitality, Fitzgerald said, "After my pilot gets me to Fairbanks, he'll be flying back past here. What kind of chocolates do you like?" Fannie quickly replied, "Schlitz." The pilot came back the next day with two cases of beer and a quart of whiskey.[10]

Joe continued to patent more mines including Star, Lucky Strike, Bright Light, Darling, Pittsburgh, Red Top, and Sulphide in 1926, the 183-acre Francis Lode in 1927, and the White Hawk in 1929.[11] When a mine is patented, the federal government passes the title of the land to the claimant and it becomes real property rather than just mining rights. Joe eventually owned several hundred acres of land in the Kantishna mining district.

Things had been shifting and changing in Kantishna and the way of life there no longer felt satisfying to Joe. He enjoyed adventure and solitude as well as being social with his friends and neighbors, but tourism was part of the plan for the park from the beginning, and there were more people coming through as time went on. Joe and Fannie were losing the original feeling of community that they had as their old friends moved away or died. By the late 1920s and into the 1930s, traders, fur farm operators, and roadhouse keepers replaced miners as the principal commercial operators on the upper Kantishna River. Roosevelt, which was 30 miles from Kantishna, was an important year-round stopover for travelers, and that brought more people into the park as well.[12]

Any romance that had been between Joe and Fannie was gone, but they were yoked together in the rugged life they had created in the foothills of Denali. As Fannie's alcoholism grew progressively worse, she continued to tell exaggerated stories to visitors and transform what had been her charming wit, and tendency to affectionately tease, into unreasonable verbal abuse and bullying. There were many who loved and admired Fannie for her good qualities, and an increasing number of people who avoided her or found her off-putting.

One story of Fannie's intimidating ways was remembered by Ruth Lawlor, the live-in nanny for Joe Crosson and his wife Lillian. Joe and Fanny were visiting Joe and Lillian Crosson in Fairbanks. Lillian was feeding their son, Joe Jr., who kept turning away because he didn't want to eat. Fannie said something to the effect of "Give me that kid, I'll get him to eat!" but included expletives in her statement that young Ruth Lawlor was too embarrassed to repeat. Ruth said that Lillian would have no part in handing the baby to Fannie because "gee whiz, he was scared of her!"[13]

Fannie was very competitive, even with Joe. One day when Joe and Fannie each went out separately to hunt, Joe came back empty-handed, while Fannie was already cleaning the game she had killed. Fannie berated him,

"You ain' fit to go huntin,'" as she tossed him her skirt.[14] "Here, you do the housework today. Gimme your pants." It's not a matter of record whether that was her harsh sense of humor or if she was sober at the time. In truth, Fannie did hunt for most of their meat, but when game was scarce, it was Joe who got the job.[15] The hard life of living off the land was wearing them out by this time. They had hoped to have gotten a big payoff from the gold mining by now, but they still didn't feel like they would get as much money from selling out at this time as they might be able to get later.

Even though they felt that they couldn't move to the States yet, Joe would leave Kantishna for weeks at a time. One of the places he went was the hot springs in Circle. His life of hard labor and the wear and tear on his body left him with some chronic pain. He felt that the hot springs were the best cure for his sciatica, and because Fannie rarely wanted to go with him, the trips also gave him a break from the tension between the two of them. One day in 1929 he decided to hitch up three dogs and "beat it" to the hot springs in Circle. He left a fourth dog, Fritz, with Fannie to keep her company. Sadly, Fritz died three days later, and Fannie had a funeral for the dog by herself.[16] Dogs were treated with respect when they died as they were in life. Joe had gone the 120 miles to Nenana with the dog sled and then dropped Fannie a postcard to tell her that all was well on his journey before he caught a plane to Circle. Fannie had no way to tell Joe that Fritz had died, and unfortunately Joe's postcard got lost in the mail. Joe's trip was taking longer than usual, and Fannie was left alone with her grief and isolation for the next six weeks until Joe made it home.

Fannie wrote to her niece Teresa in 1929 telling her that there was no news but work.[17] Their life in Kantishna required relentless hard work, and they were getting older. Joe was 60, Fannie was 58, and they were tired. It felt like time to sell out and move to a place with an easier lifestyle, but in the States the economy was in trouble, and the stock market crash of October of 1929 set off biggest depression in the history of the industrialized world. Fannie mentions in her letter that they would like to go "outside" but can't until they sell their place. She goes on to say, "Here we have the best meat and vegetables," showing that she feels a sense of safety in staying in Kantishna.

Also in 1929 Joe wrote a letter to Lloyd Quigley and the rest of the family while spending a couple of days in Fairbanks at the Hotel Alaska with Fannie. He encloses some photos, telling the family that a friend took the photographs and that he and Fannie thought they would enjoy them. The pictures must have included a shot of Denali because Joe instructs them to "tell Little Joe that we live close to the big mountain." The letter tells the family that Joe and Fannie did not get any mail from September 15, 1928, until January 15, 1929, but that then they received two mail sacks full of first-class and second-class mail all at once.

In the letter, Joe sends regards to their mutual friend Mr. Turnison and then lets the family know that he does not expect to visit the States before the next summer and may not even be able to visit then, but that he and Fannie do want to get acquainted with Little Joe. He then lets them know that he is "just getting over what they call the intestinal flu" and that they "have had quite an epidemic of flu and small pox," but that there were very few fatalities from the flu. This was a decade after the worldwide flu epidemic, and everyone still feared the flu as potentially deadly. The letter explains that "the small pox broke out in different parts of Alaska about the same time, but fortunately they got it under control at once." Joe ends the letter by saying that they had an unusually warm winter "above zero most all the time, but a little more than the average snow fall. It rained and blowed [*sic*] winds 40–55 above zero for about one week in the middle of January and the snow practically all went off there. But it snowed before we left [for Fairbanks]." He signs off with "Fannie joins me in sending love and best wishes to all, Sincerely yours Truly, J. B. Quigley, Kantishna, Alaska."

Chapter 20

Cave In

The 1930 U.S. census for Kantishna looked very different from the 1920 census. Joe is listed as a quartz miner and Fannie as a housewife. All but one of the non–Native residents were white, and all of the white people were foreign born except for Joe, Fannie, and two trappers. The rest of the population was listed as Indian. There were more people listed as being in the fur business than in mining. John and Paula Anderson had a fur farm, but the rest of the people in the fur business were trappers.[1]

Joe and Fannie were getting older, and they had expected to be able to retire to the States years earlier but continued to maintain their wilderness lifestyle. They spent little time together and Joe continued to develop his mines as he had done for nearly four decades. On Wednesday, May 21, 1930, almost exactly 39 years after he crossed the Chilkoot Pass, the kind of catastrophic accident that all miners fear happened to Joe Quigley.[2] Now 61 years old, Joe was timbering the roof of the Banjo mine when the accident occurred. Timbering is the setting of timber supports in the tunnel, and a cap is a flat piece of wood inserted between the top of a post and the roof of the mine to provide support. "I was knocking a corner of a rock off in order to cap a timber, when the rock fell all around me."[3] Joe remembered the moment as if it were slow motion.

About 3000 pounds of rock fell, crushing Joe Quigley's body. When he initially regained consciousness his right arm was "numb and useless" and he could not move it.[4] Joe's right shoulder and left leg below the hip took the main weight of the fall. The doctor in Fairbanks later said that the "main nerve had been severed." His left femur had a compound fracture, so the bone was sticking out through the skin, and the leg was "bent clear back under my body, with the toes up by my ears."[5] His right leg was covered in rocks but not broken. He used his left arm to move some rocks, and "passing out periodically," he managed to free his right leg and got his left leg straightened out. He was all alone and knew he had to get out. Each time he would struggle to get an inch or two along, he would lose consciousness, wake up and drag himself another inch or two, where he would fall unconscious again, repeating the

Chapter 20. Cave In

process over and over. After about eight hours he had managed to drag himself out from under the rocks and into the blacksmith shop at the mouth of the tunnel, where he lost consciousness again.

Joe had taken to sleeping in the blacksmith shop that he'd built near the mine, going back to the cabin where he and Fannie lived each Saturday night to prepare for the next work week, and then back to work again on Monday mornings. Fannie would bring up food mid-week so that Joe could continue to work without going back to the cabin more than once a week. If the accident had not happened on a day that she normally brought food, he could have been there for many days and would likely have died. Within 24 hours after Joe dragged himself to the shop and passed out on the floor, Fannie came by on her routine weekly trip and found him. She sensed that something was amiss as she approached the shack and noticed that there wasn't any smoke coming from the chimney. At first sight of his motionless body she feared that Joe was dead. Running over to him, she found that he was critically injured but still alive. Knowing that this situation was beyond anything she could handle alone, Fannie made Joe as comfortable as possible and went back over the four-mile trail to enlist the help of men from the small community of miners. The men came to help, and some stayed with Fannie and Joe, but Billy Taylor went to summon medical help.

Neighbors bring a stretcher to carry severely injured Joe Quigley from the shack where he dragged himself after his mining accident in 1930 (National Park Service, DENA 3509).

By all accounts there was considerable snow on the ground even though it was May. Taylor headed through the snow toward the railroad station to use the telephone to summon the doctor in Fairbanks. Quigley Ridge is about 90 miles from the railroad station, and about four or five hours into the hike to McKinley Station, Taylor, accompanied by two dogs, stopped in to Ben Cleary's mess tent to tell the people there that Joe Quigley had been badly injured. Cleary was the foreman of a road crew for the Alaska Road Commission and many members of the crew were in the tent when Taylor came in saying, "I've got some bad news, fellows. Quigley has been hurt!" Several people asked what happened and how bad the injuries were. Taylor went on to explain, "Mine caved in.... It's bad.... He's got a busted leg and a busted shoulder, but it's the leg that's the worst. Might have to amputate." Taylor then explained that he was hurrying to the railroad station to use the phone and that he believed that Joe Quigley's life could be saved if a doctor was immediately flown into the Kantishna. One of the men in the room muttered under his breath, "Joe Quigley. It couldn't happen to a nicer guy."[6] Cleary quickly gave an order for one of the men to gas up the truck and insisted that Taylor have something to eat before continuing his mission of mercy. Someone from Cleary's crew drove Taylor and his dogs to the train station, and Martin Cole,[7] a new employee at Cleary's camp, rode along. There was no road, and the Ford plowed through patches of snow in low gear, avoiding drifts. They drove across a frozen stream, passed herds of caribou, and reached McKinley Station around midnight.

Because of the time of year, there was still plenty of light, but it was midnight and the railroad agent was sleeping when Taylor arrived at the station. Taylor called Saint Joseph's Hospital in Fairbanks, summarizing the circumstances of Joe's accident, emphasizing the immediate need for a doctor and hospitalization: "His leg is a sight; you may have to amputate." Minutes later a call came back to the railroad station from Dr. Rex Schwartz, who let Taylor know that he would come to Kantishna to evaluate Joe's condition, and that if amputation was necessary, he would first have the patient flown to the hospital. Schwartz let Taylor know that Alaska Airways had already been called and as soon as possible he would be flying to Moose Creek.

Joe Crosson called next, expressing concern about landing on the sandbar at Moose Creek. He wanted to bring a Fairchild 71, a larger plane with a cabin that would accommodate seven passengers. After some deliberation it was determined that the sandbar was too short and that he would have to fly a standard biplane with open cockpits. Shortly after Taylor and Crosson hung up the phone, a reporter from the Fairbanks *Daily News-Miner* called to confirm the story with Taylor. Cole and the truck driver returned to Cleary's camp, but Taylor stayed at the station with the intention of taking the next train to Fairbanks. Crosson brought Dr. Rex Swartz to Kantishna in a Curtiss JN-4 "Jenny" biplane, arriving at three o'clock in the morning.

Chapter 20. Cave In

Getting to the phone to call the doctor, getting the doctor to Kantishna, and getting Joe to the plane took until noon on June 2. Joe's leg had 12 days to begin healing before he was taken to the plane. Joe's friends carried him on a stretcher a mile and a half to the plane. The men knew that the cockpit space was too short for Joe's six-foot-plus frame on a stretcher, so they had planned to tie the stretcher to the tail of the plane, but the space wasn't long enough. They then decided to stick his feet into the cockpit without a stretcher. They built staging beside the plane so they could lower him into the cockpit. During the attempt to transfer him into the plane, the staging slipped, and they let him fall into the cockpit. Because it had been nearly two weeks without medical care since the femur was crushed, Joe's body had time to form new cartilage around the fracture and was beginning to form new bone. When they dropped him, Joe's leg broke again "with the sound of a gunshot."[8] He was wrapped in a single blanket and had no clothes on. Although Joe tried to hold the blanket down with his good arm, he "nearly froze to death, as the Jetstream of air poured in through the cockpit."[9] When remembering the event years later, Joe said, "I don't know yet how I stood the pain and the freezing blast of air."[10] He was admitted to St. Joseph's Hospital in Fairbanks and expected to stay for three months.[11]

When Joe was first admitted to the hospital, things looked grim. He told an interviewer later, "I think I was the only one in the hospital who thought I would come out alive."[12] During his time in the hospital, Joe had a stenographer friend write business letters for him, but he avoided writing to his family about the accident until later.[13] He left the hospital as soon as he could walk on crutches and checked into a hotel until September 24. On August 23, while in Fairbanks and still on crutches, Joe was called to testify before the Senate committee for the rail hearings. He told the committee that "big tonnage" would be assured for the Alaska Railroad if there was a link across the 80 miles that separates the area from the railroad. He testified that without the link, only very high-grade ore could be shipped due to excessive transportation costs. He stated that ore going for under $150 a ton could not be shipped.[14] Joe's friends Dr. Charles Bunnell and mining engineer Earl Pilgrim testified as well.

On September 9, 1930, pilot Ed Young attempted to fly Joe home.[15] They made it to Kantishna but were unable to land. Joe saw his home below, but the bar on Moose Creek was covered with water and the plane returned to Fairbanks. Young's second attempt to get Joe home, on September 24, was successful. They took off at noon that day, hoping that the flood waters had receded enough to land, and they were relieved when the bar on Moose Creek was clear.[16] Joe was finally home, after more than three months. His activities were quite limited, but he was able to walk.

Six months after the event, on November 29, 1930, Joe wrote a letter to

Lloyd and Zelne Quigley, telling them of the accident that effectively ended his mining career. He used printed business stationery that read "J. B. Quigley, Kantishna, Alaska, The Red Top Mine." He explained that he could walk with the use of a cane and had minimal use of his right arm, but he could use it to write. He told them, "The Dr. put too much weight on my leg when he stretched it, with the result that it is now ½ inch longer than the other one." Joe said that he joked with the doctor, telling him "if it had been some little short devil that needed more leg that he would have sent him off short." Joe seemed confident that his leg would heal but was more concerned about the function of his right arm.

Boredom was difficult for Joe to handle. He expected to "not be able to do anything to speak of" before spring, writing, "Believe you me it is darned monotonous sitting in the house." He said that he hadn't written to any family members earlier because even though he had lots of relatives, he did not want to worry anyone that did care about him and did not want to give the ones who didn't care the satisfaction of knowing he'd had such a close call! He went on to say that they were having a nice winter, "a little cold at times 32 below last night," with one foot of snow on the ground, and he said that the rivers were all frozen so winter travel was good, adding, "But I dare not take a chance of hitching the dogs up yet until my leg gets a little stronger."

The letter let them know that Fannie got a moose and some caribou while he was in the hospital, and that since he had gotten home, he "sat in the door and shot two caribou." He reported that Fannie's garden had turned out fine and so "all we need now is a little tobacco and some matches and will be able to get along fine." Then he said Fannie "caught a red fox the first night after the hunting season opened, so we are safe for the tobacco and matches." Joe mentions that it "would be nice to have Little Joe up here with us for the winter" and then asks that Lloyd and Zelne tell Link and Etta that he was "pretty badly knocked out, but still in the ring." He closed the long letter by saying that he had wanted to go to California "for the winter, or until I got back into condition again," but he had read about the "bread lines and hard times" in the States and changed his mind. The Great Depression had hit the United States and Joe was cautious about future finances. It seems that he had money left to spend the winter in California, even after the costs of the accident, but thought it wiser to save money because of the economic downturn in the States.

A different version of Joe's mining accident was recounted in a few publications. Fannie told Mary Lee Davis that "they got his leg set three inches too long," which was a gross exaggeration, and that version was published in *We Are Alaskans*.[17] Fannie also talked with geologist Ira Joralemon more than a year after the accident when he visited to look at the Quigley mines. Joralemon wrote a memoir that included a garbled account of Joe's mining accident, reporting that Fannie killed a caribou, made dinner, dug Joe out from under the rocks, loaded Joe's nearly lifeless body onto a sled and drove the sled with Joe in it back to the cabin, built a fire and then went out into the night to get a neighbor, all in the same day. He also said the plane arrived to take Joe to the hospital the next day and that Fannie was alone for ten months after that.[18] Joralemon's version of the story is in complete conflict with newspaper reports from the time of the accident and photographs that were taken of the other miners carrying Joe on a stretcher. This storytelling is typical of the lack of regard for facts that some writers used to build a picture of Fannie as a frontier hero character.

The truth is that Fannie did her part in saving Joe. She found him after he dug himself out from under the rocks and dragged himself to the shack with his one good arm and one good leg. She got help and made him as comfortable as she could, rallying the neighbors to help with first aid and with carrying Joe to the cabin. She made him as comfortable as possible until, more than a week later, they carried Joe to the plane. Fannie took care of the homestead for almost four months while Joe was in the hospital in Fairbanks, and she helped him when he came home. It was a community effort to get Joe and Fannie through the crisis, and Joe himself showed astounding strength, keeping a positive attitude that helped him recover. Joe and Fannie were no longer a happily married couple, but they were still partners in many ways and were decent to each other when it mattered.

Chapter 21

Cashing Out

Joe's physical condition after the 1930 mining accident made it impossible to sustain his former lifestyle. He continued to be creative and ambitious and to grow as an individual, but his mining career was essentially over, and he could not happily stay where he was. On a personal level, these years were a tenuous time for Joe Quigley. He was 61 years old and working to recover from an accident that would have killed most people. The damage to his body took away his ability to do the rigorous work of mining and required him to devise a new plan for his livelihood. Physical therapy for such severe injuries is slow and painful and requires an intense discipline. His wife and business partner, Fannie, had become increasingly more disagreeable as her alcoholism progressed. His marriage had been disintegrating for years and by this time they fought too much to be of any comfort to one another.

During this time, Joe had to put on a brave face to attract investors to buy his life's work for as much money as he could get. There was no retirement plan, and no medical insurance. Joe was genuinely a self-made man. He managed his own resources very well and was able to save enough for contingencies. The damage from the accident went beyond financial, though. It took away his career and, in some ways, his identity. He had tapped into his seemingly bottomless supply of reserve strength and pulled himself out from under a ton and a half of rock, and now he had to do the metaphorical equivalent with his life. Reinvention of oneself at that age is not a common or easy task. This was the most significant time of change that Joe Quigley had had to face since he was in his early 20s and crossed the Chilkoot Pass.

Ten months after his accident, in March 1931, Joe was in Kantishna, still recovering from his injuries. Pilot Percy Hubbard and Emil Jacobs decided to fly in and pay a surprise visit to the Quigleys.[1] The visit was newsworthy in Fairbanks because it demonstrated how easy travel was now with small planes, and the paper reported details about conditions for landing in Kantishna. Public opinion on access to the area and how active the mining was could have some effect on Joe's ability to sell, and he wanted to present himself and his property in a positive light. The paper reported that "they had a fine time with Mr. and Mrs. Quigley. Mrs. Quigley is in the best of health, but Mr. Quigley has not yet fully recovered from the injuries he received last year." As an attempt to make the area seem productive, Joe told the men that he "expects to start work soon," even though he must have known that he would not be doing more development work. The paper also mentions that there was little activity in the Kantishna area, with the exception of a trapper who had caught 28 foxes.

Road construction was still progressing, and as the population of the Kantishna Mining District changed, the miners became friendly with the construction crews, engineers and government officials who came in. Among the people who came to visit Joe and Fannie that year was civil engineer and Alaska Road Commission Superintendent Chris Edmunds and his wife Betty. Born in Wales and moving with his family to South Africa as a young teenager, Edmunds arrived in Canada in 1908 and then Fairbanks. Edmunds became a naturalized citizen of the United States in 1919 and worked for the Alaska Engineering Commission, which was formed by Congress to construct a railroad from Seward to Fairbanks. He directed the building of the road in Mount McKinley National Park from the Alaska Railroad hotel to Wonder Lake. Chris and Betty Edmunds brought their children to the park

Mr. and Mrs. Edmunds were among the many visitors to Joe and Fannie Quigley's cabin. In this photograph from 1931, from left to right, are Chris Edmunds, Joe Quigley, Betty Edmunds, and Fannie Quigley. Chris Edmunds was the Alaska Road Commission superintendent and brought his wife and children for a stay in Mount McKinley National Park during the summer of 1931 (Alaska and Polar Regions Collections, Elmer E. Rasmuson Library, University of Alaska, Fairbanks, UAF-1980-0046-00243).

during the construction of the road for the summer of 1931, living with the road crews.[2] Although Joe and Fannie were not getting along with each other, they continued to entertain friends and prospective business contacts, including the Edmundses.

Joe was starting to stay outside of Kantishna more often and was focused on getting investors to buy his mines, but he remained connected to the park and the Kantishna community. One day he was headed back toward Kantishna from the railroad station to show his Red Top mine to an engineer who was potentially interested in buying the property. When he got to park ranger Grant Pearson's cabin at Big Timber, he noticed that Pearson's cache, with his entire winter supply of food in it, had fallen down. Pearson was out on patrol and there was no one home to save the food, which, although still dry, was scattered all around the ground. Joe promptly started the big job of gathering all the food and carrying it into the cabin to save it, although it meant that he'd miss the potential buyer for his mine. Fortunately, another park ranger, Lee Swisher, happened to show up an hour after Joe started putting the food away, and Joe was able to leave for his meeting with the engineer.[3] Pearson remembered Joe as a kind neighbor who put his friends' needs before his own.

In August of 1931 the *Fairbanks Daily News-Miner* reported that mining engineer D. L. Sawyer had written about Alaska mines for *Engineering and Mining World*, predicting increased production of gold.[4] Sawyer expressed expectations for better transportation including a highway connecting Fairbanks and Seattle, bringing increased mining productivity. He specifically mentioned Kantishna and the Quigley property. A month later, Ira B. Joralemon and A. D. McRae were reported as having looked at and been impressed with the Quigley mines.[5]

General Alexander Duncan McRae was a Canadian capitalist who investigated thousands of properties in Alaska and invested in many gold mines. He employed consulting geologist Ira B. Joralemon and others, including Ernest Patty, as mining experts. McRae himself was an expert at managing business.[6] McRae would buy options on many mines, sink shafts, get accurate assays, and test ore to decide on the development potential of the property. McCrae's arrival gave many miners false hopes. They believed that his investment was a sure sign of his faith in the claim. Wealthy investors like McCrae were dispassionately looking for prime investments, hedging their bets, knowing that there was always another prospect.[7] Individual miners like Joe Quigley were dealing with their life's work and could be crushed when a big investor tied up the property with options and then didn't develop it.

During McRae and Joralemon's first visit in 1931 Joe was in Seattle getting treatment for his injured shoulder, so Fannie showed them around the mines, but the tunnels were "filled to the roof with green ice." Joralemon couldn't see enough to tell the value of the mines, but he suspected that McRae gave

Joe spent time with his great nephews, Lloyd Joseph "Little Joe" Quigley (right) and Kenneth Quigley (left), in Oregon in 1931. Joe's namesake, "Little Joe" became a rock climber and died in a fall from St. Peter's Dome, Multnomah, Oregon, in 1957 (Kenneth Winne Quigley Collection).

Fannie an informal cash payment without a contract for an option.[8] While Joe was in Washington for treatment, he went to visit his family on the West Coast, and he finally got to meet his great nephew and namesake, Lloyd Joseph Quigley. As part of his recovery and reinvention of himself, Joe sat for a portrait at a Portland, Oregon, photography studio.

Joe Quigley was known for being as tight-lipped and discreet about his personal life as Fannie was known for sharing about hers. By the time of Joe's accident, their marriage was essentially reduced to a business arrangement, and by the end of 1931, Joe spent most of his time away from Fannie. It is likely that Joe met the woman who would become his second wife, Julia Braugh, in Seattle in 1931 when he went for treatment for his shoulder. Julia was a 45-year-old nurse who lived and worked in Seattle, was divorced and had a grown son. Even though Fannie and Joe were no longer together romantically, Fannie was infuriated that Joe met someone else. She persisted in telling people that Joe had run off with a young red-haired nurse. Joe had not run off but had begun living alone in a Fairbanks hotel most of the time. He continued to hold up his end of the business partnership with Fannie and sought out investors for the mines, but he was not willing to continue living together as husband and wife. Fannie was a more vociferous person than Joe and so news of her anger became widespread gossip.

January 1932 brought prominent Philadelphia socialite Nannie Biddle to Joe and Fannie's cabin in Kantishna. In Mrs. Biddle's quest to find meaning in her life, she planned an expedition to Alaska to research some articles and possibly a write book about the life of women there. She traveled by train to Seattle then by boat to Seward and by another train to Nenana. From Nenana, she hired Mike Cooney with his team of 17 dogs to take her to Kantishna.[9] Her driver dropped her off there, and when the Alaskan winter weather prevented her from leaving when she intended to, it made national news. The *Pittsburgh Press* reported the story and included a statement by Joe's brother, William Quigley, that Mrs. Biddle would be "suffering no hardship as long as she is with Joe and Fannie Quigley."[10] It is likely that Mrs. Biddle was there alone with Fannie while Joe was in Fairbanks, but it seems that she was well taken care of. Nannie Biddle left Kantishna and arrived by plane in Fairbanks on April 5. When interviewed by the *Fairbanks Daily News-Miner* she stated that she got along wonderfully with Fannie Quigley and that the views from the cabin were beautiful.[11]

Joe sat for a studio portrait at Davidson Studio, 465 Washington Street, during a visit to Portland, Oregon, in 1931 (Kenneth Winne Quigley Collection).

In May 1933 the *Fairbanks Daily News-Miner* announced that Joe Quigley would be at the Alaska Hotel in Fairbanks "for an extended stay."[12] Joe was living in Fairbanks by himself when McRae and Joralemon came for their next visit in August 1933, bringing Joe's friend Ernest Patty with them. McRae had hired Patty as the Alaska manager for his mining investments, and Patty was the liaison between Joe and McRae. Joe met them in Fairbanks and the group flew together to Wonder Lake. Joe and Fannie signed an option with McRae for $15,000, with a check for half the amount going to each of them. There was no question of Joe and Fannie splitting the money.[13] They were separated as a couple but were still equal business partners. Joralemon and McRae didn't believe that Fannie and Joe were legally married even though they were. Joralemon wrote in his memoirs regarding Fannie and Joe that there were concerns about the legal status of a common-law wife. He also noted that Fannie was much older looking and milder than she had been two years earlier, and that although Joe and Fannie "fought too much to live together" they were both friendly when signing the business agreement.[14]

Ernest N. Patty developed a long-term business relationship with McRae and remained friends with Joe Quigley. Patty was one of six original faculty members at the Alaska Agricultural College and School of Mines and developed the game of "rock poker" to teach prospectors the basics of geology. He and Joe Quigley became friends while Joe was a student there. After leaving his geology professorship in 1935, Patty developed several mines in Alaska and the Klondike country. Patty's family encouraged him to return to the university as president in 1953. He did and undertook an unprecedented expansion of campus facilities during the next seven years.[15]

McRae contracted for development work on the Quigley mine, hiring Joseph Snyder to drill a 1000-foot tunnel into the Red Top vein.[16] Testing showed that the ore samples were low grade and that there was not enough ore to be worth the cost of development in such a remote location, so McRae gave up his option, leaving Joe free to sell to someone else. When asked about the deal falling through Joe was optimistic, telling the press, "I have a pretty fair idea of what I have there." He was confident and seemed to be already in negotiations with another investor, saying that there were a number of promising-looking showings in the area that needed more development before the owners would be warranted in putting in milling equipment. He then announced that he would be going back to Seattle to have his arm looked at by a doctor and that Fannie would be staying at the Kantishna property.[17]

Joe took the $7,500 from his half of the McRae deal ($150,000 in 2019) and spent the winter of 1933 on a drive up the California and Oregon coasts. Joe had family and friends on the coast, and he also kept an eye out for possible investments for his own future. He had talked with his brother and nephew years earlier about investing in land and had old miner friends who invested in other businesses outside of Alaska. While he was on vacation, he looked for potential investors in his own properties. A souvenir menu from the SS *Victoria* from March 1934, given to Joe's nephew, suggests that Joe returned to Alaska on the first Alaskan cruise operated by the Seattle-based Alaska Steamship Company.

The district mining commissioner Charles Trundy was aware of the developments in the Kantishna area and expressed confidence in the region. In a statement to the press in 1934, as he passed through Fairbanks, Trundy pointed to the price of gold and the extension of the park road as major factors for potential growth. President Franklin Roosevelt had declared the dollar convertible to gold at a new price of $35 an ounce, increasing the value of gold from $20.67 an ounce, and as the larger investors were pulling out, local investors did become more interested. In 1935 Joe leased his Banjo Lode claim to local investors Ernest R. Fransen and Clifton M. Hawkins. Both were long-time hard rock miners in the Fairbanks district.[18] Gold prices were up, and the interior of Alaska was enjoying the resurgence that Commissioner Trundy hoped for as the rest of the country sunk deeper into economic depression.

The combination of the high price of gold, the coming of the railroad, cheaper fuel, and improved technologies caused mines that had been too low grade to work on to become profitable. This made the Quigley mines more attractive to Fransen and Hawkins who bought 17 patented claims from Joe in 1935 for $100,000 (equivalent to nearly $2 million in 2019), plus 10 percent of gross.[19] Joe and Fannie deposited the money in the bank. Fransen and Hawkins, along with Fairbanks businessman A. Hjalmer Nordale, formed the Red Top Mining Company, and the development of the company between 1935 and 1939 was part of the new mining boom. The new investments in

Dressed for business, Joe Quigley (left) talks with Joe Dalton. Dalton and his partner Stiles began mining in Kantishna around the same time that Joe Quigley and his partner Jack Horn made the first claims there in July 1905 (National Park Service DENA 3510).

equipment including draglines, quartz drills, tractors, bulldozers, and milling machinery made the 1937 mining season historically productive.[20]

In early January 1936, 65-year-old Fannie Quigley sustained a severe fracture of the ankle when she fell down the stairs at the home of park superintendent Harry J. Liek and his wife. During her three months in the hospital in Fairbanks, she had her friends stop by with alcohol, and when it ran out, she would scream and carry on in her "outdoor voice" disturbing the other patients and the staff.[21] While Fannie was in the hospital that winter, Joe went to Kantishna to stay and care for the homestead. Grant Pearson would visit often and said, "Joe surely put on some good meals for me, and believe me, it's a lot different cooking where you haven't a grocery store to go to!"[22] Pearson went on to describe Joe as an excellent cook and said that his sourdough bread and hot cakes were unsurpassed.

By the mid-1930s Joe decided that he had to settle up with Fannie about the terms for their divorce. He took his friend, engineer and miner Earl Pilgrim, with him to Kantishna to deliver the news. It was an emotional experience for Pilgrim and he described it to several people, saying that in the mid-1930s he and Joe flew into the Friday Creek airstrip, which was just below the mining claims held by Joe and Fannie, on Quigley Ridge. As Pilgrim remembered it, "Joe Quigley had left Fannie several years earlier while recovering from his mine accident and wanted to talk over terms of property

Joe Quigley looking at the cairn monument on Wickersham Dome sometime after the pointed capstone was missing. Cairns were sometimes used to show the boundaries of a mining claim. Wickersham Dome is close to Quigley Ridge, where Joe lived and worked his mines (Alaska and Polar Regions Collections, Elmer E. Rasmuson Library, University of Alaska, Fairbanks, UAF-1980-0046-00148).

rights pursuant to divorce." Selling the mines and coming to terms as partners was essential, and it was time to address the situation.

Pilgrim was nervous about Joe meeting up with Fannie because it was well known throughout the Alaska Territory that she was very angry with Joe and any meeting might result in violence from Fannie. He stayed with the pilot and Joe went up the hill to talk to Fannie. After waiting for about two hours, Pilgrim decided to walk up the hill and see if everything was OK. When he arrived at the cabin, he was shocked to see Joe and Fannie in a very fond embrace, both with tears in their eyes, reminiscing about their time in Kantishna. The encounter was very touching for Pilgrim and he never forgot it. Fannie and Joe had coffee with Pilgrim before he and Joe left. Pilgrim said, "Joe left with me and never returned to the Kantishna mining district."[23] Pilgrim was 23 years younger than Joe Quigley, but the two were close friends. In addition to being a miner, Pilgrim was an instructor for the School of Mines, and initiated, designed, and conducted offerings in the mine engineering curriculum. He passed away in 1987, and Pilgrim Peak in the Kantishna hills was named for him in 1990.[24]

Joe had a sense of responsibility to the people in his life and would not run away leaving loose ends. He had spent the last 30 years building a world with Fannie and his friends and would find a way to fairly and equitably move on to the next phase of his life. "Little" Johnnie Busia was the last miner to live in Kantishna and was friends with both Joe and Fannie. When asked about a picture of Joe on the wall, Busia said, "That is a picture of my oldest and dearest friend, Joe Quigley. He had no enemies. Do you know I've never heard Joe speak a bad word about anyone."[25] Looking through records of Joe's life and family letters it seems that Busia was correct and that Joe lived by the old adage of either saying something good about someone or saying nothing at all.

In August of 1937 Joe optioned mines to W. E. Dunkle for $150,000[26] (approximately $2.5 million in 2018). Like Joe Quigley, Wesley Earl Dunkle was born in western Pennsylvania and came from a family that had arrived in the new world in the 1730s. The Dunkle family was German, or "Pennsylvania Dutch," and Wesley Earl's father, John Wesley Dunkle, was elected to the position of county attorney for Warren County, Pennsylvania. Shortly after graduating from Yale, Dunkle headed for Alaska in 1910 and became involved with the famous Kennecott Copper Mines. He was a skilled pilot and became known as the Flying Miner.[27] Dunkle had been interested in the Quigley mines for years and was familiar with the Kantishna Mining District. His first flight as a pilot was a one-way trip near the Quigley mine in 1928, and he examined the Little Annie vein later that year. He remained interested in the mines over the years, and as technology advanced enough to make the Quigley property a viable investment, he bought the option from the Quigleys.

Chapter 21. Cashing Out

Little Johnny Busia (left) and Joe Quigley take a break near the creek in Kantishna. Busia was the last of the old miners to live year-round in Kantishna. He was friends with both Joe and Fannie and was the last person to see Fannie alive in 1944 (National Park Service, DENA 3513).

Joe and Fannie split the money they got from Dunkle equally. Traditionally when mining partners broke up, they simply divided the money and belongings and went their separate ways. This was as close to that arrangement as possible for a married couple and was truly the end of Joe Quigley's partnership with Fannie.

The 92-mile-long park road was finally completed in 1938 and ended at a point close to the old Quigley mines. By the fall of 1938 the Red Top Mining Company had built five miles of road, an assay shop, bunkhouses, and a blacksmith shop. W. E. Dunkle had optioned the Quigley mines and large-scale development was underway in the Kantishna Mining District. Fannie continued to live in the area, and Red Top Mining Company contractor George Bachner built a small frame house for her near the Moose Creek airstrip. While the mine was under construction and in operation, from 1938 to 1942, Fannie was able to use the mining company's flights to and from Fairbanks.

Fannie was financially very well off after the divorce but didn't change her lifestyle very much. She continued to garden and to greet tourists and other visitors. There are many photographs of her in her older years, and also a short clip of a silent home movie of her talking to a group of women in her garden. Johnnie Busia remained her friend and was the one who found her body in her cabin on August 25, 1944. She had died while preparing to build a fire in her stove, possibly of a heart attack. Her obituary praised her many talents and skills, and she was hailed as a legend after her death.[28] She was buried in Fairbanks. The arrangements for her funeral were made by her attorney, E. B. Collins.[29]

Chapter 22

Still Rovin'

Joe Quigley's "roving disposition" hadn't faded with age or with his long recovery from the mining accident. He continued to live in Fairbanks during the summer and explore "outside" during the winter. He headed for Seattle at the age of 68 in the fall of 1937. It is likely that this is when he began living with his second wife Julia, and she was probably with him for at least part of his long road trip. From Seattle he went to Michigan to pick up a brand-new Chevrolet, spending two weeks in Flint waiting for the car to be ready. It was worth the wait. He had ordered the automobile with a "good radio receiving set" and enjoyed listening to the news and other programs while driving. Joe had loved radio since the first time he heard one in Fairbanks more than a decade earlier, and he was always happy to be traveling, so for Joe this was a winning combination. He described the long drive as "lots of fun."[1]

Joe spent most of the winter of 1937 in Hot Springs, Arkansas, where he filed for divorce from Fannie.[2] There had been a divorce trade war going on since the end of World War I between Nevada, Idaho, and Arkansas. All three states made it as easy as possible to obtain a divorce, partially through a short residency requirement. Arkansas was a particularly attractive destination for Joe because in addition to a quick divorce, it offered Hot Springs National Park. Hot Springs gained notice in 1936 when President Franklin D. Roosevelt visited. Roosevelt had been an advocate of hydrotherapy since his polio diagnosis in 1921 and made a speech praising Arkansas after taking a tour of the bathhouses.

Since his mining accident, Joe had an increased interest in various therapies to improve the function of his injured right arm. The park's Fordyce Bathhouse had just installed its first whirlpool bath in January of that year, and the Hot Springs National Park museum was formally opened to the public in June.[3] It was the perfect place for Joe to get away from the harsh winter conditions, have some much-needed physical therapy for his injuries, and make his split from Fannie official. After 50 years of hard labor and business uncertainties, along with years of a stressful, disintegrating marriage, he could finally relax.

The Fordyce Bathhouse was a luxurious spa. The lobby featured marble and stained-glass transoms and ornate ceramic fountains, marble partitions separated the bath halls, and the men's bath hall had a stained-glass ceiling. The dressing rooms and men's massage rooms were on the second floor, and there was a formal bath routine with various massage therapies offered, including electrotherapy. The Fordyce included grand staterooms, a bowling alley, and a gymnasium, and it was part of a group of eight buildings called "Bathhouse Row" located in Hot Springs National Park. The eight buildings were built between 1832 and 1926 and had been included in the four parcels of land that were taken over by the government in order to preserve the hot springs.[4] The mineral waters there were especially desirable because they lacked the sulfur smell of many hot springs. Joe was indulging in some first-class relaxation and recovery.

Just as Joe's marriage to Fannie seemed like a formality, happening a decade after they began living together as a couple, filing for divorce came long after the marriage was over. Taking care of official paperwork was nothing new for Joe Quigley, but this was his first (and only) divorce and certainly different from registering a mine claim. Joe always hesitated to say something bad about anyone, but Arkansas law required that the moving party state the grounds for divorce. On the official Divorce Petition Coupon, dated Novem-

Exterior of the Fordyce bathhouse, part of "Bathhouse Row" in Hot Springs, Arkansas. The 28,000-square-foot Fordyce is the largest bathhouse on the row and opened in 1915. Joe Quigley spent time in the luxurious bathhouse when he went to Arkansas to obtain a divorce from Fannie in 1937 (National Park Service).

Chapter 22. Still Rovin'

ber 30, 1937, the petitioner is Joseph B. Quigley and the defendant is Fannie McKenzie Quigley. The "alleged cause for Petition" was "indignities."[5] There were other possible choices, including habitual drunkenness, but Joe chose the less damning "indignities." Under Arkansas supreme court guidelines, indignities is a catch-all term that is the equivalent of the term irreconcilable differences used in most states today.

Feeling a renewed energy, Joe put a total of 17,000 miles on his car that winter, driving through the West, Midwest, and Southwest, visiting the Florida Keys and Mexico City. After so many years in the cold mountains, he was ready to spend some time on a warm beach. A Fairbanks newspaper reported that on his 1937 trip, one of Joe's "greatest delights was looking for shells on the seashores of Florida and California."[6] It had been seven years since his horrendous accident and Joe was enjoying his new lease on life. Although he had stopped working as a miner, he was still interested in prospecting and never stopped looking at potential sites wherever he went. Florida, which was promoted as "the Sunshine State", had been an attractive vacation spot for people since the 1800s and it was on Joe's list of places he wanted to see. At the time that Joe visited Florida and the Keys, author Ernest Hemingway was living and writing in Key West. Hemingway had already written some of his most popular works, and it seems likely that with the rugged masculinity portrayed in Hemingway's work and Joe's penchant for reading, he would have been familiar with Hemingway's writing.

Winter is the dry season in Mexico, and Joe's drive to Mexico City that winter may have been inspired by a number of factors, including the warm weather. After the Mexican Revolution ended in 1920, Mexican culture and art became very fashionable in the United States during the 20s and 30s. The Mexican government was heavily promoting tourism, and Americans who could afford it visited. Joe's friend Charles Sheldon had made a fortune in Mexican mining decades earlier, and Joe was always interested in mining operations, so he may have wanted to look into the mining industry there, but he was also on a vacation.

Joe enjoyed the unique and colorful atmosphere in Mexico City, which was enhanced by the murals that the area is known for. Mural painting was particularly encouraged during the 1920s and the most popular mural artists gained international fame. Prominent Mexican muralist Diego Rivera was central to the movement, and his wife, another of Mexico's most well-known artists, painter Frida Kahlo, was also active then. Joe could not have missed seeing Rivera's work along with that of muralist Jose Clemente Orozco on the walls of Mexico City. The popularity of Mexican art at the time resulted in many cultural exchanges with the United States.

Having been involved with precious metals for his entire career, Joe may have noted the quality of the hand-crafted silver jewelry in Mexico. The Taxco silversmiths were an important part of Mexican culture that attracted tourists and captured the imagination of the people of the United States. The most successful of the Taxco silversmiths was William Spratling. He had a connection to Alaska. By the late 1930s Spratling had added 500 employees in Mexico to meet the demand for his work in the United States.[7] In 1945 he was asked by his friends Ernest Gruening, Alaska territorial governor, and Rene d'Harnoncourt, director of the Indian Arts and Crafts Board, to replicate his success in Alaska. He responded by establishing workshops and exhibit centers in various regions of Alaska organized into a federation of Alaska Native arts.

The pyramids just northeast of Mexico City in Teotihuacán were undoubtedly on Joe's itinerary. Having built cairns in the hills of Alaska, Joe must have paused to consider the mind-boggling stonework involved in creating the 2000-year-old, 213-foot-high pyramid of the Sun, the Avenue of the Dead, and the pyramid of the Moon at the masterfully planned Mesoamerican city. Experiencing the immense man-made structures gave him a different perspective from his lifestyle in the shadows of the magnificent mountains of the Far North. Having spent a lifetime moving massive quantities of rock, he surely had a unique appreciation for the labor involved in building the ancient city.

Joe told a Fairbanks reporter that everywhere he went people were fascinated with Alaska and would tell him that they wanted to go there.[8] Since President Warren G. Harding made an extended visit to Alaska in 1923 to celebrate the completion of the Alaska Railroad, tourists began to put Alaska on their list of places to visit.[9] Businesses in Alaska were aware of the economic boost that tourism brings. Beginning in the 1920s, steamship companies teamed up with the Alaska Railroad and Alaskan-owned motor coach companies to create package adventure tours and advertised to encourage tourism. Joe's love of Alaska and experience with living in the wilderness made him a natural promoter to anyone he met who was seeking adventure.

Between 1937 and 1942 Joe Quigley was at his financial peak. He was not the tycoon that some of his friends had become, but he had the large initial payment for his mines in the bank and was collecting royalties on the gross profits from them as well. Ever the realist, when asked if he was wealthy, Joe would answer that he was "medium rich." He was also aware that the Great Depression was still dragging on in the United States, and traveling by car, he could not avoid seeing signs of poverty everywhere. When talking with a reporter in Fairbanks Joe said, "Anybody touring the States cannot help but notice economic conditions are bad."[10]

In the cities there were long lines of unemployed people looking for food given out by charitable organizations. In rural areas, drought and wind devastated farmland and many farmers abandoned their homes. The average American family lived by the Depression-era motto "Use it up, wear it out, make do or do without."[11] At the same time that Joe was making his cross-country road trips, photographer Dorthea Lange, working for the Resettlement Administration and Farm Security Administration, was documenting poverty in the United States. In 1937, while Joe was exploring the beaches of Florida and the pyramids of Mexico, Lange was capturing many evocative portraits of destitute Americans including "Broke, baby sick, and car trouble!" the heartbreaking portrait of a Missouri woman and her baby by the side of a deserted dirt road in California. The Great Depression was an even more devastating economic downturn than the depression that Joe lived through in his youth during the late 1800s. Pervasive poverty was bringing starvation and homelessness in both rural areas and in cities. As he was the type of person who would not announce his own contributions to the needy, there is no way to know how Joe handled the disparity between his own wealth and the deprivation around him. Knowing from his past actions that Joe was of a generous and caring nature, it seems reasonable to assume that he found a way to help some people.

In 1938 Joe officially moved to Seattle and told the press in Fairbanks that he would be spending summers in Alaska. Prospector-miners all had a "ceaseless urge to make a new discovery,"[12] and being a typical prospector in many ways, Joe was still interested in prospecting even though he had stopped working as a miner. He never stopped looking at potential sites wherever he went and was particularly impressed with the Muscle Shoals development on the Tennessee River in northern Alabama. "It is a wonderful enterprise; and has to be seen to be realized."[13] Most of the old-timers never stopped prospecting. Once they'd struck it rich, some of them continued to look for gold and other minerals in milder climates than the arctic conditions that they'd endured to attain their wealth. Some also got involved in the oil industry, and some stayed in Alaska continuing to look for strikes.

That winter Joe drove his car another 14,000 miles, touring from the Pacific coast to Chicago, Detroit and along the southern Atlantic seaboard. He drove back through Nevada, Arizona and other western states, touring mines and other industries and visiting old miner friends from Alaska who had retired to the States. He stayed in touch with old Fortymiler friends and reported the current status of many of them to the *Fairbanks Daily News-Miner* when he went back to Alaska. He seems to have visited Jim Chronister who lived in San Francisco. Chronister was a well-known old-timer bartender who had killed brawling bully Jim Washburn in self-defense back in the early Fortymile days. At the time of the killing, he offered himself up to a miners' meeting trial and was acquitted in 20 minutes.[14] Chronister had spent some time after leaving the Far North living with another veteran of the Yukon goldfields, Howard Hamilton Hart. Although Hart had made moderate stakes back in the gold rush days, he found his fortune in oil, and when he died, he was one of the wealthiest of all the old prospectors.

Another acquaintance from Joe's early days in the Yukon Order of Pioneers, Skiff Mitchell, was living in Eureka, California, when Joe passed through the area. In Arizona, Joe visited with Billy Leake, who had done very well during the gold rush and continued his success after moving to the States in both oil and mining. While driving through Arizona Joe was surprised to bump into pioneer newspaper man Frank Coulter. Coulter stayed in the publishing business but was also interested in mining in Arizona.

In an interview for his 70th birthday, the *Fairbanks Daily News-Miner* described Joe as "active as a man in his 50's." He did stay active in his fraternal organizations and kept up with his old friends. In addition to visiting his old prospector friends in the States, he kept track of any of his old Fortymiler friends who were still alive and still in the Far North. He told a reporter that Bill Leggit had moved to California, Gordon Bettles was living with his second wife on an island between Seward and Valdez, and Jerry Baker was in the Flat, Alaska, mining area. B. A. Davis was still prospecting and trapping near the mouth of the Tolovana, Frank Bennett was prospecting near Woodchopper Creek, and Casper Ellingen was still working near Circle. Joe's old partner Jack Horn was ranching and operating a small sawmill on his homestead on the Chena River, 15 miles above Fairbanks. There weren't very many of the old-timers left by 1939, but those that were all had the same "roving disposition" as Joe Quigley and never stopped looking for the next big strike.

Joe was dividing his time according to the seasons, spending the winter months each year living in Seattle and traveling through other states, and spending his summers visiting and prospecting in Alaska. He told a newspaper reporter that during his travels, he went to the fair in San Francisco several times.[15] He was referring to the Golden Gate International Exposition, a world's fair which opened on February 18, 1939. The fair was a spectacular event, held on San Francisco's Treasure Island, an artificial island built during 1936 and 1937 especially for the exposition. San Francisco was celebrating its two masterpieces, the San Francisco–Oakland Bay Bridge which opened in 1936, and the Golden Gate Bridge which opened in 1937. The theme of the exposition was "Pageant of the Pacific." The expositions showcased goods from countries that bordered the Pacific Ocean, bringing attention to goods from Asia and Latin America.[16]

The fair provided a temporary escape from the mood of the Great Depression by looking into other cultures. World's fairs were cities within cities, built to work both symbolically and practically, with a planned infrastructure that could accommodate thousands of visitors. The architecture at the fair was a dynamic combination of modernism and Beaux-Arts, with buildings of varying scale, creating a heterogeneous atmosphere. It was designed so that visitors entered from the parking lot, through the 40-acre midway, to an entertainment zone called the gayway. High culture was presented along with bawdy entertainment. Spectators could spend a quarter to view Sally Rand's Nude Ranch featuring 20 "cowgirls" wearing only G-strings and boots as they tossed horseshoes or swung lariats and then move on to see a $40 million art exhibition with works borrowed from European museums. Fair visitors could watch Mexican mural painter Diego Rivera paint what is now a theater lobby at the City College of San Francisco's Ocean Avenue campus.[17]

In addition to visiting the fair during the winter of 1939–1940, Joe spent time in Oregon looking at the John Day mining district. The district was getting attention from prospectors because it hadn't been worked over since 1858.[18] In those early years, $20 million in placer gold was found there, and it was thought that with modern equipment and methods some of the creeks in the district might be worth working again. Joe reported that there was one dredge in operation in the district in 1940.

There are no records showing if Joe was alone on the road trips he took during the late 30s and early 40s or if Julia was along for some of them. When he talked to the Fairbanks newspaper about his activities he only spoke of his own experiences. The only photograph found of Joe and Julia Quigley together was too poor quality to reprint.[19] The caption under the photograph is "Joseph B. and Julie Quigley." The couple are standing in snow in front of small airplane fitted with skis for landing and a fabric cover over the engine. Joe is wearing an overcoat and fedora, and Julia is a very feminine, if somewhat matronly, looking woman, wearing a stylish ladies' hat and fur-trimmed coat over a mid-calf-length dress. Both Joe and Julia have pleasant looks on their faces and appear to be enjoying themselves.

Chapter 23

Seattle

Joe Quigley made his permanent residence in Seattle, Washington. Seattle was connected to Alaska by design. During the 19th century, growth and development of Seattle was radically changed by the gold rush in California and then later the gold rush in Alaska. Even in the depressed years of the mid-1890s Seattle and other Northwest cities saw a few gold miners and supplied them with food and equipment. In early 1896, months before the Klondike discoveries, miners showed up in Seattle in increasing numbers, taking passage for Circle City and Cook Inlet, following news of gold strikes. The Seattle Chamber of Commerce created a campaign to capture the Alaska trade, and Seattle reached out to claim Alaska as its hinterland, moving to solidify the economic ties between the city and Alaska. By 1905, the city directory labeled Seattle "the Gateway to Alaska and the Orient."[1] Joe was not the only gold miner to retire in Seattle. There were so many that there was a Yukon Order of Pioneers chapter in Seattle, founded by George Carmack and George Snow in 1912.[2]

Just as Joe's beginning with Fannie is a mystery, so is most of Joe's relationship with his second wife, Julia. Years of back-breaking toil and being married to a verbally abusive alcoholic left him lonely but resigned to the path he had chosen. In Joe and Fannie's earlier years together, he planned for Fannie to retire with him on the outside, but it became apparent over time that he would be on his own. Meeting Julia was a pleasant turn of events and made him happy.

Julia has been described as a "young nurse,"[3] which is a little different than it sounds. It is true that she was a nurse, and she was 16 years younger than Joe, but it is also true that in 1930, Julia Amelia Braugh was a 45-year-old divorcee with a grown son when 61-year-old Joe Quigley had his accident. Sometime before 1920 she had been divorced and she worked as a nurse, raising her son Leroy Reed on her own in Seattle.[4] Julia's parents were Canadians who moved to Michigan during the late 1870s and then to Oregon around 1890. She had many siblings who lived in Washington, Oregon and California. By the time Joe moved to Seattle to live with Julia full-time, her son lived on his own in Seattle.

Chapter 23. Seattle

The house that Joe bought for his life in Seattle with Julia was a conventional middle-class suburban home by the standards of the day but luxurious compared to the cabin Joe and Fannie shared in Kantishna. Joe bought the house at 16344 Linden Avenue on October 25, 1939, in an unincorporated area of King County outside Seattle called Highland Acres. It had been built in 1925 and had a garage, laundry, a fireplace, electricity, central heat, seven rooms, and two porches on an acre of land. Joe enjoyed his garden and grew roses and apple and peach trees. He loved his car and maintained it meticulously. Seeing no reason to replace it, as long as it was working, Joe kept the car he had picked up in Michigan in 1938 for the rest of his life. He described the vehicle in a 1953 interview, "Chevrolet, and it works like new, though I put in a new engine at 108,000 miles. Now have 124,000 miles on it and wouldn't trade it for a 1953 model."[5]

Joe's sister-in-law, Lincoln's wife Marietta Quigley, had passed away in 1936. Link stayed in Vancouver, Washington, and his son Lloyd, daughter-in-law Zelne and their two children Ken and "Little Joe" all lived in Vancouver as well. Joe had written many letters to this branch of his family throughout his years in Kantishna when he lived more than 2000 miles from them. Now that he lived only 150 miles away from them, the letter writing stopped, but Joe and Julia did send holiday cards to the family and visited with them sometimes. Both of Joe's parents and most of his siblings back in Pennsylvania had passed away during his years in the Far North, and no letters from Joe to them after his 1923 visit have resurfaced.

16344 Linden Avenue in Highland Acres outside of Seattle, Washington. Joe Quigley bought the house on October 25, 1939, for himself and his second wife, Julia, to live in. The house also had a garage for Joe's beloved 1937 Chevrolet (1937 Washington State Archives, 329370-0160, house, 1937.tif).

Seattle was a bustling metropolis of nearly 370,000 when Joe moved there in 1938, but the Great Depression had hit the city hard. Unemployment insurance was still a thing of the future in the early 1930s, and by 1931 homelessness and extreme poverty reached unprecedented levels. Tent camps and shack towns began to appear, including one large encampment that the residents called Hooverville after the president that they blamed for their poverty. City authorities ordered Hooverville to be burned, but it was quickly rebuilt and at one time had nearly 1000 residents. It remained occupied until the government ordered it torn down in 1941.[6]

When Franklin Roosevelt assumed office in 1933 the federal government employed emergency measures, which helped the state economy begin to recover. By 1937, the year before Joe Quigley moved there, the Seattle economy had reached 93 percent of the 1929 levels.[7] There was an economic surge after Japan's attack on Pearl Harbor in 1941 when the Seattle branch of the Boeing company received contracts to build aircraft for use in World War II.[8] The Seattle shipyards supported 22,000 employees and produced 45 destroyers and other ships for the war effort.[9] The city was the largest Joe had ever lived in and had a diverse population. He continued to travel after he purchased his home, making trips to other parts of Washington and Oregon to investigate promising mining regions.[10]

Joe kept active ties in Alaska and returned to Fairbanks often. The *Fairbanks Daily News-Miner* reported that on June 15, 1940, he left Seattle for Seward on the SS *Aleutian*. Julia is not listed as a passenger and it is unknown if he ever took her to Alaska with him. While he was in the Far North, recognition for his photography came when Joe won a photography contest at the Tanana Valley Fair in September 1940.[11]

World War II had a negative impact on Joe's personal wealth when President Franklin D. Roosevelt closed down gold mining for the war effort in 1942. Part of the reason the Quigley mines sold for the price they did was because, in an attempt to stimulate the flagging economy in 1933, President Roosevelt increased the price of gold from $20.67 to $35 per ounce, which led to more gold mining in Alaska. That expansion continued until the early years of World War II when federal order E-208 shut down gold mines throughout the United States because gold mining was not considered critical to the war effort. Joe was proud of his life's work and how well his mines did for the new owners: "The new owners put in a fifty-ton mill and did very well until closed down by Federal Order.... I was paid for the mine, but no longer get my royalties until they can operate again."[12] He was optimistic that gold mining would resume, bringing income from his royalty agreement, but that did not happen in his lifetime.

The lack of royalties did not bring Joe's income down enough to interrupt the comfortable lifestyle that he and Julia had in suburban Seattle. Julia was 16 years younger than Joe and they probably expected her to outlive him, but on her 65th birthday, December 3, 1950, she was taken to the doctor for chronic pyelonephritis (kidney disease) and congestive heart failure. She died at Swedish Hospital ten days later, and an autopsy was performed, showing that the kidney disease was the condition directly leading to death. Her obituary listed her survivors as her husband Joseph, her son Leroy, brothers Charles, Joseph, Edward, Alex, and James, and a sister, Mrs. Nema Stoves. After Julia died, Joe Quigley's group associations and friends were a source of comfort to him. He never let go of his strong connection to Alaska and many of his Seattle friends also had roots in Alaska.

In 1953 Joe was interviewed by Hazel Lindberg for a book she intended to write on the gold rush pioneers.[13] The notes were thought by the Pioneers of Alaska to be from Joe Quigley's diary. When the original documents are examined it becomes apparent that it is not exactly a diary written by Joe Quigley, but copious notes taken by Lindberg from an interview with Joe. Most of the document is a transcription of Joe telling his own life story. Although he wrote many letters, there is no known diary written by Joe Quigley.

Lindberg describes Joe at 84: "Joe is a widower, with no children. Has a merry twinkle and gets a kick out of life. Tall and husky yet, except for the injured arm, which he can now use for light work. He likes flowers and gardens and has planted peach and apple trees and is content." Even after more than 20 years of chronic pain and some disability from his old injuries, Joe was a lively man with a pleasant disposition. His health began to deteriorate shortly after his interview with Lindberg, but he maintained a positive outlook.

On April 12, 1954, Joe corresponded with Forbes L. Baker, the secretary for Tanana Lodge N. 162, F&AM, about a proxy that he had failed to mail. Joe explained in the letter that he found it "already filled out and signed" but had failed to mail it. The *"only excuse I have is I am getting a bit old and absent minded."*[14] He had always been a conscientious person and was embarrassed that he had forgotten about the correspondence. At age 85, Joe was realizing that his memory wasn't as sharp as it had been. Eight months later, a letter dated December 18, 1954, was sent to Joe informing him that the lodge had approved a "paid-up Life Membership in Tanana Lodge N. 162." The letter was cordial, with Baker adding, "It is my very great pleasure to enclose a life member card in your name. We all join in wishing you a very Merry Christmas and a Happy New Year and hope to hear from you often." The letter is signed "Yours Sincerely and Fraternally, Forbes L. Baker, P.M., Secty."

Almost a year after receiving the letter announcing that Joe had a paid-up lifetime membership, on November 24, 1955, Joe wrote to Baker again, enclosing his $15 dues for 1954. Joe explained that he had been intending to go to Fairbanks the previous summer but had contracted "a very bad case of the shingles. Which I have not got over yet." He went on to explain that the condition was leaving him in a very weakened condition, making him unable to make another trip to Alaska "for a long time." Shingles is a viral infection that affects the nerve tissue near the spinal cord, and it causes a painful rash on the body. Joe had moved from his home into the nearby home of Juanita and Reginald Jensen by 1954. Mrs. Jensen was his caretaker and was later appointed as his guardian. Always looking for the positive side of his situation, Joe added in his letter to Baker, "I have many good neighbors here and guess I am as happy as any old codger my age should hope to be, but it will help a lot better when I get over the shingles." He signed off with a wish that the lodge was still prosperous and the hope that everyone would have a very merry Christmas and happy new year.

In 1957 Joe filled out a Personal Record for the Alaska Yukon Pioneers for an upcoming event they were planning that would include biographies of several members. Line 8 of the form requests "the names, place and date of birth of your children born in the North, if any." Joe's answer was "None—No Savvy,"[15] and he continued to fill out the space with "I crossed the Chilkoot Pass, headed for 40 mile River on the Yukon, spent many years prospecting." He was 88 years old, and when assessing his own life, he felt that the years he would have been raising children were the years he first arrived in the Far North. That same year, on September 15, 1957, Joe Quigley's great nephew and namesake, Lloyd Joseph "Little Joe" Quigley, died. Little Joe had become an avid mountain climber. He and a friend, Don McKay, died in a 200-foot plunge on the seldom-climbed St. Peter's Dome in the Columbia River Gorge near Medford, Oregon. The pair were both experienced climbers and were trying the climb by a new route. Little Joe was 32 years old at the time of his death.[16]

In a later letter to Forbes Baker, Joe sent a proxy and explained that his health had deteriorated further, saying, "would like to write more but am now in my 87th year and my health is not the best." Joe knew that he was near the end of his life. He was still a gracious and thoughtful man, sending "kindest regards to all my friends in Alaska," and he expressed his disappointment with being too ill to go to Alaska again: "Would liked to have made some more trips to the north but don't think I could stand to make the them anymore." He ends the letter with "Good luck and good health to all my old friends in Alaska." This appears to be Joe Quigley's last letter to Baker.

In December 1958 Forbes Baker sent a letter to Mr. C. B. Dameron, Executive Secretary, Masonic Service Bureau in Seattle, informing Dameron that Joe had died a few weeks earlier and asking for follow-up information about burial for the Tanana Lodge records. Dameron's response is dated December 22, 1958, and explains that "Brother Quigley passed away November

23, 1958 at Christiansen's Nursing Home, Seattle." He went on to say that the funeral services were held at Green Lake Chapel, followed by cremation. Mr. Dameron expressed his disappointment that the office was not informed of his passing, explaining that they had contacted Joe several times over the previous two years. Dameron assured Baker that "Wor. Bro. Ferrier, past master of Richmond 248, was his neighbor at the Linden Avenue address and saw him often." The letter ended with the sad news that "about four months ago due to physical and mental impairment Brother Quigley was taken to a hospital and later to the Nursing Home. His condition required that he be kept under restraint at all times and he did not recognize his former friends. Further visits seemed useless as he appeared to have adequate care."

Although some of Joe Quigley's family was still alive, the only relatives listed in his obituary were Vern Quigley of Portland, Oregon, and a niece, Mrs. Joseph Morgan of Pasadena, California. All 13 of his siblings predeceased him. He had nieces and nephews and their children in both Pennsylvania and on the West Coast who had lost touch with him. He had no children, but near the end of his life, he described his caretaker and guardian Juanita Jensen as "a woman who treats me like her own father." His will, which he wrote in 1953, named Mrs. Jensen as the executrix of his estate, and the entire estate was left to her. In the event that Mrs. Jensen predeceased him, his entire estate was to go to the Shriners Crippled Children's Hospital in Portland, Oregon. In the end, after all of his expenses were paid and real estate sold, Mrs. Jensen received about $6000 ($50,000 in 2019). His cremation remains were released to Mrs. Jensen.

Chapter Notes

Chapter 1

1. Polar Regions Archives, Lindberg Collection, University of Alaska, Fairbanks, Hazel Lindberg Box 7, Folder 7.

2. Tom Walker, *Kantishna Mushers, Miners, Mountaineers: The Story Behind Mt. McKinley National Park* (Missoula, MT: Pictorial Histories, 2005).

3. "Mosquitoes in Alaska: How to Avoid the Bugs," Alaska.org, accessed May 12, 2019. http://www.alaska.org/advice/mosquitoes-in-alaska.

4. "Historic Resources and Site Survey Report," Treadwell Mining Complex—Juneau, accessed May 10, 2019. http://www.juneau.org/history/treadwell/TMCHRS.pdf.

5. Mercury was used in small-scale gold mining to separate gold from the other minerals it is mixed with by forming a mercury-gold amalgam which was heated, vaporizing the mercury to obtain the gold.

6. Melody Webb, *The Last Frontier* (Albuquerque: University of New Mexico Press, 1985).

7. Polar Regions Archives, Lindberg Collection, University of Alaska, Fairbanks, Hazel Lindberg Box 7, Folder 7.

8. Melody Webb, *The Last Frontier* (Albuquerque: University of New Mexico Press, 1985).

9. "Ton of Goods," National Parks Service, accessed May 10, 2019. https://www.nps.gov/klgo/learn/historyculture/tonofgoods.htm.

10. "The Chilkoot Trail Cultural Landscape Report for the Chilkoot Trail Historic Corridor," produced by the Cultural Landscapes Program, Alaska, in cooperation with Klondike Gold Rush National Historical Park. 2011. NPS History.

11. "Golden Places: The History of Alaska-Yukon Mining (Chapter 4)," National Parks Service, accessed May 10, 2019. https://www.nps.gov/parkhistory/online_books/yuch/golden_places/chap4.htm.

12. "Klondike Gold Rush National Historical Park (U.S. National Park Service)," National Parks Service, accessed May 10, 2019. https://www.nps.gov/klgo/index.htm.

13. Pierre Berton, *Klondike: The Life and Death of Last Great Gold Rush* (London: W.H. Allen, 1960).

14. "Ton of Goods," National Parks Service, accessed May 10, 2019. https://www.nps.gov/klgo/learn/historyculture/tonofgoods.htm.

15. Polar Regions Archives, Lindberg Collection, University of Alaska, Fairbanks, Hazel Lindberg Box 7, Folder 7.

16. Craig Medred, "Deadly Cold," Craig Medred, January 8, 2019, accessed May 10, 2019. https://craigmedred.news/2019/01/07/deadly-cold/.

17. Hudson Stuck, *Ten Thousand Miles with a Dog Sled: A Narrative of Winter Travel in Interior Alaska* (London, 1914).

18. Polar Regions Archives, Lindberg Collection, University of Alaska, Fairbanks, Hazel Lindberg Box 7, Folder 7.

19. Polar Regions Archives, Lindberg Collection, University of Alaska, Fairbanks, Hazel Lindberg Box 7, Folder 7.

20. Polar Regions Archives, Lindberg Collection, University of Alaska, Fairbanks, Hazel Lindberg Box 7, Folder 7.

21. A Sourdough was someone considered a seasoned expert.

22. Cheechako is Chinook for newcomer. Chechaker is the way that Joe Quigley pronounced it, with his western Pennsylvania accent.

23. Polar Regions Archives, Lindberg Collection, University of Alaska, Fairbanks, Hazel Lindberg Box 7, Folder 7.
24. Polar Regions Archives, Lindberg Collection, University of Alaska, Fairbanks, Hazel Lindberg Box 7, Folder 7.
25. "As Precious as Gold," Smithsonian National Postal Museum, postalmuseum.si.edu.
26. Polar Regions Archives, Lindberg Collection, University of Alaska, Fairbanks, Hazel Lindberg Box 7, Folder 7.
27. Grant H. Pearson, "Joe Quigley, Sourdough," *The Alaska Sportsman* 16, no. 3 (1950).
28. Grant H. Pearson, "Joe Quigley, Sourdough," *The Alaska Sportsman* 16, no. 3, (1950).
29. Polar Regions Archives, Lindberg Collection, University of Alaska, Fairbanks, Hazel Lindberg Box 7, Folder 7.
30. Pierre Berton, *Klondike: The Life and Death of Last Great Gold Rush* (London: W.H. Allen, 1960).
31. Polar Regions Archives, Lindberg Collection, University of Alaska, Fairbanks, Hazel Lindberg Box 7, Folder 7.

Chapter 2

1. J. N. Bowman, "Driving the Last Spike," *California Historical Society Quarterly* XXXVI, no. 2 (June 1957), pp. 96–106, and XXXVI, no. 3 (September 1957), pp. 263–274. cprr.org.
2. Polar Regions Archives, Lindberg Collection, University of Alaska, Fairbanks, Hazel Lindberg Box 7, Folder 7.
3. Robert Walter Smith, *History of Armstrong County, Pennsylvania* (Chicago: Waterman, Watkins, 1883).
4. Thinley Kalsang Bhutia, *Encyclopedia Brittanica, United States History, California Gold Rush*. November 2017. Britannica.com.
5. Robert Walter Smith, *History of Armstrong County, Pennsylvania* (Chicago: Waterman, Watkins, 1883).
6. Robert Walter Smith, *History of Armstrong County, Pennsylvania* (Chicago: Waterman, Watkins, 1883).
7. *Stories from PA History, Agriculture and Rural Life*, 2011, ExplorePAhistory.com.
8. People who followed the 1849 California Gold Rush were known as 49ers.
9. U.S. Appointments of Postmasters, Armstrong County Pennsylvania, 12 June 1883.
10. Samuel T. Wiley, historian and editor, *Biographical and Historical Cyclopedia of Indiana and Armstrong Counties, Pennsylvania* (Philadelphia: John M. Greshan & Co., 1891).
11. In the centennial year for the Homestead Act, 1962, President John F. Kennedy called the act "the single greatest stimulus to national development ever enacted."
12. *Butler Citizen*, Butler, Pennsylvania, 4 January 1906.
13. "Salty Sentence for Quigley," *Butler Citizen*, Butler, Pennsylvania, 28 June 1912.
14. *Butler Citizen*, Butler, Pennsylvania, 25 October 1917.
15. U.S. City Directories, Pennsylvania, Butler, 1906.
16. "Children's Lives at the Turn of the Twentieth Century," Primary Source Sets | Teacher Resources—Library of Congress, accessed May 10, 2019. https://www.loc.gov/teachers/classroommaterials/primarysourcesets/.
17. "County Schools Closing," *Simpson's Leader-Times*, Kittanning, Pennsylvania, 28 April 1930.
18. California State Library, California History Section; Great Registers, 1866–1898; Collection Number 4–2A; CSL Roll Number 22; FHL Roll Number:976931

Chapter 3

1. Mary Lee Davis, *We Are Alaskans* (Boston: W. A. Wilde Company, 1931).
2. Myron P. Gutman and Sara M. Pullum-Pinon, "Three Eras of Young Adult Home Leaving in Twentieth-Century America," Department of History and Population Research Center, University of Texas at Austin, accessed May 10, 2019. https://liberalarts.utexas.edu/prc/_files/pdf/workingpapers/00-01-01.pdf.
3. Polar Regions Archives, Lindberg Collection, University of Alaska, Fairbanks, Hazel Lindberg Box 7, Folder 7.
4. Polar Regions Archives, Lindberg Collection, University of Alaska, Fairbanks, Hazel Lindberg Box 7, Folder 7.
5. Polar Regions Archives, Lindberg Collection, University of Alaska, Fairbanks, Hazel Lindberg Box 7, Folder 7.
6. The Far North can refer to Alaska or

Canada and has to do with proximity to the Arctic Circle rather than political boundaries.

7. Douglas O. Linder, "The Haymarket Riot and Trial: An Account," Famous Trials, accessed May 10, 2019. https://famous-trials.com/.

8. Editors, History.com, "Haymarket Riot," History.com, December 16, 2009, accessed May 10, 2019. https://www.history.com/topics/19th-century/haymarket-riot.

9. Jay P. Dolan, *The Irish Americans: A History* (New York: Bloomsbury, 2010).

10. "Whites Massacre Chinese in Wyoming Territory," History.com, November 16, 2009, accessed May 23, 2019. https://www.history.com/this-day-in-history/whites-massacre-chinese-in-wyoming-territory.

11. Diane Purvis, excerpt from University of Nebraska Press for "Ragged Coast, Rugged Cove: Labor, Culture, and Politics in Southeast Alaska Canneries from the Russian Mercantile Era to the Cold War," email with author, May 11, 2019.

12. Polar Regions Archives, Lindberg Collection, University of Alaska, Fairbanks, Hazel Lindberg Box 7, Folder 7.

13. Bill Ganzel, "Riding the Rails," Wessels Living History Farm, accessed May 10, 2019. https://livinghistoryfarm.org/farminginthe30s/water/riding-the-rails/.

14. "19th-Century Blacksmithing," Old Sturbridge Village, accessed May 10, 2019. https://www.osv.org/.

15. "Indian Country Today," IndianCountryToday.com, accessed May 10, 2019. https://newsmaven.io/indiancountrytoday/.

16. Polar Regions Archives, Lindberg Collection, University of Alaska, Fairbanks, Hazel Lindberg Box 7, Folder 7.

17. "Seeing the Forest for the Trees: Placing Washington's Forests in Historical Context," Center for the Study of the Pacific Northwest, Accessed May 10, 2019. http://www.washington.edu/uwired/outreach/cspn/Website/Classroom Materials/Curriculum Packets/Evergreen State/Section II.html.

18. Polar Regions Archives, Lindberg Collection, University of Alaska, Fairbanks, Hazel Lindberg Box 7, Folder 7.

19. Pierre Berton, *Klondike: The Life and Death of Last Great Gold Rush* (London: W.H. Allen, 1960).

20. "Kittanning Native Helps Mrs. Biddle," *Pittsburgh Press*, Pittsburgh, Pennsylvania, Thursday, 24 March 1932.

21. Polar Regions Archives, Lindberg Collection, University of Alaska, Fairbanks, Hazel Lindberg Box 7, Folder 7.

Chapter 4

1. "Alaska Native Heritage Center," Alaska Native Heritage Center, December 13, 2018, accessed May 10, 2019. https://www.alaskanative.net/.

2. J. Ellis Ransom, "Derivation of the Word 'Alaska,'" *American Anthropologist*, October 28, 2009, accessed May 10, 2019. https://anthrosource.onlinelibrary.wiley.com/doi/abs/10.1525/aa.1940.42.3.02a00340.

3. "Aleut History," Aleut Corporati on, accessed May 10, 2019. https://www.aleutcorp.com/.

4. "Colonialism Wreaked Havoc on Alaska Native Peoples," *Anchorage Daily News*, 31 May 2016.

5. Jim McDowell and José Narváez, *José Narváez: The Forgotten Explorer: Including His Narrative of a Voyage on the Northwest Coast in 1788* (Spokane: Clark, 1998).

6. "A Brief History of Hudson Bay Company," Hudson Bay Company Heritage, accessed May 10, 2019. http://www.hbcheritage.ca/history/company-stories/a-brief-history-of-hbc.

7. Alaska Humanities Forum, Alaska History & Cultural Studies, Interior Alaska. http://www.akhistorycourse.org/interior-alaska/1800-1869-the-russians-and-english-meet.

8. Alaska Humanities Forum, Alaska History & Cultural Studies, Interior Alaska. http://www.akhistorycourse.org/interior-alaska/1800-1869-the-russians-and-english-meet.

9. William Iggiagruk Hensley, "Smithsonian 150 Year Treaty of Cession Celebration," September 16, 2017.

10. Melody Webb, *The Last Frontier* (Albuquerque: University of New Mexico Press, 1985).

11. "March 30: On This Day in History," On This Day, accessed May 10, 2019. https://www.onthisday.com/day/march/30.

12. "Modern Alaska," AKHF, accessed May 10, 2019. https://www.akhf.org/#!.

13. Arthur C. Banet, "Oil and Gas Development on Alaska's North Slope: Past Results and Future Prospects," Bureau of Land Management, March 1991.

14. "Alaska Becomes a State," The Learning Network, learning.blogs.nytimes.com, January 3, 2012.
15. The Kantishna post office was established in 1905, but the Board on Geographic Names didn't officially name it Kantishna until 1944.

Chapter 5

1. Polar Regions Archives, Lindberg Collection, University of Alaska, Fairbanks, Hazel Lindberg Box 7, Folder 7.
2. Polar Regions Archives, Lindberg Collection, University of Alaska, Fairbanks, Hazel Lindberg Box 7, Folder
3. Polar Regions Archives, Lindberg Collection, University of Alaska, Fairbanks, Hazel Lindberg Box 7, Folder 7.
4. Michael Gates, "Life Was Harsh for the Early Pioneers in the Yukon," Yukon-news.com, November 20, 2009.
5. Polar Regions Archives, Lindberg Collection, University of Alaska, Fairbanks, Hazel Lindberg Box 7, Folder 7.
6. Jane G. Haigh, *Searching for Fannie Quigley: A Wilderness Life in the Shadow of Mount McKinley* (Athens: Swallow Press/Ohio University Press, 2007).
7. Polar Regions Archives, Lindberg Collection, University of Alaska, Fairbanks, Hazel Lindberg Box 7, Folder 7.
8. Melody Webb, *The Last Frontier* (Albuquerque: University of New Mexico Press, 1985).
9. Polar Regions Archives, Lindberg Collection, University of Alaska, Fairbanks, Hazel Lindberg Box 7, Folder 7.
10. Polar Regions Archives, Lindberg Collection, University of Alaska, Fairbanks, Hazel Lindberg Box 7, Folder 7.
11. Peterborough was a Canadian brand name that became a generic term for a specific type of lightweight canoe that one person could carry.
12. Pierre Berton, *Klondike: The Life and Death of Last Great Gold Rush* (London: W.H. Allen, 1960).
13. Pierre Berton, *Klondike: The Life and Death of Last Great Gold Rush* (London: W.H. Allen, 1960).
14. Grant H. Pearson, "Joe Quigley, Sourdough," *The Alaska Sportsman* 16, no. 3 (1950).
15. "Gold Placers of the Historical Fortymile River Region, Alaska," Pubs.usgs.gov.
16. Melody Webb, *The Last Frontier* (Albuquerque: University of New Mexico Press, 1985).
17. Pierre Berton, *Klondike: The Life and Death of Last Great Gold Rush* (London: W.H. Allen, 1960).
18. "Log Cabin Metropolis: Circle City," National Parks Service, accessed May 10, 2019. https://www.nps.gov/yuch/learn/historyculture/circle-city.htm.
19. Melody Webb, *The Last Frontier* (Albuquerque: University of New Mexico Press, 1985).
20. Pierre Berton, *Klondike: The Life and Death of Last Great Gold Rush* (London: W.H. Allen, 1960).
21. Pierre Berton, *Klondike: The Life and Death of Last Great Gold Rush* (London: W.H. Allen, 1960).
22. Pierre Berton, *Klondike: The Life and Death of Last Great Gold Rush* (London: W.H. Allen, 1960).
23. Claire Rudolf Murphy and Jane G. Haigh, *Gold Rush Women* (Kenai, AK: Hillside Press, 2012).
24. Polar Regions Archives, Lindberg Collection, University of Alaska, Fairbanks, Hazel Lindberg Box 7, Folder 7
25. Claire Rudolf Murphy and Jane G. Haigh, *Gold Rush Women* (Kenai, AK: Hillside Press, 2012).
26. Heather Steinhagen, "History & Evolution," Yukon Order of Pioneers, accessed May 10, 2019. http://yukon-seniors-and-elders.org/index.php/yoop-about/yoop-history.

Chapter 6

1. Polar Regions Archives, Lindberg Collection, University of Alaska, Fairbanks, Hazel Lindberg Box 7, Folder 7.
2. Polar Regions Archives, Lindberg Collection, University of Alaska, Fairbanks, Hazel Lindberg Box 7, Folder 7.
3. Polar Regions Archives, Lindberg Collection, University of Alaska, Fairbanks, Hazel Lindberg Box 7, Folder 7.
4. Polar Regions Archives, Lindberg Collection, University of Alaska, Fairbanks, Hazel Lindberg Box 7, Folder 7.
5. Pierre Berton, *Klondike: The Life and Death of Last Great Gold Rush* (London: W.H. Allen, 1960).
6. "Perfectly Yukon," Dawson City,

Yukon, accessed May 10, 2019. https://dawsoncity.ca/.

7. Margaret E. Murie, Olaus J. Murie, and Terry Tempest Williams, *Two in the Far North* (Portland, OR: Alaska Northwest Books, 1997).

8. "Children of the Gold Rush," Stories of the Gold Rush, Accessed May 10, 2019. https://education.alaska.gov/temp_lam_pages/library/goldrush/stories/home.htm.

9. Polar Regions Archives, Lindberg Collection, University of Alaska, Fairbanks, Hazel Lindberg Box 7, Folder 7.

10. Les McLaughlin, "Inspector Charles Constantine," Hougen Group, accessed May 10, 2019. http://hougengroup.com/yukon-history/yukon-nuggets/inspector-charles-constantine/.

11. Pierre Berton, *Klondike: The Life and Death of Last Great Gold Rush* (London: W.H. Allen, 1960).

12. Pierre Berton, *Klondike: The Life and Death of Last Great Gold Rush* (London: W.H. Allen, 1960).

13. "As Precious as Gold," Smithsonian National Postal Museum, postalmuseum.si.edu.

14. Polar Regions Archives, Lindberg Collection, University of Alaska, Fairbanks, Hazel Lindberg Box 7, Folder 7.

15. David A. James, "Mail Carriers a Vital Part of Alaska History," *Fairbanks Daily News-Miner*, 19 May 2012.

16. Polar Regions Archives, Lindberg Collection, University of Alaska, Fairbanks, Hazel Lindberg Box 7, Folder 7.

17. Polar Regions Archives, Lindberg Collection, University of Alaska, Fairbanks, Hazel Lindberg Box 7, Folder 7.

18. Claus-M. Naske and Herman E. Slotnick, *Alaska: A History of the 49th State* (Norman: University of Oklahoma Press, 1987).

Chapter 7

1. "Rich Strike Made in the Tanana," *The Yukon Sun*, 17 January 1903.

2. Jane G. Haigh, *Searching for Fannie Quigley: A Wilderness Life in the Shadow of Mount McKinley* (Athens: Swallow Press/Ohio University Press, 2007).

3. Jane G. Haigh, *Searching for Fannie Quigley: A Wilderness Life in the Shadow of Mount McKinley* (Athens: Swallow Press/Ohio University Press, 2007).

4. Claus-M. Naske and Herman E. Slotnick, *Alaska: A History of the 49th State* (Norman: University of Oklahoma Press, 1987).

5. Denali National Park Historic Resource Study, "Challenge of the Mountain," nps.gov.

6. "Wickersham State Historic Site," Alaska Department of Natural Resources, accessed May 30, 2019. http://dnr.alaska.gov/.

7. Polar Regions Archives, Lindberg Collection, University of Alaska, Fairbanks, Hazel Lindberg Box 7, Folder 7.

8. Jane G. Haigh, *Searching for Fannie Quigley: A Wilderness Life in the Shadow of Mount McKinley* (Athens: Swallow Press/Ohio University Press, 2007).

9. Polar Regions Archives, Lindberg Collection, University of Alaska, Fairbanks, Hazel Lindberg Box 7, Folder 7.

10. Chris Allen, "Kantishna Gold! (U.S. National Park Service)," National Parks Service, accessed May 10, 2019. https://www.nps.gov/articles/kantishna-gold.htm.

11. "As Precious as Gold," Smithsonian National Postal Museum, postalmuseum.si.edu.

12. "Challenge of the Mountain," Denali Historic Resources Study, nps.gov.

13. The temporary name Mount McKinley was officially returned to its original name, Denali, by President Barack Obama in 2015.

14. Tom Walker, *Kantishna Mushers, Miners, Mountaineers: The Story Behind Mt. McKinley National Park* (Missoula, MT: Pictorial Histories, 2005).

15. James Wickersham, *Old Yukon: Tales—Trails—and Trials* (Washington, D.C.: Washington Law Book Co., 1938).

16. James Wickersham, *Old Yukon: Tales—Trails—and Trials* (Washington, D.C.: Washington Law Book Co., 1938).

17. James Wickersham, *Old Yukon: Tales—Trails—and Trials* (Washington, D.C.: Washington Law Book Co., 1938).

18. James Wickersham, *Old Yukon: Tales—Trails—and Trials* (Washington, D.C.: Washington Law Book Co., 1938).

19. Jane G. Haigh, *Searching for Fannie Quigley: A Wilderness Life in the Shadow of Mount McKinley* (Athens: Swallow Press/Ohio University Press, 2007).

20. Polar Regions Archives, Lindberg Collection, University of Alaska, Fairbanks, Hazel Lindberg Box 7, Folder 7.

21. Polar Regions Archives, Lindberg Collection, University of Alaska, Fairbanks, Hazel Lindberg Box 7, Folder 7.

Chapter 8

1. "Golden Places: The History of Alaska-Yukon Mining (Chapter 14)," National Parks Service, accessed May 10, 2019. https://www.nps.gov/parkhistory/online_books/yuch/golden_places/chap14.htm.
2. Grant Pearson, History of Mount McKinley National Park, National Park Service, 1953.
3. "Golden Places: The History of Alaska-Yukon Mining (Chapter 14)," National Parks Service, accessed May 10, 2019. https://www.nps.gov/parkhistory/online_books/yuch/golden_places/chap14.htm.
4. Pierre Berton, *Klondike: The Life and Death of Last Great Gold Rush* (London: W.H. Allen, 1960).
5. Pierre Berton, *Klondike: The Life and Death of Last Great Gold Rush* (London: W.H. Allen, 1960).
6. James Wickersham, *Old Yukon: Tales—Trails—and Trials* (Washington, D.C.: Washington Law Book Co., 1938).
7. Tappan Adney, *The Klondike Stampede of 1897–1898* (Fairfield, WA: Ye Galleon Press, 1968).
8. Jennifer Raffaeli, Denali National Park and Preserve, Kennels.
9. The Thule were proto–Inuit people and ancestors of the modern Inuit
10. Thom "Swanny" Swan, "Marche: Sled Dogs in the North West Fur Trade," tworiversak.com.
11. Tappan Adney, *The Klondike Stampede of 1897–1898* (Fairfield, WA: Ye Galleon Press, 1968).
12. Grant H. Pearson, "Joe Quigley, Sourdough," *The Alaska Sportsman* 16, no. 3 (1950).
13. Helen Hegener, "Early Days of Mushing," Northern Light Media, accessed May 20, 2019. https://northernlightmedia.wordpress.com/2015/03/05/the-early-days-of-mushing/.
14. Polar Regions Archives, Lindberg Collection of the University of Alaska, Fairbanks, Hazel Lindberg, Box 7, Folder 7.
15. Bill Cotter, professional musher, email with the author.
16. Hudson Stuck, *Ten Thousand Miles with a Dog Sled: A Narrative of Winter Travel in Interior Alaska* (London, 1914).
17. Hudson Stuck, *Ten Thousand Miles with a Dog Sled: A Narrative of Winter Travel in Interior Alaska* (London, 1914).
18. Chris Allen, "Kantishna Gold! (U.S. National Park Service)," National Parks Service, ccessed May 10, 2019. https://www.nps.gov/articles/kantishna-gold.htm.
19. Grant H. Pearson, "Joe Quigley, Sourdough," *The Alaska Sportsman* 16, no. 3 (1950).
20. Polar Regions Archives, Lindberg Collection of the University of Alaska, Fairbanks, Hazel Lindberg, Box 7, Folder 7.
21. Jane G. Haigh, *Searching for Fannie Quigley: A Wilderness Life in the Shadow of Mount McKinley* (Athens: Swallow Press/Ohio University Press, 2007).
22. Stephen R. Capps of the U.S. Geological Survey, 1919, 75–76.
23. Jane G. Haigh, *Searching for Fannie Quigley: A Wilderness Life in the Shadow of Mount McKinley* (Athens: Swallow Press/Ohio University Press, 2007).
24. Government of Yukon, "Energy, Mines and Resources," How It Works—Energy, Mines and Resources—Government of Yukon, Accessed May 16, 2019. http://www.yukonplacersecretariat.ca/howitworks.html.
25. Tom Walker, *The Seventymile Kid: The Lost Legacy of Harry Karstens and the First Ascent of Mount McKinley* (Seattle: Mountaineers Books, 2013).
26. Jane G. Haigh, *Searching for Fannie Quigley: A Wilderness Life in the Shadow of Mount McKinley* (Athens: Swallow Press/Ohio University Press, 2007).
27. "Golden Places: The History of Alaska-Yukon Mining," National Parks Service, accessed May 10, 2019. https://www.nps.gov/parkhistory/online_books/yuch/golden_places/.
28. Chris Allan, "Kantishna Gold! (U.S. National Park Service)," National Parks Service, accessed May 26, 2019. https://www.nps.gov/articles/kantishna-gold.htm.
29. Jane G. Haigh, *Searching for Fannie Quigley: A Wilderness Life in the Shadow of Mount McKinley* (Athens: Swallow Press/Ohio University Press, 2007).

Chapter 9

1. David Charles Beyreis, "Middle Class Masculinity and the Klondike Gold Rush," Oklahoma State University, 2005.
2. Katherine Hughes, bl.uk/romantics-and-victorians, May 2014.
3. William Makepeace Thackeray, "The Angel of the House," Academic.Brooklyn.cuny.edu.
4. "The Gibson Girl's America," www.loc.gov.
5. Department of the Interior Census Office Report, "Population and Resources of Alaska," Eleventh Census 1890.
6. Sara Bornstein, "Women of the 1898 Alaska Gold Rush," 2009 Senior History Thesis, Bryn Mawr.
7. 1900 Census.
8. Jane G. Haigh, *Searching for Fannie Quigley: A Wilderness Life in the Shadow of Mount McKinley* (Athens: Swallow Press/ Ohio University Press, 2007).
9. Jane G. Haigh, *Searching for Fannie Quigley: A Wilderness Life in the Shadow of Mount McKinley* (Athens: Swallow Press/ Ohio University Press, 2007).
10. Jane G. Haigh, *Searching for Fannie Quigley: A Wilderness Life in the Shadow of Mount McKinley* (Athens: Swallow Press/ Ohio University Press, 2007).
11. Chris Allen, "Kantishna Gold! (U.S. National Park Service)," National Parks Service, accessed May 10, 2019. https://www.nps.gov/articles/kantishna-gold.htm.
12. Jane G. Haigh, *Searching for Fannie Quigley: A Wilderness Life in the Shadow of Mount McKinley* (Athens: Swallow Press/ Ohio University Press, 2007).
13. Jane G. Haigh, *Searching for Fannie Quigley: A Wilderness Life in the Shadow of Mount McKinley* (Athens: Swallow Press/ Ohio University Press, 2007).
14. *Klondike Nugget*, December 1901
15. Tom Walker, *Kantishna Mushers, Miners, Mountaineers: The Story Behind Mt. McKinley National Park* (Missoula, MT: Pictorial Histories, 2005).
16. Jane G. Haigh, *Searching for Fannie Quigley: A Wilderness Life in the Shadow of Mount McKinley* (Athens: Swallow Press/ Ohio University Press, 2007).
17. Jane G. Haigh, *Searching for Fannie Quigley: A Wilderness Life in the Shadow of Mount McKinley* (Athens: Swallow Press/ Ohio University Press, 2007).
18. Chris Allen, "Kantishna Gold! (U.S. National Park Service)," National Parks Service, accessed May 10, 2019. https://www.nps.gov/articles/kantishna-gold.htm.
19. Grant H. Pearson and Philip Newill, *My Life of High Adventure* (Englewood Cliffs, NJ: Prentice-Hall, 1962).
20. Jane G. Haigh, *Searching for Fannie Quigley: A Wilderness Life in the Shadow of Mount McKinley* (Athens: Swallow Press/ Ohio University Press, 2007).
21. Mary Lee Davis, *We Are Alaskans* (Boston: W.A. Wilde, 1931).
22. Tom Walker, *Kantishna Mushers, Miners, Mountaineers: The Story Behind Mt. McKinley National Park* (Missoula, MT: Pictorial Histories, 2005).
23. Jane G. Haigh, *Searching for Fannie Quigley: A Wilderness Life in the Shadow of Mount McKinley* (Athens: Swallow Press/ Ohio University Press, 2007).
24. Mary Lee Davis, *We Are Alaskans* (Boston: W.A. Wilde, 1931).

Chapter 10

1. Hudson Stuck, *Ten Thousand Miles with a Dog Sled: A Narrative of Winter Travel in Interior Alaska* (London, 1914).
2. Ravenna Koenig, "'Fairbanks' Famously Severe Cold Snaps Are Getting Less Cold and More Rare," *Fairbanks Daily News-Miner*, 9 January 2019.
3. Global Climate Change, Vital Signs of the Planet, NASA, climate.nasa.gov, 2019.
4. Tom Walker, *Kantishna Mushers, Miners, Mountaineers: The Story Behind Mt. McKinley National Park* (Missoula, MT: Pictorial Histories, 2005).
5. "In mining law. A contract between two parties by which one undertakes to furnish the necessary provisions, tools, and other supplies, and the other to prospect for and locate mineral lands and stake out mining claims thereon, the Interest in the property thus acquired inuring to the benefit of both parties, either equally or in such proportions as their agreement may fix. Such contracts create a qualified or special partnership" (thelawdictionary.org).
6. "National Park Service: Golden Places: The History of Alaska-Yukon Mining (Chapter 13)," National Parks Service, accessed May 26, 2019. https://www.

nps.gov/parkhistory/online_books/yuch/golden_places/chap13.htm.

7. Stephen R. Capps of the U.S. Geological Survey, 1919, 75–76.

8. Tom Walker, *Kantishna Mushers, Miners, Mountaineers: The Story Behind Mt. McKinley National Park* (Missoula, MT: Pictorial Histories, 2005).

9. Murray Lundberg, "Living in the North, Exploring the World," The ExploreNorth Blog, accessed May 26, 2019. http://explorenorth.com/wordpress/.

10. "Old Fortymilers Now Form Last Guard of Earliest Yukon Camp," *Fairbanks Daily News-Miner*, 8 May 1939.

11. Polar Regions Archives, Lindberg Collection, University of Alaska, Fairbanks, Hazel Lindberg Box 7, Folder 7.

12. Polar Regions Archives, Lindberg Collection, University of Alaska, Fairbanks, Hazel Lindberg Box 7, Folder 7.

13. Tom Bundtzen, mining engineer, president of AMHF in personal correspondence with author.

14. Ch'ung-yu Wang, *Antimony: Its History, Chemistry, Mineralogy, Geology, Metallurgy, Uses* (Charles Griffin & Company, 1909).

15. "Golden Places: The History of Alaska-Yukon Mining (Chapter 14)," National Parks Service, accessed May 10, 2019. https://www.nps.gov/parkhistory/online_books/yuch/golden_places/chap14.htm.

16. "Golden Places: The History of Alaska-Yukon Mining (Chapter 14)," National Parks Service, accessed May 10, 2019. https://www.nps.gov/parkhistory/online_books/yuch/golden_places/chap14.htm.

17. Jane G. Haigh, *Searching for Fannie Quigley: A Wilderness Life in the Shadow of Mount McKinley* (Athens: Swallow Press/Ohio University Press, 2007).

18. "A History of the Denali—Mount McKinley Region, Alaska," Chapter 4, The Kantishna and Nearby Mining Districts, npshistory.gov.

Chapter 11

1. Correspondence between the author and Simon Hamm, long-time Denali area resident and innkeeper.

2. Ken Burns, "The National Parks: America's Best Idea," PBS, 2009.

3. Charles Sheldon and Paul D. Webster, *The Wilderness of Denali: Explorations of a Hunter-Naturalist in Northern Alaska* (Clinton, NJ: Amwell Press, 1983).

4. Worldhistory.us, "Charles Sheldon: One Man's Quest to Create the Alaskan Park."

5. Charles Sheldon and Paul D. Webster, *The Wilderness of Denali: Explorations of a Hunter-Naturalist in Northern Alaska* (Clinton, NJ: Amwell Press, 1983).

6. Charles Sheldon and Paul D. Webster, *The Wilderness of Denali: Explorations of a Hunter-Naturalist in Northern Alaska* (Clinton, NJ: Amwell Press, 1983).

7. Charles Sheldon and Paul D. Webst er, *The Wilderness of Denali: Explorations of a Hunter-Naturalist in Northern Alaska* (Clinton, NJ: Amwell Press, 1983).

8. Charles Sheldon and Paul D. Webster, *The Wilderness of Denali: Explorations of a Hunter-Naturalist in Northern Alaska* (Clinton, NJ: Amwell Press, 1983).

9. Charles Sheldon and Paul D. Webster, *The Wilderness of Denali: Explorations of a Hunter-Naturalist in Northern Alaska* (Clinton, NJ: Amwell Press, 1983).

10. San Diego Zoo, "Lynx and Bobcat," animals.sandiegozoo.org/animals/lynx-and-bobcat.

11. Ann Kain, "Scientific Legacy of Denali," www.nps.gov.

12. nps.gov, "Contemplating Denali, Origin of Denali National Park and Preserve."

13. Charles Sheldon Papers, Series 1: Correspondence File, 1893–1933, Box 3, Folder 9, Quigley, Joe and Fannie 1909–1913.

14. Charles Sheldon Papers, Series 1: Correspondence File, 1893–1933, Box 3, Folder 9, Quigley, Joe and Fannie 1909–1913.

15. "Adolph Murie: Wildlife Biologist, Conservationist," www.nps.gov.

16. "Adolph Murie: Wildlife Biologist, Conservationist," www.nps.gov.

17. Ann Kain, "Scientific Legacy of Denali," *Series: Alaska Park Science* 5, Issue 1, U.S. National Park Service.

18. "Edgar Brooker, Jr. Memoirs," Edgar Brooker, Jr., to John Dalle-Molle, July 23, 1984, Denali National Park and Preserve, Alaska.

19. David Attenborough, Planet Earth 2, "Grassland," BBC.

20. Kyle Joly, Jeff Rasic, Rachel Mason, and Maija Lukin, "History, Purpose, and Status of Caribou Movements in Northwest

Alaska," *Series: Alaska Park Science* 17, Issue 1, Migration: On the Move in Alaska.

21. Ann Kain, "Scientific Legacy of Denali," *Series: Alaska Park Science* 5, Issue 1, U.S. National Park Service.

Chapter 12

1. Grant H. Pearson, "Joe Quigley, Sourdough," *The Alaska Sportsman* 16, no. 3 (1950).
2. Margaret E. Murie, Olaus J. Murie, and Terry Tempest Williams, *Two in the Far North* (Portland, OR: Alaska Northwest Books, 1997).
3. "A Long History for Alaska Media: News Industry Has Grown Alongside the Last Frontier," *Fairbanks Daily News-Miner*, 21 April 2017.
4. Margaret E. Murie, Olaus J. Murie, and Terry Tempest Williams, *Two in the Far North* (Portland, OR: Alaska Northwest Books, 1997).
5. Margaret E. Murie, Olaus J. Murie, and Terry Tempest Williams, *Two in the Far North* (Portland, OR: Alaska Northwest Books, 1997).
6. Igloo history, pioneersofalaska.org/igloo_history.
7. Igloo history, pioneersofalaska.org/igloo_history.
8. *Fairbanks Daily Times*, 31 December 1911.
9. Margaret E. Murie, Olaus J. Murie, and Terry Tempest Williams, *Two in the Far North* (Portland, OR: Alaska Northwest Books, 1997).
10. Mary Ann Clawson, "Nineteenth-Century Women's Auxiliaries and Fraternal Orders," *Signs* 12, no. 1 (Autumn 1986).
11. Jane G. Haigh, *Searching for Fannie Quigley: A Wilderness Life in the Shadow of Mount McKinley* (Athens: Swallow Press/Ohio University Press, 2007).
12. Tom Walker, *Kantishna Mushers, Miners, Mountaineers: The Story Behind Mt. McKinley National Park* (Missoula, MT: Pictorial Histories, 2005).

Chapter 13

1. Mary Lee Davis, *We Are Alaskans* (Boston: W.A. Wilde, 1931).
2. Terrence Cole, *The Sourdough Expedition* (Portland, OR: Alaska Northwest Publishing 1985).
3. Terrence Cole, *The Sourdough Expedition* (Portland, OR: Alaska Northwest Publishing 1985).
4. Terrence Cole, *The Sourdough Expedition* (Portland, OR: Alaska Northwest Publishing 1985).
5. Tom Walker, *Kantishna Mushers, Miners, Mountaineers: The Story Behind Mt. McKinley National Park* (Missoula, MT: Pictorial Histories, 2005).
6. Tom Walker, *Kantishna Mushers, Miners, Mountaineers: The Story Behind Mt. McKinley National Park* (Missoula, MT: Pictorial Histories, 2005).
7. W. F. Thompson, "The Story Behind the Story," *New York Times Sunday Magazine*, June 5, 1910.
8. Americanart.si.edu, Smithsonian American Art Museum, "Belmore Browne."
9. Belmore Browne, "The Conquest of Mount McKinley," from the compilation *Denali: Deception, Defeat, & Triumph* (Seattle: Mountaineers Books, 2001).
10. Belmore Browne, "The Conquest of Mount McKinley," from the compilation *Denali: Deception, Defeat, & Triumph* (Seattle: Mountaineers Books, 2001).
11. Cassandra Conyers, Kathleen Cubley, and Donna DeShazo, editors, *Glorious Failures*, Mountaineers Anthology Series 1 (Seattle: Mountaineers Books, 2001).
12. William E. Brown, historian, "A History of the Denali–Mount McKinley Region, Alaska, NPS, 1991.
13. Charles Sheldon Papers, Series 1: Correspondence File, 1893–1933, Box 3, Folder 9, Quigley, Joe and Fannie, 1909–1913.
14. "Cold Weather Records Shattered in the East," *Alaska Citizen*, Fairbanks, 15 January 1912.
15. Charles Sheldon Papers, Series 1: Correspondence File, 1893–1933, Box 3, Folder 9, Quigley, Joe and Fannie, 1909–1913.
16. Tom Walker, *The Seventymile Kid: The Lost Legacy of Harry Karstens and the First Ascent of Mount McKinley* (Seattle: Mountaineers Books, 2013).
17. Jane G. Haigh, *Searching for Fannie Quigley: A Wilderness Life in the Shadow of Mount McKinley* (Athens: Swallow Press/Ohio University Press, 2007).
18. Hudson Stuck, D.D., Archdeacon of the Yukon, *The Alaskan Missions of the Episcopal Church* (New York: Domestic and

Foreign Missionary Society, 1920), available at Project Canterbury website.
19. Tom Walker, *Kantishna Mushers, Miners, Mountaineers: The Story Behind Mt. McKinley National Park* (Missoula, MT: Pictorial Histories, 2005).
20. Hudson Stuck, "The Ascent of Denali," from the compilation *Denali: Deception, Defeat, & Triumph* (Seattle: Mountaineers Books, 2001).
21. Tom Walker, *The Seventymile Kid: The Lost Legacy of Harry Karstens and the First Ascent of Mount McKinley* (Seattle: Mountaineers Books, 2013).
22. Tom Walker, *Kantishna Mushers, Miners, Mountaineers: The Story Behind Mt. McKinley National Park* (Missoula, MT: Pictorial Histories, 2005).
23. Tom Walker, *Kantishna Mushers, Miners, Mountaineers: The Story Behind Mt. McKinley National Park* (Missoula, MT: Pictorial Histories, 2005).
24. Tom Walker, *The Seventymile Kid: The Lost Legacy of Harry Karstens and the First Ascent of Mount McKinley* (Seattle: Mountaineers Books, 2013).
25. Tom Walker, *The Seventymile Kid: The Lost Legacy of Harry Karstens and the First Ascent of Mount McKinley* (Seattle: Mountaineers Books, 2013).
26. "Dr. Stuck Relates Mt. M'Kinley Climb," *The Sun*, New York, Saturday, 6 September 1913.
27. Hudson Stuck quoted in the *Fairbanks Daily News-Miner*, 4 December 1918.
28. Yvonne Mozee, Walter Harper's niece, "Walter Harper," from the compilation *Denali: Deception, Defeat, & Triumph* (Seattle: Mountaineers Books, 2001).
29. Yvonne Mozee, Walter Harper's niece, "Walter Harper," from the compilation *Denali: Deception, Defeat, & Triumph* (Seattle: Mountaineers Books, 2001).

Chapter 14

1. Margaret E. Murie, Olaus J. Murie, and Terry Tempest Williams, *Two in the Far North* (Portland, OR: Alaska Northwest Books, 1997).
2. *Fairbanks Daily Times*, Sunday, 16 February 1913.
3. *Fairbanks Daily Times*, Sunday, 18 May 1913.
4. *Fairbanks Daily Times*, Thursday, 15 April 1915.
5. *Fairbanks Daily Times*, Thursday, 3 June 1915.
6. "Natives Are in Want, Say People from Kantishna," *Fairbanks Daily Times*, Tuesday, 17 March 1914.
7. William Schneider, AHS Blog, "The 1915 Tanana Chiefs Meeting," Alaskahistoricalsociety.org, 2015.
8. William L. Hensley, "Why the Natives of Alaska Have a Land Claim," speech given November 1969, Alaskool.org.
9. David Jarvis, customs agent at Eagle, to Senator Dillingham's Senate committee investigating conditions in Alaska, 1903.
10. Tom Walker, *Kantishna Mushers, Miners, Mountaineers: The Story Behind Mt. McKinley National Park* (Missoula, MT: Pictorial Histories, 2005).
11. "Edgar Brooker, Jr. Memoirs," Edgar Brooker, Jr., to John Dalle-Molle, July 23, 1984, Denali National Park and Preserve, Alaska.
12. Denali History, Chapter 6, Conditions in Alaska in the World War I and Postwar Periods, npshistory.com, 2004.
13. Tom Walker, *Kantishna Mushers, Miners, Mountaineers: The Story Behind Mt. McKinley National Park* (Missoula, MT: Pictorial Histories, 2005).
14. *Fairbanks News Miner*, 25 June 1914.
15. Denali History, Chapter 6, Conditions in Alaska in the World War I and Postwar Periods, npshistory.com, 2004.
16. Robert Kessler, "Outbreak: Pandemic Strikes," ecohealthalliance.org.
17. Jane G. Haigh, *Searching for Fannie Quigley: A Wilderness Life in the Shadow of Mount McKinley* (Athens: Swallow Press/Ohio University Press, 2007).
18. Alaska Division of Public Health, Health Analytics and Vital Records, 1918, Pandemic Influenza Mortality in Alaska, http://dhss.alaska.gov/dph/VitalStats/Documents.
19. "100 Years Ago, Spanish Flu Devastated Alaska Native Villages," peninsulaclarion.com, June 22, 2018.
20. Denali History, Chapter 6, Conditions in Alaska in the World War I and Postwar Periods, npshistory.com, 2004.
21. Jane G. Haigh, *Searching for Fannie Quigley: A Wilderness Life in the Shadow of Mount McKinley* (Athens: Swallow Press/Ohio University Press, 2007).

Chapter 15

1. Charles Sheldon Papers, Series 1: Correspondence File 1893–1933, Box 3, Folder 9, Quigley, Joe and Fannie 1909–1913.
2. "Dear Folks," Joseph Buffington Quigley to Mr. and Mrs. Lloyd Quigley, November 29, 1930, Kantishna, Alaska.
3. Stephen R. Capps, Field Notebook, August 1916.
4. Frank Norris, *Crown Jewel of the North: Denali National Park and Preserve*, vol. 2, National Park Service, 2006.
5. United States Department of the Interior, Bureau of Land Management, Alaska State Office.
6. Denali History, Chapter 6, Conditions in Alaska in the World War I and Postwar Periods, npshistory.com, 2004.
7. "Quick History of the National Park Service (U.S. National Park Service)," National Parks Service, accessed May 28, 2019. https://www.nps.gov/articles/quick-nps-history.htm.
8. Boone and Crockett Club, "Boone and Crockett Club," accessed May 28, 2019. http://www.boone-crockett.org/.
9. Marriage Certificate, United States of America, Territory of Alaska, February 2, 1918
10. "Edgar Brooker, Jr. Memoirs," Edgar Brooker, Jr., to John Dalle-Molle, July 23, 1984, Denali National Park and Preserve, Alaska.
11. In the article "Light Unearths Evidence Against Nulato Bad Men," it is stated, states, "a white man is charged with illicit cohabitation, but the wire did not state whether it was with a white or a native woman." *Fairbanks Daily Times*, 10 January 1914.
12. Theodore Roosevelt, "The Strenuous Life," 1899 speech on strenuous effort and overcoming hardships as ideals to be embraced by Americans for the betterment of the world.
13. Jane G. Haigh, *Searching for Fannie Quigley: A Wilderness Life in the Shadow of Mount McKinley* (Athens: Swallow Press/Ohio University Press, 2007).
14. Tom Walker, *Kantishna Mushers, Miners, Mountaineers: The Story Behind Mt. McKinley National Park* (Missoula, MT: Pictorial Histories, 2005).
15. Grant H. Pearson, "Joe Quigley, Sourdough," *The Alaska Sportsman* 16, no. 3 (1950).
16. Grant H. Pearson, "Joe Quigley, Sourdough," *The Alaska Sportsman* 16, no. 3 (1950).
17. Tom Walker, *Kantishna Mushers, Miners, Mountaineers: The Story behind Mt. McKinley National Park* (Missoula, MT: Pictorial Histories, 2005).

Chapter 16

1. Congressman Charles E. Hooker, as quoted by Helen Hegener, *The Alaska Railroad*, Northern Light Media 2017.
2. Denali History, Chapter 6, Conditions in Alaska in the World War I and Postwar Periods, npshistory.com, 2004.
3. Jane G. Haigh, *Searching for Fannie Quigley: A Wilderness Life in the Shadow of Mount McKinley* (Athens: Swallow Press/Ohio University Press, 2007).
4. Helen Hegener, *The Alaska Railroad*, Northern Light Media, 2017.
5. Sam Bishop, "A Mine for Learning." UAF News and Information, September 14, 2017, accessed May 28, 2019. https://news.uaf.edu/a-mine-for-learning/.
6. Polar Regions Archives, Lindberg Collection, University of Alaska, Fairbanks, Hazel Lindberg Box 7, Folder 7.
7. Grant H. Pearson and Philip Newill, *My Life of High Adventure* (Englewood Cliffs, NJ: Prentice-Hall, 1962).
8. Polar Regions Archives, Lindberg Collection, University of Alaska, Fairbanks, Hazel Lindberg Box 7, Folder 7.
9. International Library of Technology, "Blowpiping, Mineralogy, Geology, Prospecting," Scranton International Textbook Company, 1908.
10. "A History of Alaska Population Settlement," Alaska Government Labor Statistics, April 2013. http://live.laborstats.alaska.gov/pop/estimates/pub/pophistory.pdf.
11. Department of Commerce and Labor, Bureau of the Census, Thirteenth Census of the United States, Population—Alaska, taken from December 25, 1909, to January 7, 1910, by Ernest J. Foster
12. Department of Commerce and Labor, Bureau of the Census, Fourteenth Census of the United States, Population—Alaska, taken on March 10, 1920, by Fred B. Drane.
13. Denali History, Chapter 6, Conditions in Alaska in the World War I and Postwar Periods, npshistory.com, 2004.

14. United States Department of the Interior, Bureau of Land Management, Alaska State Office. www.blm.gov.
15. Jane G. Haigh, *Searching for Fannie Quigley: A Wilderness Life in the Shadow of Mount McKinley* (Athens: Swallow Press/ Ohio University Press, 2007).
16. United States Department of the Interior, Bureau of Land Management, Alaska State Office.
17. *Nenana Daily News*, 13 October 1919.
18. Jane G. Haigh, *Searching for Fannie Quigley: A Wilderness Life in the Shadow of Mount McKinley* (Athens: Swallow Press/ Ohio University Press, 2007).
19. Tom Walker, *The Seventymile Kid: The Lost Legacy of Harry Karstens and the First Ascent of Mount McKinley* (Seattle: Mountaineers Books, 2013).
20. "Welcome to McKinley Station," National Parks Service, accessed May 28, 2019. https://www.nps.gov/dena/learn/photosmultimedia/station01.htm.
21. "Mount McKinley Park Hotel," National Parks Service, accessed May 28, 2019. https://www.nps.gov/dena/learn/photosmultimedia/station03.htm.
22. *Fairbanks Daily News-Miner*, 14 July 1926.
23. Polar Regions Archives, Lindberg Collection, University of Alaska, Fairbanks, Hazel Lindberg Box 7, Folder 7.
24. "Hand Drilling and Breaking Rock for Wilderness Trail," accessed May 28, 2019. https://www.fs.fed.us/t-d/pubs/pdfpubs/pdf84232602/pdf84232602pt01.pdf.
25. Polar Regions Archives, Lindberg Collection, University of Alaska, Fairbanks, Hazel Lindberg Box 7, Folder 7.
26. "History of Alcohol Control in Alaska," Commerce.alaska.gov, accessed May 28, 2019. https://www.commerce.alaska.gov/web/amco/History.aspx
27. "History of Alcohol Control in Alaska," commerce.alaska.gov, accessed May 28, 2019. https://www.commerce.alaska.gov/web/amco/History.aspx
28. "Edgar Brooker, Jr. Memoirs." Edgar Brooker, Jr., to John Dalle-Molle, July 23, 1984, Denali National Park and Preserve, Alaska.
29. "Edgar Brooker, Jr. Memoirs." Edgar Brooker, Jr., to John Dalle-Molle, July 23, 1984, Denali National Park and Preserve, Alaska.
30. "Edgar Brooker, Jr. Memoirs." Edgar Brooker, Jr., to John Dalle-Molle, July 23, 1984, Denali National Park and Preserve, Alaska.
31. Erik Johnson, National Register of Historic Places, United States Department of the Interior, National Park Service, February 16, 2018.

Chapter 17

1. Professor Emeritus Rick Musser, "History of American Journalism," University of Kansas, School of Journalism & Mass Communications, history.journalism.ku.edu.
2. Jane G. Haigh, *Searching for Fannie Quigley: A Wilderness Life in the Shadow of Mount McKinley* (Athens: Swallow Press/ Ohio University Press, 2007).
3. Jane G. Haigh, *Searching for Fannie Quigley: A Wilderness Life in the Shadow of Mount McKinley* (Athens: Swallow Press/ Ohio University Press, 2007).
4. Jane G. Haigh, *Searching for Fannie Quigley: A Wilderness Life in the Shadow of Mount McKinley* (Athens: Swallow Press/ Ohio University Press, 2007).
5. Phyllis Demuth Movius, *A Place of Belonging* (Fairbanks: University of Alaska Press, 2010).
6. "Dear Folks," Joseph Buffington Quigley to Mr. and Mrs. Lloyd Quigley, November 29, 1930, Kantishna, Alaska.
7. Lois McGarvey, *Along Alaska Trails*, 19 60 (Pathfinder Books, Kindle version 2017).
8. Walter Dean, "The Lost Meaning of 'Objectivity.'" American Press Institute, accessed May 29, 2019. https://www.americanpressinstitute.org/journalism-essentials/bias-objectivity/lost-meaning-objectivity/.
9. Mary Lee Davis, *We Are Alaskans* (Boston: W.A. Wilde, 1931).
10. Lewis Jacobs, *The Documentary Tradition* (New York: W. W. Norton and Company, 1979).
11. "Edgar Brooker, Jr. Memoirs." Edgar Brooker, Jr., to John Dalle-Molle, July 23, 1984, Denali National Park and Preserve, Alaska.
12. Mary Lee Davis, *We Are Alaskans* (Boston: W.A. Wilde, 1931).
13. "Quigley to Be on Sick List Next 3 Months," *Fairbanks Daily News-Miner*, 5 June 1930.

Chapter 18

1. Polar Regions Archives, Lindberg Collection, University of Alaska, Fairbanks, Hazel Lindberg Box 7, Folder 7.
2. "Hundreds View Airplane When Boat Comes In," *Fairbanks Daily Times*, 22 June 1913.
3. "The Day We Celebrate," *Fairbanks Daily Times*, 1 July 1913.
4. Dermot Cole, "First Flight Launched Alaska into Aviation Age 100 Years Ago," *Fairbanks Daily News-Miner*, 30 June 2013.
5. Polar Regions Archives, Lindberg Collection, University of Alaska, Fairbanks, Hazel Lindberg Box 7, Folder 7.
6. Dirk Tordoff, *Mercy Pilot: The Joe Crosson Story* (Seattle: Epicenter Press, 2002).
7. Polar Regions Archives, Lindberg Collection, University of Alaska, Fairbanks, Hazel Lindberg Box 7, Folder 7.
8. Dirk Tordoff, *Mercy Pilot: The Joe Crosson Story* (Seattle: Epicenter Press, 2002).
9. "Alaska and the Airplane : A Century of Flight." November 11, 2018, accessed May 29, 2019. https://www.worldcat.org/title/alaska-and-the-airplane-a-century-of-flight/oclc/824726922.
10. Celia M. Hunter, "Women Play Significant Roles in Aviation in Alaska; World War II Provided Impetus," *Fairbanks Daily News-Miner*, 20 November 1957.
11. United States Department of the Interior, Bureau of Land Management, Alaska State Office.

Chapter 19

1. Jane G. Haigh, *Searching for Fannie Quigley: A Wilderness Life in the Shadow of Mount McKinley* (Athens: Swallow Press/Ohio University Press, 2007).
2. "Dear Sir," Joseph Buffington Quigley to Mr. Lloyd Joseph Quigley, July 26, 1926, Kantishna, Alaska. From the Kenneth Quigley collection.
3. "Dear Sir," Joseph Buffington Quigley to Mr. Lloyd Joseph Quigley, July 26, 1926, Kantishna, Alaska. From the Kenneth Quigley collection.
4. "Dear Sir," Joseph Buffington Quigley to Mr. Lloyd Joseph Quigley, July 26, 1926, Kantishna, Alaska. From the Kenneth Quigley collection.
5. Grant H. Pearson and Philip Newill, *My Life of High Adventure* (Englewood Cliffs, NJ: Prentice-Hall, 1962).
6. NPS, "Paula Anderson, " Denali National Park and Preserve, 2017. nps.gov/articles/akwomen-paula-anderson.htm.
7. Erik Johnson, "Johnnie Busia Mayor of Kantishna," NPS, 2018. nps.gov/articles/dena-history-busia.htm.
8. Grant h. Pearson and Philip Newill, *My Life of High Adventure* (Englewood Cliffs, NJ: Prentice-Hall, 1962).
9. Grant H. Pearson, "Joe Quigley, Sourdough," *The Alaska Sportsman* 16, no. 3 (1950).
10. Grant H. Pearson and Philip Newill, *My Life of High Adventure* (Englewood Cliffs, NJ: Prentice-Hall, 1962).
11. U.S. Department of the Interior, Bureau of Land Management, General Land Office Records.
12. U.S. Deptartment of the Interior, Bureau of Land Management, Alaska State Office.
13. Dirk Tordoff, *Mercy Pilot: The Joe Crosson Story* (Seattle: Epicenter Press, 2002).
14. Lastfrontiermagazine.com, "Fanny Quigley—An Alaskan Folk Hero," October 2, 2014.
15. Grant H. Pearson, "Joe Quigley, Sourdough," *The Alaska Sportsman* 16, no. 3 (1950).
16. "Quigley to Be on Sick List Next 3 Months," *Fairbanks Daily News-Miner*, 5 June 1930.
17. Jane G. Haigh, *Searching for Fannie Quigley: A Wilderness Life in the Shadow of Mount McKinley* (Athens: Swallow Press/Ohio University Press, 2007).

Chapter 20

1. United State Census, 1930.
2. Letter from Joe Quigley to family, written November 29, 1930, describes accident and gives date of cave in.
3. Polar Regions Archives, Lindberg Collection, University of Alaska, Fairbanks, Hazel Lindberg Box 7, Folder 7.
4. Polar Regions Archives, Lindberg Collection, University of Alaska, Fairbanks, Hazel Lindberg Box 7, Folder 7.
5. Polar Regions Archives, Lindberg Collection, University of Alaska, Fairbanks, Hazel Lindberg Box 7, Folder 7.

6. Martin Cole, "Journey to Caribou Land," Cole Revocable Trust 1983.
7. Martin Cole, "Journey to Caribou Land," Cole Revocable Trust 1983.
8. Polar Regions Archives, Lindberg Collection, University of Alaska, Fairbanks, Hazel Lindberg Box 7, Folder 7.
9. Polar Regions Archives, Lindberg Collection, University of Alaska, Fairbanks, Hazel Lindberg Box 7, Folder 7.
10. Polar Regions Archives, Lindberg Collection, University of Alaska, Fairbanks, Hazel Lindberg Box 7, Folder 7.
11. "Quigley to Be on Sick List Next 3 Months," *Fairbanks Daily News-Miner*, 5 June 1930.
12. Polar Regions Archives, Lindberg Collection, University of Alaska, Fairbanks, Hazel Lindberg Box 7, Folder 7.
13. Letter to family, Ken Quigley collection.
14. "Rail Hearings Adjourn Sunday," *Fairbanks Daily News-Miner*, 25 August 1930.
15. "Plane Unable to Land," *Fairbanks Daily News-Miner*, 10 September 1930.
16. "Quigley on Way Home," *Fairbanks Daily News-Miner*, 24 September 1930.
17. Mary Lee Davis, *We Are Alaskans* (Boston: W.A. Wilde, 1931).
18. Ira Jorlemon, "Adventure Beacons," Society of Mining Engineers of AIME New York, 1976.

Chapter 21

1. "Quiggley's Have Afternoon Callers Come by Air," *Fairbanks Daily News-Miner*, 28 March 1931.
2. Walter Van Horn and Bruce Parham, "Edmunds, Morgan Christopher," Cook Inlet Historical Society, *Legends & Legacies, Anchorage, 1910–1940*, http://www.alaskahistory.org.
3. Grant H. Pearson and Philip Newill, *My Life of High Adventure* (Englewood Cliffs, NJ: Prentice-Hall, 1962).
4. "D. L. Sawyer Writes About Alaska Mines," *Fairbanks Daily News-Miner*, 8 August 1931.
5. "Engineers See Quartz Future for Interior," *Fairbanks Daily News-Miner*, 24 September 1931.
6. Ira Beaman Joralemon, *Adventure Beacons* (New York: Society of Mining Engineers of AIME for the Mining and Metallurgical Society of America, 1976).
7. Jane G. Haigh, *Searching for Fannie Quigley: A Wilderness Life in the Shadow of Mount McKinley* (Athens: Swallow Press/Ohio University Press, 2007).
8. Ira Beaman Joralemon, *Adventure Beacons* (New York: Society of Mining Engineers of AIME for the Mining and Metallurgical Society of America, 1976).
9. Jane G. Haigh, *Searching for Fannie Quigley: A Wilderness Life in the Shadow of Mount McKinley* (Athens: Swallow Press/Ohio University Press, 2007).
10. "Kittanning Native Helps Mrs. Biddle," *Pittsburgh Press*, 24 March 1932.
11. Jane G. Haigh, *Searching for Fannie Quigley: A Wilderness Life in the Shadow of Mount McKinley* (Athens: Swallow Press/Ohio University Press, 2007).
12. "Joseph Quigley at the Hotel Alaska," *Fairbanks Daily News-Miner*, 2 May 1933.
13. Ira Beaman Joralemon, *Adventure Beacons* (New York: Society of Mining Engineers of AIME for the Mining and Metallurgical Society of America, 1976).
14. Ira Beaman Joralemon, *Adventure Beacons* (New York: Society of Mining Engineers of AIME for the Mining and Metallurgical Society of America, 1976).
15. "UAF Home | University of Alaska Fairbanks." UAF Home | University of Alaska Fairbanks, accessed May 29, 2019. http://www.uaf.edu/.
16. Jane G. Haigh, *Searching for Fannie Quigley: A Wilderness Life in the Shadow of Mount McKinley* (Athens: Swallow Press/Ohio University Press, 2007).
17. Jane G. Haigh, *Searching for Fannie Quigley: A Wilderness Life in the Shadow of Mount McKinley* (Athens: Swallow Press/Ohio University Press, 2007).
18. Jane G. Haigh, *Searching for Fannie Quigley: A Wilderness Life in the Shadow of Mount McKinley* (Athens: Swallow Press/Ohio University Press, 2007).
19. Jane G. Haigh, *Searching for Fannie Quigley: A Wilderness Life in the Shadow of Mount McKinley* (Athens: Swallow Press/Ohio University Press, 2007).
20. Jane G. Haigh, *Searching for Fannie Quigley: A Wilderness Life in the Shadow of Mount McKinley* (Athens: Swallow Press/Ohio University Press, 2007).
21. Jane G. Haigh, *Searching for Fannie Quigley: A Wilderness Life in the Shadow of*

Mount McKinley (Athens: Swallow Press/ Ohio University Press, 2007).

22. Grant H. Pearson, "Joe Quigley, Sourdough," *The Alaska Sportsman* 16, no. 3 (1950).

23. As told to Tom Bundtzen and Jim Lounsbury by Earl Pilgrim, and sent to the author by Tom Bundtzen.

24. "Alaska Mining Hall of Fame Foundation Home," Alaska Mining Hall of Fame Foundation Home, accessed May 29, 2019. http://alaskamininghalloffame.org/.

25. Grant H. Pearson, "Joe Quigley, Sourdough," *The Alaska Sportsman* 16, no. 3 (1950).

26. Jane G. Haigh, *Searching for Fannie Quigley: A Wilderness Life in the Shadow of Mount McKinley* (Athens: Swallow Press/ Ohio University Press, 2007).

27. Charles Caldwell Hawley, *Wesley Earl Dunkle: Alaska's Flying Miner* (Fairbanks: University of Alaska Press, 2006).

28. Charles Caldwell Hawley, *Wesley Earl Dunkle: Alaska's Flying Miner* (Fairbanks: University of Alaska Press, 2006).

29. "Frances "Fannie" Sedlacek Quigley (1870–1944)," Find a Grave, accessed May 29, 2019. https://www.findagrave.com/memorial/66478485/frances-quigley.

Chapter 22

1. "Quigley Has Long Car Trip," *Fairbanks Daily News-Miner* 24 April 1939.

2. "Out for Winter," *The Alaska Miner*, Fairbanks, Tuesday, 20 September 1938, page 24.

3. "Bathhouse Row Today," National Parks Service, accessed May 21, 2019. https://www.nps.gov/hosp/learn/historyculture/bathhouse-row-today.htm.

4. "Bathhouse Row Today," National Parks Service, accessed May 21, 2019. https://www.nps.gov/hosp/learn/historyculture/bathhouse-row-today.htm.

5. State of Arkansas, official document, Divorce Petition Coupon, November 30, 1937.

6. *Fairbanks Daily News-Miner*, 8 May 1939.

7. Penny C. Morrill and Carole A. Berk, *Mexican Silver: Modern Handwrought Jewelry & Metalwork* (Atglen, PA: Schiffer, 2007).

8. "Quigley Has Long Car Trip," *Fairbanks Daily News-Miner*, Monday, 24 April 1939, page 7.

9. Dermot Cole, "Since Harding in 1923, Presidential Stops in Alaska Have Brought the Unexpected and Memorable," *Anchorage Daily News*, 28 September 2016.

10. "Quigley Has Long Car Trip," *Fairbanks Daily News-Miner*, Monday, 24 April 1939, page 7.

11. Lindsey Konkel, "Life for the Average American Family During the Great Depression," A&E Television Networks, April 19, 2018. history.com/news/life-for-the-average-family-during-the-great-depression.

12. "Old Fortymilers Now Form Last Guard of Earliest Yukon Camp," *Fairbanks Daily News-Miner*, 8 May 1939.

13. "Quigley Has Long Car Trip," *Fairbanks Daily News-Miner*, Monday, 24 April 1939, page 7.

14. Jane Gaffin, "They Grubstaked a Goldrush," *The Yukoner Magazine* 32 (2006).

15. "Quigley Has Long Car Trip," *Fairbanks Daily News-Miner*, Monday, 24 April 1939, page 7.

16. Andrew Michael Shanken, *Into the Void Pacific: Building the 1939 San Francisco Worlds Fair* (Berkeley: University of California Press, 2015).

17. Gary Kamiya, "The '39 World's Fair: An Island of Joyus Excess," *San Francisco Gate*, 17 August 2013.

18. "Quigley Back from Oregon Gold Region," *The Alaska Miner*, Fairbanks, 25 June 1940.

19. Warren Wolff, "The Quigley Family," family genealogy document.

Chapter 23

1. Kathryn Morse, "The Klondike Gold Rush," Curriculum Materials for Washington Schools, Center for the Study of the Pacific Northwest, University of Washington Department of History.

2. University of Washington Libraries Digital Collectiona, accessed May 29, 2019. https://digitalcollections.lib.washington.edu/

3. Claire Rudolf Murphy and Jane G. Haigh, *Gold Rush Women* (Kenai, AK: Hillside Press, 2012).

4. U.S. Census 1920, Seattle.

5. Polar Regions Archives, Lindberg

Collection, University of Alaska, Fairbanks, Hazel Lindberg Box 7, Folder 7.

6. James Gregory, The Great Depression in Washington State, accessed May 21, 2019. http://depts.washington.edu/depress/.

7. James Gregory, The Great Depression in Washington State, accessed May 21, 2019. http://depts.washington.edu/depress/.

8. "World War II Home Front on Puget Sound," World War II Home Front on Puget Sound, accessed May 29, 2019. https://www.historylink.org/File/1664.

9. "World War II Home Front on Puget Sound," World War II Home Front on Puget Sound, accessed May 29, 2019. https://www.historylink.org/File/1664.

10. "Quigley Back from Oregon Gold Region," *Fairbanks Daily News-Miner*, 21 June 1940.

11. *The Alaska Miner*, Fairbanks, 10 September 1940.

12. Polar Regions Archives, Lindberg Collection, University of Alaska, Fairbanks, Hazel Lindberg Box 7, Folder 7.

13. "Mining in Alaska Primary Source Collections: Home," Libraries, Archives, & Museums, accessed May 29, 2019. https://lam.alaska.gov/miningprimarysources.

14. "Joe Quigley to Secretary of Masonic Service Bureau," Joseph Buffington Quigley to Forbes Baker, April 12, 1954.

15. "No savvy" means "I do not understand." Collins English Dictionary, HarperCollins.

16. "Two Climbers Killed in Columbia Plunge," *Medford Mail Tribune*, Medford Oregon, 16 September 1957

Bibliography

Books

Adney, Tappan. *The Klondike Stampede of 1897–1898*. Fairfield, WA: Ye Galleon Press, 1968.

Berton, Pierre. *Klondike: The Life and Death of Last Great Gold Rush*. London: W.H. Allen, 1960.

Browne, Belmore. "The Conquest of Mount McKinley," from the compilation *Denali: Deception, Defeat, & Triumph*. Seattle: Mountaineers Books, 2001.

Cole, Terrence. *The Sourdough Expedition*. Portland, OR: Alaska Northwest Publishing 1985.

Conyers, Cassandra, Kathleen Cubley and Donna DeShazo, editors. *Glorious Failures*, Mountaineers Anthology Series 1. Seattle: Mountaineers Books, 2001.

Davis, Mary Lee. *We Are Alaskans*. Boston: W.A. Wilde, 1931.

Dolan, Jay P. *The Irish Americans: A History*. New York: Bloomsbury, 2010.

Haigh, Jane G. *Searching for Fannie Quigley: A Wilderness Life in the Shadow of Mount McKinley*. Athens: Swallow Press/Ohio University Press, 2007.

Hawley, Charles Caldwell. *Wesley Earl Dunkle: Alaska's Flying Miner*. Fairbanks: University of Alaska Press, 2006.

Hegener, Helen. *The Alaska Railroad*. Northern Light Media, 2017.

Jacobs, Lewis. *The Documentary Tradition*. New York: W. W. Norton and Company, 1979

Joralemon, Ira Beaman. *Adventure Beacons*. New York: Society of Mining Engineers of AIME for the Mining and Metallurgical Society of America, 1976.

McDowell, Jim, and José Narváez. *José Narváez: The Forgotten Explorer: Including His Narrative of a Voyage on the Northwest Coast in 1788*. Spokane: Clark, 1998.

Movius, Phyllis Demuth. *A Place of Belonging*. Fairbanks: University of Alaska Press, 2010.

Mozee, Yvonne. "Walter Harper," from the compilation *Denali: Deception, Defeat, & Triumph*. Seattle: Mountaineers Books, 2001.

Murie, Margaret E., Olaus J. Murie and Terry Tempest Williams. *Two in the Far North*. Portland, OR: Alaska Northwest Books, 1997.

Murphy, Claire Rudolf, and Jane G. Haigh. *Gold Rush Women*. Kenai, AK: Hillside Press, 2012.

Naske, Claus-M., and Herman E. Slotnick. *Alaska: A History of the 49. State*. Norman: University of Oklahoma Press, 1987.

Pearson, Grant H., and Philip Newill. *My Life of High Adventure*. Englewood Cliffs, NJ: Prentice-Hall, 1962.

Shanken, Andrew Michael. *Into the Void Pacific: Building the 1939 San Francisco Worlds Fair*. Berkeley: University of California Press, 2015.

Sheldon, Charles, and Paul D. Webster. *The Wilderness of Denali: Explorations of a Hunter-naturalist in Northern Alaska*. Clinton, NJ: Amwell Press, 1983.

Smith, Robert Walker. *History of Armstrong County, Pennsylvania*. Chicago: Waterman, Watkins, 1883.

Stuck, Hudson. *Ten Thousand Miles with a Dog Sled: A Narrative of Winter Travel in Interior Alaska*. London, 1914.

Tordoff, Dirk. *Mercy Pilot: The Joe Crosson Story*. Seattle: Epicenter Press, 2002.

Walker, Tom. *Kantishna Mushers, Miners, Mountaineers: The Story Behind Mt. McKinley National Park*. Missoula, MT: Pictorial Histories, 2005.

Walker, Tom. *The Seventymile Kid: The Lost

Legacy of Harry Karstens and the First Ascent of Mount McKinley. Seattle: Mountaineers Books, 2013.
Wang, Ch'ung-yu. *Antimony: Its History, Chemistry, Mineralogy, Geology, Metallurgy, Uses.* Charles Griffin & Company, 1909.
Webb, Melody. *The Last Frontier.* Albuquerque: University of New Mexico Press, 1985.
Wickersham, James. *Old Yukon: Tales—Trails—and Trials.* Washington, D.C.: Washington Law Book Co., 1938.
Wiley, Samuel T., historian and editor. *Biographical and Historical Cyclopedia of Indiana and Armstrong Counties, Pennsylvania.* Philadelphia: John M. Greshan & Co., 1891.

Newspapers

The Alaska Miner, Fairbanks
Butler Citizen, Butler, Pennsylvania
Fairbanks Daily News-Miner
Fairbanks Daily Times
Medford Mail Tribune, Medford, Oregon
Peninsula Clarion, Soldotna, Alaska
Pittsburgh Press, Pittsburgh, Pennsylvania
San Francisco Gate
The Sun, New York
Yukon News, Whitehorse, Yukon

Websites

Alaska.org. http://www.alaska.org/.
Alaska Department of Education. https://education.alaska.gov.
Alaska Department of Natural Resources. http://dnr.alaska.gov/.
Alaska Division of Public Health. http://dhss.alaska.gov.
Alaska Historical Society. https://Alaskahistoricalsociety.org.
Alaska Humanities Forum. https://www.akhf.org/.
Alaska Mining Hall of Fame. http://alaskamininghalloffame.org.
Alaska Native Heritage Center. https://www.alaskanative.net/.
Aleut Corporation. https://www.aleutcorp.com/.
American Anthropologist. https://anthrosource.onlinelibrary.wiley.com/.
American Press Institute. https://www.americanpressinstitute.org.
Boone and Crockett Club. http://www.boone-crockett.org/.
British Broadcasting Company. https://www.bbc.com/.
British Library. https://www.bl.uk/.
Brooklyn College. http://www.brooklyn.cuny.edu/.
California State Library. https://www.library.ca.gov/.
Central Pacific Railroad Museum. http://cprr.org/.
The Conversation. https://theconversation.com/.
Craig Medred. https://craigmedred.news.
Dawson City. https://dawsoncity.ca/.
Eco Health Alliance. https://www.ecohealthalliance.org/.
Encyclopedia Britannica. https://www.britannica.com/.
Explore North. http://explorenorth.com/wordpress/.
Explore Pennsylvania History http://explorepahistory.com/.
Famous Trials. https://famous-trials.com.
Find a Grave. https://www.findagrave.com.
History.com. https://www.history.com/.
Hougen Group. http://hougengroup.com.
Hudson Bay Company Heritage. http://www.hbcheritage.ca/.
Indian Country Today. https://newsmaven.io/.
Juno.org. http://www.juneau.org.
Last Frontier Magazine. https://lastfrontiermagazine.com/.
Library of Congress. www.loc.gov.
National Park Service. https://www.nps.gov/.
The New York Times Learning Network. https://www.nytimes.com.
Oklahoma State University. https://go.okstate.edu/.
Old Sturbridge Village. https://www.osv.org.
On This Day. https://www.onthisday.com.
Public Broadcasting System. www.pbs.org.
San Diego Zoo. https://zoo.sandiegozoo.org/.
Smithsonian American Art Museum. https://americanart.si.edu/.
Smithsonian National Postal Museum. https://postalmuseum.si.edu.
State of Alaska Commerce, Community and Economic Development. https://www.commerce.alaska.gov.
United States Forest Service. https://www.fs.fed.us.
University of Alaska, Fairbanks. www.uaf.edu.

University of Chicago Press. https://www.journals.uchicago.edu.
University of Kansas. https://ku.edu/
University of Texas, Austin. https://liberalarts.utexas.edu.
University of Washington. https://www.washington.edu.
Wessels Living History Farm. https://livinghistoryfarm.org/.
World History. https://worldhistory.us/.
WorldCat. https://www.worldcat.org/.
Yukon Government. http://www.yukonplacersecretariat.ca.
Yukon Order of Pioneers. http://www.yukon-seniors-and-elders.org/.
Yukoner Magazine. https://www.yukoner.com.

Correspondence

Brooker, Edgar, Jr., to John Dalle-Molle. Denali National Park and Preserve, Alaska. July 23, 1984.
Bundtzen, Thomas, mining engineer, president of AMHF. Emails with author. 2018–2019.
Hamm, Simon, long-time Denali area resident and innkeeper. Email with author. December 13, 2018.
Purvis, Diane. Excerpt from University of Nebraska Press for "Ragged Coast, Rugged Cove: Labor, Culture, and Politics in Southeast Alaska Canneries from the Russian Mercantile Era to the Cold War." Email with author. May 11, 2019.
Quigley, Joe, to Forbes L. Baker, Secretary, Tanana Lodge No. 162, F&AM, Fairbanks, Alaska, written 1953–1954.
Quigley, Joe, to Lloyd and Zelne Quigley, written January, 1926–November, 1930. From the Kenneth Winne Quigley collection.
Charles Sheldon Papers, Series 1: Correspondence File, 1893–1933, Box 3, Folder 9, Quigley, Joe and Fannie 1909–1913.

Index

Abby, Denise 107
Abramsky, Billy 61
Adams, Charles 50
Adrian, Pennsylvania 19, 20
Aitken, Thomas P. 113, 114
Alabama 159
Alaska College of Agriculture and School of Mines 101
Alaska Commercial Company 39
Alaska Dispatch 118
Alaska Engineering Commission 109, 112, 145
Alaska Natives 1–3, 7, 9, 27, 31–33, 52, 53, 63, 73, 85, 91, 92, 95–99, 112, 121, 122, 158
Alaska Railroad 109, 114, 141, 145, 158
Alaska Range 55, 94
Alaska Road Commission 114, 128, 140, 145
Alaska Territorial Legislation 101
Alaska Territory 10, 96, 97, 109, 152
Alaska Times 80
alcohol 20, 62, 64, 106, 115, 135, 144, 151, 162
Allakariallak 121
Allegheny River 16, 17, 26
Alpha Claim 101
American-Yukon Navigation Company 113
Anderson, John 79, 128, 133, 138
Anderson, Paula 133, 138
Anderson, Pete 86, 87
antimony 70, 71, 114
Arbeiter-Zeitung 23
Arctic Brotherhood Lodge 83
Are You Rockin' Every Day? (song) 97
Armstrong County, Pennsylvania 16, 19, 21, 22, 26, 129
assaying 110, 111, 146, 153
assessment work 37, 66, 70, 71
Athabascans 3, 8, 53, 84, 92

Bagoy, Pete 107
Baker, Forbes L. 165–167
Baker, Jerry 37, 38, 43, 44, 160
banjo mine 138, 150
Barnett, E.T. 50, 51
Barnett, Isabelle 50
Barnette's Cache 50
Beam, Bob 47

Bearpaw River 53, 60, 113, 114
Bears 12, 13, 33, 35, 36, 72, 122, 131
Benbenneck, Gus 58, 61
Bennett, Frank 160
Benson, Joe 58, 61
Bering, Vitus 31
Bering Straits 32
Betticher, Charles, Jr. 91, 96
Bettles, Gordon 160
Biddle, Nannie 148
Birch Creek 37–39
Birds and Mammals of Mount McKinley National Park, Alaska 78
Blackburn 51
blacksmithing 17, 22, 26, 107, 113, 139, 153
boat poling 12, 43, 48
Bonanza's Pup 44
Bone Dry law 115
boomtowns 6, 27, 28, 42, 45, 48, 52, 61, 81
Boone and Crockett Club 102
Bright Light mine 135
Brochu, Joseph 68
Brooker, Edgar, Jr. 103, 116, 117, 121
Brooker, Edgar, Sr. 101, 103, 116
Brooks, Alfred Hulse 33, 55, 77
Browne, Belmore 88–90, 107
Brynteston, John 48
bull teams 28
Bunnell, Charles 110, 141, 110
Burning Daylight 91
Burns, Joe 116
Busia, Johnnie 133, 152, 154

Cabin Creek 75
cairns 73, 74 151
Call of the Wild (Jack London) 56
Canada 6, 8, 10, 31, 35, 37, 39, 41, 45, 47, 50, 56, 88, 112, 212, 145
Cape Simpson 33
Capps, Stephen Reid 76, 99
caribou 13, 14, 61, 77, 78, 79, 88, 108, 132–134, 140, 142, 143
Caribou Creek 58, 59, 68, 101
Carlson, Slim 97
Carmack, George 43, 86, 162

189

Carmack, Kate (Shaaw Tlaa) 43
cheechako 43, 99
Chena (town) 52
Chena River 50, 160
Chena Slough 50, 81
Cherokee Strip 28
Chicago 23, 24, 40, 41, 159
children 16, 17, 18, 20, 21, 22, 27, 32, 42, 45, 53, 65, 81, 92, 95, 96, 129, 130, 132, 145, 163, 165, 166, 167
Chilkats 8
Chilkoot Pass 5, 7, 8, 10, 42, 91, 138, 144, 166
Chinese Exclusion Act 25
Chitsia Creek 53, 54
Chitsia Mountain 53
Chronister, Jim 61, 159
Church 17, 20, 40, 82, 84, 91, 93, 109
Circle City 37-40, 42, 48, 136, 160, 162
Circle Hot Springs 136
Clear Creek 65
Cleary, Ben 140
Cole, Martin 140
Columbia University 89
Constantine, Charles 46, 47
Cook, Albert 87
Cook, Dr. Frederick 87-89
Cook, James 32
Cook, Thomas 44, 45
Cook Inlet 32, 162
Cooney, Mike 148
Cooney Hotel 98
Copper Center 48
Cordova Times 118
Coulter, Frank 160
Croschket 55
Crosson, Joe 125-128, 135, 140
Crosson, Lillian 127, 135
Crosson, Marvel 128
Cudahy, Jack 40
Cudahy, Michael 40
curling 117

Dall sheep 75, 78
Dalton, Joe 59, 61, 119, 133, 150
Dameron, C.B. 166, 167
dance halls/dance hall girls 41, 52, 63
Darling mine 135
Davis, B.A. 160
Davis, John Allen 119
Davis, Mary Lee 119, 121, 122, 142
Dawson, George Mercer 45
Dawson City 39, 45-48, 50, 54, 56, 58, 59, 64, 75, 81, 90
Denali National Park and Preserve (McKinley National Park) 1, 2, 34, 69, 73, 74, 76, 77, 78, 93, 102, 103, 133, 134, 139, 145, 150, 153
Densmore, Frank 55
Department of the Interior 102
d'Harnoncourt, Rene 157
Diamond City 60, 68

Dickey, W.A. 55
discovery claim 15, 37, 43, 59, 61
disease 31, 36, 41, 52, 96-99, 123, 165
distemper 95, 96
divorce 20, 146, 151-153, 155, 156, 162
Dixon, Joseph 78
dogs 7, 12, 15, 50, 54, 56, 57-60, 66-69, 72, 75, 78, 85, 91, 92, 95, 100, 109, 119, 121, 122, 133, 136, 140, 142, 148
drift mining 37
Dunkle, Wesley Earl 152, 153
Durand, Vic 116
Dyea 6-8

East Franklin Township, Pennsylvania 16, 17, 129
economic depression 10, 26, 136, 142, 150, 158-160, 164
Edmunds, Betty 145
Edmunds, Chris 145
Eisenhower, Pres. Dwight D. 33
Eldorado Creek 15, 44, 45, 49, 101
Eldridge, George 55
Ellingen, Casper 160
Episcopal Church 84, 91, 92, 93, 109
Eureka, California 160
Eureka Creek 113, 58, 59, 63, 70, 72, 113
Exhibition Park, Fairbanks 124

Fair, Carrie B. 20
Fair, Cora Henry 20
Fair, Frank 2, 20, 21
Fair, James Franklin 20
Fair, John 19, 20, 129
Fair, Lawrence Homer "Irish" 20
Fairbanks (city) 50-64, 66, 68, 69, 78, 80-84, 86-89, 91, 95-98, 100, 101, 103-105, 110, 111, 114, 116-119, 123-126, 131, 134-138, 140, 141, 143-146, 148-151, 153-155, 157-161, 164, 166
Fairbanks, Charles W. 51
The Fairbanks Daily News 80
Fairbanks Daily News-Miner 80, 81, 123, 124, 140, 146, 148, 159, 160, 164
Fannie the Hike 63, 71, 106
Farrar, Mace 101
Federation of Organized Trades and Labor 23
First Nations Wars 27
Fitzgerald, Father 134
Five Finger Rapids 12
Flaherty, Robert 121
Florida 157, 159
Flume Creek 58
Fordyce Bathhouse 155, 156
Fort Reliance 39
Fort Yukon 32, 94
Fortymile City 39, 42, 45
Fortymile River 5, 8, 12, 39
49er 17, 18
Frampton, Charley 5, 6, 10
Francis Lode 135

Index

Fransen and Hawkins 150
Fraternal orders 82, 105
Fredson, John 92
Freemasons 84
Friday Creek 59, 61, 70, 72, 95, 103, 104, 116, 117, 151
frostbite/hypothermia 9, 57, 58, 68, 109

George, Esaias 92
Georgia 90
Gillette, Louise 78
Glacier (town) 60, 68
Glacier Creek 35, 58, 73, 76, 84, 92
Gold Dollar mine 117
Gold Eagle mine 117
Golden Gate Bridge 160
Golden Gate International Exposition 160
Golden Staircase 10
Gould, Hanna 18
The Great Mountain (Denali, McKinley) 51, 52, 53, 55, 66, 72, 86, 93
Green Lake Chapel 167
Grinnell, George Bird 102
Grubstake Bill 110, 111
Gruening, Ernest 158

hard rock mining (quartz mining) 6, 70–72, 101
Harper, Arthur 39, 91
Harper, Walter 91–94
Hart, Howard Hamilton 159
Haymarket Affair 24
Healy (place) 112
Healy, John 7, 8, 40
Hegg, Eric 10, 46, 47
Henderson, Nels 111
Homestead Act 26
Horn, Jack 33, 46, 54, 56–59, 61, 64, 69, 150, 160
Hot Springs, Arkansas 155
Hot Springs National Park 155, 156
Hotel Alaska 130, 131, 136
Hubbard, Percy 144
Hudson Bay 97, 121
Hudson Bay Tea 97
Hunker Creek 48, 64
Hurricane Gulch 112

immigrants 17, 24, 25, 64
influenza 97, 98, 137
Inuit 121
Inupiat 3
Irvine, Lily 124

Jacobs, Emil 144
Jeffery, George A. 52
Jensen, Juanita 166, 167
Jim Crow Laws 24
John Day mining district 161
Johnson, Pres. Andrew 21, 32, 33
Johnson, John W. 68

Johnstown, Pennsylvania 29
Joralemon, Ira 142, 143, 146, 148, 149
Juneau 5, 6, 7, 9, 29, 94

Kahlo, Frida 157
Kantishna Hydraulic Mining Company 101
Kantishna mining district
Kantishna river
Karstens, Harry 60, 73, 75, 77, 88, 90–93, 114, 133
Karstens-Stuck expedition 88, 91, 92, 93
Kaufman, Billy 5, 6, 10, 11
King, George 126
King Charles II of England 32
Kittanning, Pennsylvania 17, 23, 29
Klondike 2, 5, 7, 10, 15, 43, 44, 45, 47, 50, 58, 69, 86, 97, 149, 162
Klondike River 43, 47
Klondike Treasure Ships 69
Knights of Labor 23, 24
Koonah 53
Koyukon 92
Krishy, John 47, 48
Kuskokwim River 52, 55

Lady Eagles 84
Lady Moose Club 84
Lake Bennett 11, 12
Lake Creek 128
Lake Lindeman 11
Lake Minchumina 55
Lange, Dorthea 159
Last Chance mine 70
LaVoy, Merl 89
Lawlor, Ruth 135
Leake, Billy 160
Like, Harry J. 151
Lincoln, Abraham 21, 22
Lindberg, Hazel 3, 36, 165
Lindberg, Jafet 48
Lindblom, Eric 48
Lindstrom, Miss 111
Little Annie claims 101, 113, 152
Little Witch of Denali 119
Lloyd, Billy 97
Lloyd, Tom 70, 86–88
logging 18, 26, 28, 29
London, Jack 25, 91
Lucky Strike mine 135
Lynn Canal 8, 94

mail service 39, 48, 60, 69, 86, 91, 108, 122, 124, 126, 133, 134, 136
Malden, Adam 14
Manifest Destiny 27
market hunting 38, 77, 78, 114
Martha Q mine 20, 98, 117
Martin, James V. 124
Mason, Skookum Jim 43
Mateer, Alice Jane 18

Index

Mather, Stephen 102
Mayo, Alfred 39, 91, 92
McGarvey, Lois 120
McGonagall, Charlie 60, 86–88, 91, 92
McKenzie, Angus 64, 84, 104
McKinley, Pres. William 49, 51–52
McKinley Park Hotel 114
McKinley River 35
McKinley Station 114, 116, 133, 140
McKinley town 61, 68
McLeod, John 52
McPhee, William 81, 86, 87
McQuesten, Leroy "Jack" 39, 40, 42, 91, 92
McRae, A.D. 146, 148, 149
mercury 6
Mexia, Inez 79
Mexico 75, 156–159
Meyers, Harry M. 122, 123
Miles Canyon 11
Mineral Ridge 71
miner's code 40
mining the miners 6, 45
missionaries 31, 32, 91, 93, 134
Mitchell, Skiff 14, 15, 46, 160 (photo)
Mizner, Wilson 41
Moody, George 113, 114
Moore, James 113, 114
moose 13, 35, 38, 53, 78, 79, 81, 90, 107, 119, 120, 122, 142, 153
Moose Club 84
Moose Creek 53, 58, 60, 68, 101, 113, 125, 127, 128, 140, 141
Morino, Maurice 114
Mount Foraker 94
Mount McKinley (Denali) 51–55, 81, 86–92, 99, 126
Mount McKinley Gold Placer Company 101
Mount McKinley National Park (Denali National Park and Preserve) 76–78, 92, 102, 133, 134, 145
Muldrow, Robert 55
Mulligan, Carrie 41
Mulligan, John 41
Murie, Adolf 77, 78
Murie, Olaus 77, 78

Nabesna River 48
Nachereah 53
Nanook of the North 121
National Geographic 77
National Park movement 102
Native Americans 27
Nebraska 20, 22, 26, 27, 63, 64, 84, 107, 118
Nelson, Aven 79
Nelson, Dr. E.W. 102
Nelson, Pete 133
Nelson, Ruth Ashton 79
Nenana river 55, 112
Nenana town 52, 57, 95, 96, 98, 109, 110, 113, 114, 116, 126, 136, 148

New York 25, 88, 90
The New York Sun 93
Nome 45, 48, 50, 51, 54, 97
Nordale, A. Hjalmer 150
North Pole 87
North-West Mounted Police 13, 45, 47, 51
Nyberg, Fritz 78, 133

Oklahoma 20, 27, 28
Oklahoma Land Rush 27
Order of Alaska Pioneers 97
Order of Pioneers of the Yukon 97
Order of the Eastern Star 84
Oregon 21, 27, 130, 147–149, 161, 162, 164, 166, 167
Orozco, Clemente 157
Overheiser, Charlie 48

Paiute 27
Park Service 102, 114
Parker, Herschel 89
Parker-Browne expedition 88, 89
Patmore, Coventry 62
Patty, Ernest 110, 146, 148, 149
Paxton, U.J. 91
Payne, Frances 79
Pearson, Grant 14, 58, 78, 108, 110, 133, 134, 146, 151
Pedro, Felix (Felice Pedroni) 50
Pemberton, Pete 116
Pennsylvania 1, 3, 16–23, 25, 29, 65, 82, 84, 90, 98, 122, 129, 130, 152, 163, 167
Peter's Glacier 53
photography 2, 108, 164
Pierce, Lew 5, 6, 10, 11
Pilgrim, Earl 141, 151, 152
Pinchot, Gifford 102
Pioneer Women of Alaska 84
Pioneers of Alaska 82–84, 101, 165
Pittman, Key 102
Pittsburgh, Pennsylvania 17, 23, 25, 26, 29, 98
Pittsburgh mine 135
Pittsburgh Press 29, 148
Placer mining 12, 13, 36, 58, 60, 70, 72, 114
population 6, 16, 17, 24–28, 31, 33, 38, 40, 45, 48, 51, 63, 68, 69, 82, 85, 96–98, 110–113, 133, 138, 145, 164
Post, Wiley 127
SS *Princess Sophia* 94
Prohibition 115

quartz mining (hard rock mining) 6, 13, 60, 70, 114, 138, 151
Quigley, Benjamin 18, 130
Quigley, Benjamin Cook 17
Quigley, David Cook 17
Quigley, Emmaline Delene 18–20, 63, 129, 130
Quigley, Fannie Sedlacek McKenzie 52, 62–66, 71–73, 75–77, 82, 84, 86, 89–92, 99–101,

Index

103–113, 115, 116, 118–123, 125–127, 129–139, 142–153, 155–157, 162, 163
Quigley, James Sharron 20, 22, 26, 27
Quigley, Jane 20
Quigley, John 18
Quigley, Julia Braugh 147, 155, 161–165
Quigley, Kenneth 131, 147
Quigley, Lee David 20
Quigley, Lincoln Johnson 21, 130, 132, 142, 163
Quigley, Lloyd Joseph "Little Joe" 130,–132, 136, 137, 142, 147, 163, 166
Quigley, Lloyd Lincoln 21, 78, 130–132, 136, 142, 163, 166
Quigley, Marietta Mulkey 21, 130, 132, 142, 163
Quigley, Martha 20, 98 130
Quigley, Mary 20
Quigley, Mary Oliver 16, 18
Quigley, Pauline 20
Quigley, Robert O., Jr. 20
Quigley, Robert Orr, Sr. 16, 21, 23
Quigley, Roseanna 20
Quigley, Sarah 20
Quigley, Vernetta 132
Quigley, Vernon Orr 21, 132, 167
Quigley, William H. 23
Quigley, William Houston 21, 130
Quigley, Zelne 130–132, 142, 163
Quigley Creek 47
Quigley Gulch 47
Quigley Ridge 71–74, 98, 101, 104, 109, 116–118, 125, 140, 151

Rag Time Kid 41
Rand, Sally 161
Red Top mine 101, 117, 135, 142, 146, 149, 150, 153
Renwick Gallery 88
Riley Creek 112
Rivera, Diego 157, 161
Robertson, Nan 118, 119
Rogers, Will 128
Roosevelt (town) 60, 61, 68, 111, 113, 114, 118, 135
Roosevelt, Franklin 150, 155, 164
Roosevelt, Theodore 60, 102
Rowe, Peter Trimble
Ruby Record Citizen 93
Russo-Japanese war 71
Ryan, Miss 111

St. Joseph's Hospital 141
St. Mark's Episcopal Mission 92, 109
San Francisco, California 17, 28, 32, 37, 56, 159–161
Savage, Tom 95
Sawyer, D.L. 146
Schwartz, Rex 140
scurvy 15, 99
Seattle 33, 45, 56, 69, 146–149, 155, 159, 160, 162–167

Sedlacek, James 91
Seventymile Creek 91
Seventymile River 39, 91
Seward (town) 114, 145, 148, 160, 164
Seward, William H. 32
Seyn-dahn, (Jennie Albert) 92
Sheldon, Charles 73, 75–77, 85, 90, 92, 93, 99, 102, 108, 121, 132, 157
Sherman, William Tecumseh 102
Shesoie 53
silver 70, 75, 113, 114, 157
Simpson, Thomas 33
Sitka 80
Sixtymile River 15, 35, 39
Skagway 8
sketch maps 58
Skookum 14, 43
smallpox 31, 137
Smithsonian 3, 32, 79, 88
Snow, Anna 42
Snow, Crystal Brilliant 42
Snow, George Thornton 42, 162
Snow, Montgomery 42
Sourdough Expedition 81, 86, 88, 89, 91
South Dakota 27
Southern Hotel 98
Spratling, William 158
Squaw Rapids 12
Star mine 135
starvation 8, 14, 24, 38, 95, 159
steamships 5, 40, 41, 52, 53, 59, 69, 80, 98, 101, 113, 149, 158
Steller, Georg Wilhelm 31
Sterling, Hawley 117
Stevens, Morton I. 52
stibnite 70, 71
Stiles, Joe 59, 61, 150
Stuck, Hudson 9, 67, 87, 88, 91–94, 96, 121
sulphide mine 135
Summit Lake 10
Susitna River 112
Sway, Joe 111
Swisher, Lee 146

Tacoma 69, 101, 113
Tagish 43
Tanacross 48
Tanana Lodge 165, 166
Tanana River 37, 48, 50, 51, 55, 57, 59, 81, 91, 93, 101, 113
Tanana Valley 37, 50, 51, 52, 91, 164
Tatum, Robert 91, 92
Taylor, Billy 70, 71, 86–88, 91, 139, 140
Tena 53
Tenana Chiefs 96
The Third Territorial Legislature 101
Thomas, Mardie 78
Thompson, W. 124
Tlingit 8
Toklat River 57, 77

Tortella School 96, 109
Transcontinental Railroad 16
Treadwell, John 6
Treadwell Mining Complex 6
Treasure Island 160
Trundy, Charles 150
tuberculosis 36
Turnison 131, 137
typhoid 52, 64, 94
Tyrell, Edith 45

U.S. Army engineers 109
United States Congress 25, 32, 33, 77, 102, 145
United States Mine 118
University of Alaska, Fairbanks 2, 3, 40, 46, 101, 110
University of California 79
University of Copenhagen 87
University of the South 91
University of Wyoming 79

Valdez 160
Vanderbilt Reef 94
Van Orsdel 103
Van Slyke, Lee 61, 68, 69
vigorous masculinity 62
virtuous masculinity 62

Wada, Jujiro 50, 51
Washburn, Jim 159
Washington (state) 21, 27, 29, 78, 101, 131, 132, 147, 162–164
Washington D.C. 76, 97, 102
Washington Saloon 86
We Are Alaskans 119, 142

Weare, Portus 40
Webb, Charley 52
Wein Air Alaska 125
Wells, Frances 94
Western Union Telegraph Company 17
White Hawk mine 135
White Horse Rapids 12
Wickersham, James 51, 52, 53, 54, 55, 56, 61, 68, 71, 73, 74, 81, 96, 102, 151
Wickersham Dome 73, 74, 151
Wickersham Wall 53
Willow Flats 47
Wilson, Ruth 118, 119
Wilson, Pres. Woodrow 102
women 27, 29, 30, 41, 45, 51, 62, 63, 64, 65, 73, 84, 105, 118–120, 128, 134, 148, 154
Women's Transcontinental Air Races 128
Wonder Lake 53, 70, 128, 133, 145, 149
World War I 97, 101, 155
World War II 164
Wounded Knee 27
Wrangell–St. Elias Mountains 48
Wright, George 78
Wyoming 25, 27, 79, 102

Yakima 132
Yako 53
Yale 73, 152
Young, Ed 141
Yukon 5,-9, 12, 13, 31–33, 37, 39, 42–44, 47, 49, 51–53, 63, 69, 91, 94, 159, 166
Yukon Order of Pioneers 42, 46, 47, 54, 58, 82, 83, 86, 97, 160, 162
Yukon River 8, 12, 31, 37, 39, 43, 44, 101, 113

www.ingramcontent.com/pod-product-compliance
Ingram Content Group UK Ltd.
Pitfield, Milton Keynes, MK11 3LW, UK
UKHW042009140426
5217IPUK00015B/1064